Commando Gene

Commando General

The Life of Major General Sir Robert Laycock KCMG, CB, DSO

Richard Mead

Foreword by Major General Julian Thompson CB, OBE

Pen & Sword
MILITARY

First published in Great Britain in 2016 by
Pen & Sword Military
an imprint of
Pen & Sword Books Ltd
47 Church Street
Barnsley
South Yorkshire
S70 2AS

ISBN 978 1 47385 407 9

A CIP catalogue record for this book is available from the British Library

Typeset in Ehrhardt by
Mac Style Ltd, Bridlington, East Yorkshire
Printed and bound in the UK by CPI Group (UK) Ltd,
Croydon, CRO 4YY

Pen & Sword Books Ltd incorporates the imprints of Pen & Sword Archaeology, Atlas, Aviation, Battleground, Discovery, Family History, History, Maritime, Military, Naval, Politics, Railways, Select, Transport, True Crime, and Fiction, Frontline Books, Leo Cooper, Praetorian Press, Seaforth Publishing and Wharncliffe.

For a complete list of Pen & Sword titles please contact
PEN & SWORD BOOKS LIMITED
47 Church Street, Barnsley, South Yorkshire, S70 2AS, England
E-mail: enquiries@pen-and-sword.co.uk
Website: www.pen-and-sword.co.uk

Contents

List of Maps

Foreword

Robert Laycock was the youngest British or Commonwealth officer to be promoted to the rank of major general in the Second World War, at the age of thirty-six. But as Richard Mead tells us, 'Bob', as he calls him, 'never went on to higher command in the field or in grand strategy', so he cannot be counted among the truly great soldiers of the Second World War. Instead, Richard Mead believes, with good reason, that Laycock deserves to be remembered for his key role in the evolution of the Commandos from their tentative beginnings into the elite formation they are today. He was one of the first Commandos, and it is to his credit that the inheritors of the concept launched in June 1940, are the Royal Marines. This was made clear to me, a young subaltern in 40 Commando Royal Marines in Malta in 1957, when the Governor, Major General Sir Robert Laycock, visited us. Our commanding officer, and many of the majors and captains had served in commandos in the Second World war, which had ended a mere twelve years before. They all held 'Lucky' Laycock in high esteem. As none of us was insubordinate enough to address him thus, we did not know that he disliked the nickname for its insinuation that he owed his position to luck rather than merit. One could argue that in many cases luck in the form of opportunity recognized and seized is one of the attributes of a good commander, and in that sense Laycock was both lucky and a good commander. The notice asking for volunteers to join the Commandos coming out just before he was due to leave Britain for a posting in Egypt; his escape and evasion after the abortive 'Rommel Raid'; and his appointment to succeed Mountbatten as Chief of Combined Operations are just three examples of how the wings of Laycock's luck beat over his head on numerous occasions.

He was most certainly *not* lucky to be sent to command the commandos of Layforce in the Middle East; although only the gift of foresight could have told him that. That they were misused was not his fault; anymore than the debacle in Crete, in which Layforce was involved at the very end, was his fault. Given a choice, and again equipped with a crystal ball, he would probably have opted for command of one of the four Special Service (Commando) brigades in the more fulfilling period of late 1943 onwards. But other than a very successful twelve days commanding the Special Service Brigade in Sicily and Italy in mid-1943, this was not to be. His appointment as CCO put paid to that. But the beneficiaries of the decision to make him CCO were the commandos, and especially the Royal Marines. The frustrating time experienced by the Royal Marines during the first half of the Second World War is given due coverage by Richard Mead. The Admiralty were the architects of the muddle and frustration and to some extent a few senior Royal Marines were as well. Mountbatten and Laycock saved the Royal Marines from the oblivion that would have been their fate after the Second World War. In his foreword to the *Green Beret: The Story of the Commandos*, Mountbatten refers to Laycock as 'one of the original Commando soldiers – and in my opinion perhaps the greatest of them all'. That accolade, written in 1949, surely refers not just to Laycock's achievements in action, but even more so to his work as CCO from mid-October 1943 to June 1947. It is fitting that it does so.

Several well known personalities appear in the book, among them Evelyn Waugh whom Laycock allowed to serve in the Special Service Brigade, in the role of court jester, long after he had overstayed his welcome. Several officers who served with him have expressed the view that although personally brave, Waugh was the type of officer who should never be allowed near troops.

Commando General is a balanced and perceptive biography of a soldier whose work endures to this day. It is also a window on a world that has all but disappeared, and the glimpses we are given are entertaining and revealing. The author is to be congratulated on a very enjoyable and informative work, which moves along apace.

Julian Thompson

Introduction

In early June 1940 Great Britain was on the back foot. The British Expeditionary Force had been ejected from the continent of Europe and, although the majority of its men had been rescued, all its heavy weapons and transport had been abandoned at Dunkirk. France, the country's only ally outside the British Empire, was a broken reed and would shortly capitulate to the Germans. The prospect of invasion seemed all too likely and, unsurprisingly, the focus of the armed forces was exclusively on defence.

Winston Churchill, Prime Minister for just a month, was determined to find some way to take the battle to the enemy rather than simply wait to be attacked. The main obstacle was water. Germany was already in control of the coastline of Europe from North Cape to the Pas-de-Calais and would shortly extend its rule to the Spanish frontier. The chances of crossing the intervening seas in significant strength in the immediate future were minimal, but Churchill saw an opportunity for small-scale operations to show the enemy that he was not safe in Fortress Europe but could be attacked at any time. He demanded from his military leaders a force which could mount frequent raids on that long coastline.

Thus were born the direct ancestors of today's 3 Commando Brigade, an elite formation which has continued to prove itself since the Second World War, in Korea, at Suez, in the Falklands, Iraq and Afghanistan and a number of other smaller campaigns.

However, whilst a very small number of Royal Marines were recruited into the original Commandos in mid-1940, the new force was essentially an Army affair, and it was not until early in 1942 that the first RM Commando was formed. Amongst the officers selected to raise the Army Commandos was a thirty-three-year-old captain in the Royal Horse Guards, Robert Laycock. Just over three years later he would become the youngest general officer in the British Army and the Chief of Combined Operations, sitting at the head of the organization which, more than any other, made possible the landings which put the Western Allies back in strength onto the continent of Europe.

I have long been fascinated by Bob Laycock's wartime career. The eighteen months which followed his selection to raise 8 Commando were for the most part a story of disappointment, failure, even disaster. Yet in early 1942 he was appointed to the most senior position within the overall Commando force and, following a short period of active service in 1943, was the surprise choice to follow Lord Louis Mountbatten at Combined Operations. I decided to look more closely at how this rapid elevation had been achieved.

I knew before I began that Bob had left behind some potentially very useful material, which was deposited in the Liddell Hart Archives at King's College, London. These papers turned out to be voluminous, containing mostly official and semi-official documents, but also many of a more personal nature. When I approached his surviving children, who were supportive from the outset, they told me that he never threw anything away, a trait which I, as a biographer, could only thoroughly commend!

It turned out that a lot of other important papers had been retained by the family. Bob only kept a proper diary during the early years of his military career, initially as a cadet at Sandhurst and then as a subaltern in the Royal Horse Guards; at first glance it is of rather more interest to a social historian than a military one, but on a closer look it is indicative of the level of professionalism, or lack of it, in the British Army in the late 1920s and early 1930s. The diary of his voyage in a four-masted barque around the Cape of Good Hope in 1932, whilst on extended leave from his regiment, is fascinating and throws a great deal of light on his character.

The most exciting find, however, was his draft memoirs. These were unearthed only shortly before I began to write, which in retrospect was a very good thing as I might otherwise have been tempted to skimp on some of the research. It was known that he was working on them and, indeed, I had found fragments at King's College; but apparently he thought that they were rather dull and appears to have made no attempt to have them published. The memoirs are, in fact, far from dull. Bob wrote excellent prose, and his keen sense of humour makes them very entertaining. They cover his pre-War career relatively sketchily until he left his regiment in 1937, but thereafter are full of both information and opinion, adding depth to what I had already discovered and correcting a few misconceptions. Unfortunately, they come to an abrupt end in the autumn of 1941, so do not cover some important parts of Bob's military career, including his participation in the raid on what was believed to be General Rommel's headquarters in North Africa, his period of active service in Sicily and Italy and his term as Chief of Combined Operations. There are jottings for the missing years in the Liddell Hart Archives, but they take the form of cryptic aide-memoires, which are of little real value. What the memoirs do include of particular significance are his own accounts of his selection for the Commandos and of events on Crete.

The very brief period which Bob spent on Crete, an incident-packed five days in all, was the most controversial of his career. The controversy, however, did not see the light of day until half a century later, long after Bob had died. It emerged in Antony Beevor's book, *Crete – The Battle and the Resistance*, published in 1991. The issues were firstly, whether Bob disobeyed orders that Layforce should be the last to be evacuated from the island, and secondly, whether he should have left himself, whilst the majority of his command remained to be taken prisoner. Beevor, whilst stating that there was no question of cowardice on Bob's part, was critical of his decisions; his view has been repeated in subsequent accounts and has arguably tarnished Bob's reputation.

Bob, however, has had at least one champion, in the person of Professor Donat Gallagher of James Cook University, who has consistently sought to justify his decisions and actions. The debate between Gallagher and Beevor, largely conducted through articles and letters in various learned journals, depends heavily on the timing of certain events and the interpretation of the interaction between Bob and his superiors. Whilst highly interesting to me, the arguments are likely to be very tedious to most of my readers. I have, accordingly, decided not to set out the two points of view but to make up my own mind on the subject based on the evidence available. I have had the advantage over the two eminent historians of reading Bob's memoirs, which give a detailed account of the battle and the circumstances of his evacuation. Whether these would have made any difference to Beevor or Gallagher, I cannot say. One might argue on the one hand that they are a primary source, but on the other that they were written many years later, when memory was inevitably less accurate, and that they were specifically designed to be a defence of the decisions taken at the time.

Whilst Bob's wartime career will be of most interest to readers and thus occupies the greater part of this book, it took up only ten per cent of his life. Inevitably, his family background and his education were important ingredients in making him the man he was. However, there are only a few clues as to how the carefree young subaltern of the late 1920s, seemingly more interested in field sports and social life than in his military duties, developed into the highly professional soldier of the 1940s. One of the most telling documents unearthed for me by the family was a notebook, the front part of which contained Bob's personal appointments diary for 1942, whilst the back, evidently transcribed from other sources in 1945 and then continued until three days before he died in 1968, listed every book he had read from 1928 onwards. It is clear that, at a time when the average cavalry subaltern would have probably confined his reading to *The Field* and *Tatler*, Bob was extraordinarily widely read. In 1928, the year after he joined the regiment from Sandhurst, the list included not only light fiction by John Buchan, 'Sapper' and R. S. Surtees, but much more serious works by Bertrand Russell, Sigmund Freud, André Maurois and Basil Liddell Hart. A similar mix continued until the War, during which the balance shifted markedly to the lighter end of the spectrum. The year 1940, for instance, was heavily dominated by P. G. Wodehouse, perhaps unsurprisingly given the background of current events. Although history and biography in particular subsequently reappeared in the reading list, Bob's taste thereafter, albeit very catholic, remained biased towards fiction.

Bob's family provided a rock-solid foundation to his life. The major source of information on his forebears was a slim volume published privately in 1936 by his aunt, Barbara Mitchell-Innes, which focused on his father, Joe, but went back some way into previous generations. By an incredible stroke of luck I managed to acquire for myself a copy of the privately printed log of the first major voyage of Joe's yacht, the *Valhalla*. Joe was the most important influence on Bob's early life, and I decided to cover him in some detail in the book, but it is clear from both Mitchell-Innes and Bob's diaries that his parents, brothers and sisters, aunts, uncles and near cousins were always very close, seeing a great deal of each other both at the family home at Wiseton in Nottinghamshire and in London. Bob himself went on to have a very successful marriage to Angela Dudley Ward, and they and their children remained as close as had previous generations.

Bob's resignation from the Army in 1947 was probably caused, like many others', by a lack of jobs for senior officers in a rapidly contracting peacetime organization. He had just turned forty, with plenty of time to embark on a new and productive career, but he chose not to do so until he was suddenly invited to become Governor of Malta, an appointment which, after two extensions, lasted for nearly five years. These were difficult times for the island, but they are at least well chronicled both in the press and in various archives. Bob's own views can be found in some of his letters to Angie on the occasions when they were parted. His wartime letters to her are also of interest, but they suffer from the requirements of the censor that nothing of any military moment should be mentioned, so are largely confined to domestic matters.

Bob Laycock's main claim to fame remains his role in the creation and development of the Commandos. At the time of his appointment to 8 Commando, few had any real idea of how they were to be employed. As it turned out, they were largely misused during their first two years, a litany of failure only alleviated by a few modest successes, in many ways reflecting the story of the British Army as a whole. Nevertheless, much was achieved during this period, especially in the design of a rigorous training regime, not so different from that of the modern Commandos, and in the devising of techniques for amphibious landings whose implementation came to fruition in the last three years of the War. Bob was at the heart of these initiatives, as he was in the debates which led to a complete reorganization of the Commandos in late 1943 and their transformation from an exclusively raiding force to one which would thenceforward largely act in support of conventional troops. As the post-War Chief of Combined Operations, he was instrumental in the retention and composition of 3 Commando Brigade, which still exists today, albeit somewhat larger in size and enhanced in capability.

Bob always insisted that the word 'Commando' should apply to the unit and not to the individual soldier who served in it. I have decided to stick to this practice, which was certainly the correct one at the time of which I write, although from the early days both the men themselves and the general public began to use the word interchangeably.

I hoped originally to be able to call the book *The First Commando General*. It became clear to me at an early stage, however, that there were two other contenders for the title, Charles Haydon, who led the Commandos as a brigadier and, as a senior officer at Combined Operations HQ, was subsequently promoted to general officer rank before Bob, and Robert Sturges, a major general already at the time of his appointment to command the Special Services Group. Bob himself would not have cared. He was immensely proud to have been in at the beginning and still there when peace was declared, as a general, but also as a Commando soldier.

Prologue

Darkness enveloped the landing craft as it headed towards the shore. Standing close to the coxswain, the brigadier could see little and hear nothing over the sound of the engines. Suddenly, from behind the vessel, the sky was illuminated as dozens of naval guns fired simultaneously, and within less than a minute he could see responding flashes away on the starboard beam. For a few moments all remained quiet ahead, but then he heard the sharp crack of guns from the destroyer lying offshore and saw explosions as the shells struck their targets. He knew that his advanced detachment was about to hit the beach and that he was hard on their heels.

Not for the first time, the brigadier was about to land on an enemy-held shore but this time it was different, the return to the mainland of Europe after years of frustration and disappointment. Like all those around him he had learnt earlier that night about the Italian surrender, but unlike most of them he believed that the opposition would still be ferocious. Nevertheless, as the landing craft began its final run-in to the beach, he was confident that the plan was good, that morale was high and that the seemingly endless months of training had furnished the skills for the job ahead. The fighting would be hard, but the outcome was not in doubt.

Chapter 1

Joe

By the early eighteenth century the Laycock family had been established in the West Riding of Yorkshire for many generations, their name supposedly deriving from that of a village near Keighley. More than one of their members acted as Agent to the Dukes of Devonshire at Bolton Abbey. In 1732 Joseph Laycock moved north to Winlaton, County Durham, to work as the manager of Crowley's Iron Works. His grandson, also Joseph, was born there in 1798 and, after serving an apprenticeship at Crowley's, entered business on his own account when the iron works closed, succeeding initially in obtaining a contract from the Royal Navy for the manufacture of chains and anchors. When the Newcastle & Carlisle Railway was founded in 1825, he bid for and obtained the contract to supply 500 goods wagons, which began to run on the railway when it was opened in 1834. He also bought land on which he believed railways would have to be built, as turned out to be the case. In due course he became Chairman of the Blyth & Tyne Railway and then, after its acquisition by the much larger North Eastern Railway, a director of the latter. In 1852, by which time he had become an extremely wealthy man, he acquired Low Gosforth House, near Newcastle, with an estate of 287 acres. A longstanding member of the Newcastle Corporation, he became the city's Mayor in 1858 and in the same year acquired the Seghill Colliery

Robert Laycock, Joseph's only child by his marriage to Barbara Nicholson, was born in 1833. After graduating from Trinity College, Cambridge, he was called to the Bar and practised for a time on the Northern Circuit, but by 1866 he was working for his father, in which capacity he was asked to arrange a visit to Seghill by a party of Austrian businessmen. They were accompanied by a young lady called Annie Allhusen, with whom he fell in love and subsequently married. Her father, Christian Allhusen, was a remarkable man, who had been born in Kiel, at that time in Denmark, in 1805. With Europe in deep depression after the Napoleonic Wars he was sent by his family to live and work in Newcastle, in the first instance as an apprentice grain merchant. In due course he found an opportunity to trade on his own account, before moving on to the manufacture of caustic soda, which earned him a considerable fortune, some of which was spent in the purchase of of Elswick Hall, a large estate not far from Low Gosforth. Allhusen became a British citizen in 1835 through a Private Act of Parliament.

By the time of the wedding Robert was not getting on at all well with his father, who was evidently a difficult man, 'a bully to his workmen and a tyrant to those dependent on him'.[1] Joseph told his son that on his marriage he would buy him an estate, but it would have to be at least 100 miles away from Gosforth, the only condition being that he would have his grandchildren back at Low Gosforth for their holidays. The selected property was Wiseton Hall, a substantial country house in North Nottinghamshire, which had been originally built in 1771 and was much enlarged subsequently. It had earlier been the home of the Acklom family, whose heiress had married Earl Spencer, a leader of the campaign to pass the Reform Bill in 1832. Having bought the house and furnished it as cheaply as possible, Joseph declared that no further money would be forthcoming to the newlyweds, who would have to live on the income of the Home Farm of some 400 acres. All hopes of a brilliant social life disappeared, and Robert turned to politics, but failed to be elected as one of the two Members of Parliament for North Nottinghamshire in 1868 and for Nottingham in 1874.

Robert and Annie produced a family very quickly, Joseph Frederick, known to all as Joe, being born in 1867 and Barbara in 1868. Whilst their parents remained disappointed with their lot, the youngsters had a happy childhood, relying on their own wits and the company of the village children. Joe in particular was highly inventive with respect to games and, as he grew up, became fascinated by machinery, on one occasion appropriating a steam plough whilst the farm workers were at lunch, and driving it into a ditch. He was in due course sent off to prep school at Temple Grove, in East Sheen, before going on to Eton. Holidays were duly spent at Low Gosforth, where Joe's grandfather kept a pony for him to ride, and at a family house in Tynemouth.

Tensions continued at Wiseton, with debts mounting up due to Robert's extravagance and Annie's inability to economize. Annie very nearly ran away, stopped from doing so only because she could not bear to leave her daughter. Shortly afterwards Robert was asked to stand again for Parliament in the 1880 general election, but this time for North Lincolnshire. Like his father he was a committed Liberal, but North Lincolnshire had two sitting Conservative members, although one of the seats had been held by a Liberal member from 1857 to 1874. Initially Robert refused to let his name go forward for a third time, but he was persuaded to do so by Annie, who felt that it would give him a goal and, if he was successful, an occupation, and might very well change their fortunes. He lodged his nomination at Brigg Town Hall with minutes to spare, disappointing the two Conservative candidates, who were expecting a walkover.

Robert fought a strong campaign, denouncing the policies of Disraeli and advocating reform, particularly of the land laws. The election resulted in a Liberal landslide nationally, and in North Lincolnshire Robert received the largest number of votes in the constituency, to the dismay of one of the Conservative candidates. Robert was delighted and Annie was ecstatic. Even his father was pleased, reimbursing Robert for the costs of his campaign. The only mild disappointment was that the house which Robert and Annie took in Mayfair, in order for him to be able to undertake his duties at Westminster, had to be shared with his parents.

A year later disaster struck. First of all, Joseph died. Nine days later Robert was suddenly taken ill in Eastbourne and died in a hotel there. Annie was left alone with two relatively young children, but for the first time in her marriage she had no financial worries, although the estate was to go substantially to Joe once he had attained his majority. At the time he was still at Eton, where he was socially successful but academically hopeless. Annie was keen that he should go on to Oxford, but neither Eton nor two successive crammers could produce the required results. Annie then suggested that he should join the Royal Horse Guards, but Joe persuaded her that the Yeomanry would be much more appropriate, since it would leave him time to look after the estate, which still included significant holdings of land and industrial businesses in the North East.

In 1887 Annie remarried, this time to Lord D'Arcy Osborne,[2] who, unlike some of her suitors, was approved of by her children. Joe attained his majority in the following year, upon which he assumed full control of his fortune from his trustees and set up his household at Wiseton Hall, with Barbara acting as his hostess. They were keen entertainers and devoted both to field sports, taking a house for the season in Bicester Hunt country, and to cricket, creating a splendid ground in front of the house which remains in use to this day.

Brother and sister had by then also developed a considerable enthusiasm for sailing. They started with a small schooner of 150 tons, the *Nore*, which was rapidly followed by a larger vessel of 250 tons, the *Lady Sibell*. In 1892 Joe, who had always been interested in ship design, produced some outline plans for a 230ft, 1,500 ton clipper, which was in essence a three-quarter sized version of the *Cutty Sark*. The basic design for the *Valhalla* was handed over to a well known naval architect, W. C. Storey, who produced detailed plans, including auxiliary steam power. The main construction contract was placed with Rammage & Ferguson of Leith, and the vessel was fitted out in Southampton. The critics were dubious, but she turned out to have excellent sailing qualities. The crew numbered 95, the majority of whom had served previously in the Royal Navy, and the vessel was well armed with two Hotchkiss cannons and a Maxim machine gun, as well as an assortment of rifles, pistols and cutlasses. The maiden voyage, between 22 March and 1 August 1893, took Joe and ten other 'idlers' from Southampton to Madeira and then into and around the Mediterranean to Constantinople, across the Black Sea to Sevastopol and back in due course to Cowes, a distance of 9,632 miles. The stay in port at Cannes was timed to coincide with Barbara's wedding there to Edward Mitchell-Innes, a barrister who later became a King's Counsel. In order to gain further experience, in 1894 Joe sailed to Australia in the clipper *Pericles*, insisting on carrying out the job of every man aboard during the long voyage.

Having declined his mother's suggestion that he should obtain a regular commission, Joe was as good as his word about joining the Yeomanry and was duly commissioned as a subaltern in his local regiment, the Sherwood Rangers. He was a keen and assiduous member, attending all the necessary courses and the annual camps. On one occasion during the latter, he led a squadron successfully across Salisbury Plain by night, a manoeuvre which brought him to the attention of John French, a coming officer in the Regular Army and himself a cavalryman. The two men formed a friendship, and French promised that, should there be a war in which he was involved, he would take Joe with him in some capacity.

In the summer of 1899 tensions between the British Government in South Africa and the two Boer republics in the Transvaal and the Orange Free State materially increased. The main issue at stake was voting rights for the 'Uitlanders', the largely British inhabitants of Johannesburg, Kimberley and other gold and diamond mining towns. The Boers were fearful that any concession would in due course result in a non-Boer majority, at least in the Transvaal, and regarded this as part of a ploy by the British to bring the two republics into a new federation under their control. The talks broke down and, on 9 October, the Government of the Transvaal delivered an ultimatum to the British to withdraw all troops on their borders and those of the Orange Free State, failing which war would be declared.

Even before this, British reinforcements had been arriving in South Africa. French had been earmarked to command a cavalry brigade and, true to his promise, sent Joe a telegram in mid-September, asking if he would like to join him on a ship leaving Southampton in a few days. Joe responded immediately: 'Delighted to come, can you get me recognized?' He was not part of French's official staff, neither at that time was his regiment earmarked to provide a contingent, although it did so later. He had no alternative, therefore, but to travel as a private individual and trust that French would be able to engineer his official appointment in due course.

French and his staff, who were led by Major Douglas Haig, embarked in RMS *Norman* on 23 September 1899 and arrived in Cape Town, via Madeira, on 11 October, just as war was declared. As the cavalry which he would be commanding was yet to arrive, French was sent temporarily to Ladysmith, where troops under Lieutenant General Sir George White were facing a large force of Boers. On the very morning of their arrival on 20 October, French, accompanied by Haig and Joe and with a mixed force including an infantry brigade under Ian Hamilton, was sent to Elandslaagte to investigate reports that the Boers had taken the town. In order to push them back French carried out a textbook manoeuvre, involving a cavalry reconnaissance, an infantry attack and then a cavalry charge, which resulted in a decisive victory. Joe was employed as a supernumerary staff officer, with a roving commission around the battlefield on French's behalf. This enabled him to participate in Hamilton's attack, in which he distinguished himself in disabling two Boer guns by dismantling their breech-blocks and carrying them back to the British lines. He also enabled news of the victory to be communicated to White by tapping the telephone lines alongside the railway.

Notwithstanding this success, White ordered French's force to fall back on Ladysmith. With the Boers closing in around the town, French, who saw no role for the cavalry in a siege, asked permission to withdraw. Against the wishes of White, the order came through from Cape Town for him to do so, and he and his staff escaped on the last train in a first-class compartment at the end of a luggage van. The carriage was hit by rifle fire, but the occupants escaped without injury to Durban, where on 4 November they embarked for Cape Town.

Joe had been mentioned in despatches for his role at Elandslaagte, and his position on the staff was now regularized. He accompanied French and Haig to De Aar, where French was to take command of a force covering the Colesberg area. On 10, 11 and 15 December the British suffered severe defeats at Stormberg, Magersfontein and Colenso, in what would come to be called 'Black Week'. Joe was highly critical of the performance of the British Army, writing to his mother: 'The school in which our leaders have been taught is the worst in the world: fighting against Zulus, Dervishes, etc. seems to make them forget all about tactics and strategy.'[3]

The disasters led to the overall command of the British troops in South Africa being transferred from Sir Redvers Buller to Lord Roberts. French, untarnished by the events of 'Black Week', had been engaged in a number of indecisive actions, but at least was active and was thus one of the few senior commanders retained by the new C-in-C. In the middle of January 1900, he sent Joe to see Roberts in Cape Town with despatches and maps to explain the position in his sector. Joe was also protesting, on French's behalf, at the appointment of Lord Erroll, one of Roberts's 'Ring', as his chief staff officer instead of Haig. The attempt failed and Erroll was appointed, but Haig stayed on as French's guest. Erroll was far from competent, so Joe found himself doing much of the work. Haig was subsequently given a column to command and asked Joe to join him, but Joe refused to leave French.

Roberts was now ready to begin his main offensive. On 14 February French, commanding the Cavalry Division, launched a wide turning movement to relieve Kimberley, taking the Boers by surprise, defeating the relatively modest opposition he encountered as a result and entering the town on the evening of the following day, in time for him and his staff to be entertained to dinner by Cecil Rhodes. A week later he began his advance on Bloemfontein, the capital of the Orange Free State, which fell on 13 March. Lack of supplies and a great deal of illness, largely typhoid, delayed a further advance, but it resumed in mid-May, with Johannesburg falling on 31 May and Pretoria, the capital of the Transvaal, on 5 June. Three days later Joe had lunch in the latter with the Duke of Marlborough and his cousin, Winston Churchill, who had earlier escaped from the POW camp in the city, which he took Joe to inspect. Joe already knew Churchill, having met him in Ladysmith before his capture. The two men were to become good friends.

Most people, not least Joe, now thought that the war was over; consequently, he booked a return passage on RMS *Dunottar Castle* in early July 1900, his fellow passengers including Churchill. He had done exceptionally well on French's staff, distinguishing himself on a number of occasions, including one on which he had ridden through the night, accompanied only by a sergeant, to get an urgent message from French to Roberts. On another he found himself behind the Boer lines and was able to report to the troops facing them that the enemy was not nearly as strong as they had supposed. For these and his other services he was awarded the Distinguished Service Order. He had also made some very influential friends, not only French, Haig, Hamilton and Edmund Allenby, but also Churchill and a young officer on Roberts's staff, 'Bendor' Grosvenor,[4] who had recently succeeded his grandfather as Duke of Westminster.

The relief of Mafeking, Kimberley and Ladysmith had been accompanied in the United Kingdom by an outpouring of patriotic rejoicing, and those returning from the conflict were welcomed as heroes. Joe received an illuminated address from his neighbours in Nottinghamshire as the first volunteer from the Sherwood Rangers, whilst a shield, accompanied by an even more magnificent and illuminated parchment, was presented to him by the NCOs and other ranks of the Newark Troop of the regiment.

Joe was now aged thirty-three and it was time for him to marry. Numerous beautiful and highly eligible young women had crossed the threshold of Wiseton Hall over the years, but the two to whom he became attracted, Daisy, Countess of Warwick, who had previously been the mistress of the Prince of Wales, and Kitty, Marchioness of Downshire, were both married. He fathered two children by the former, but, after operating a *ménage à trois* with the latter, successful divorce proceedings by Kitty's husband forced his hand and he was honour bound to marry her. Born Katherine Hare in 1872, she was the daughter of the Hon. Hugh Hare, himself the younger son of the Earl of Listowel. She had married another scion of the Irish aristocracy, Arthur Hill, 6th Marquess of Downshire, in 1893, and the couple had had three children, Arthur, who was later to succeed his father, Francis and Kathleen, the last of whom was born in 1898.

Following her marriage to Joe in 1902, Kitty came with Kathleen to live at Wiseton. In the following year the couple's first child, Christian, was born, followed by Rosemary in 1905. Whilst Kitty was expecting Rosemary she had a terrible motor accident in France, as a result of which one of her legs was amputated. She recovered very fast and refused to allow the disability to alter her life in any way, continuing to hunt, indeed establishing a reputation as a particularly hard rider, and even to play tennis. She also continued to bear children, and her third child, Robert Edward Laycock, was born in London on 18 April 1907.

Chapter 2

Bob

Bob Laycock was born into a life of wealth and privilege. The landed gentry, of which the Laycocks were members notwithstanding their relatively recent social ascent, were the backbone of rural England, although much of their wealth derived from the industrial towns of the Midlands and North. Joe himself certainly maintained a close interest in the Seghill Colliery and the family's other agricultural and business interests, which he used to visit regularly. He also retained a connection with the artisan skills of his forebears through his keen interest in engineering and, in particular, by working on a lathe which he had installed at Wiseton, on which he turned not only wooden but also ivory artefacts. The rest of the family, on the other hand, were far removed from the lives of those who created their wealth.

The family continued to grow, with a second daughter, Josephine, always called Joyce, being born in 1908, followed by Peter in 1910 and Michael in 1914. Tragedy struck, however, when the eldest child, Christian, died of appendicitis at Christmas in 1911. Described by his aunt as a 'darling, intelligent little fellow of eight, with very winning ways',[1] his death came as a great blow to Joe and Kitty.

Kitty was known to all the children and to others in the immediate family as 'Anne', named after a fictional mother rabbit who had so many offspring that she did not know what to do with them. This was an age when upper class mothers spent little time with their children, delegating the responsibility initially to a nanny, followed in due course by governesses for the girls, whilst the boys were despatched to boarding school at the age of eight or nine. This was true at Wiseton as well, but nevertheless this was a close and happy family, with a good deal of social interchange between the generations. Barbara Mitchell-Innes described Joe as 'the best friend to all of them, boys and girls alike. They all go to him for companionship and fun, as well as for advice, and there is no interest that they don't share with him.'[2] Kitty was decidedly more partial to the boys than the girls.

From an early age the leisure interests of the children, as with their parents, were centred around horses. Joe kept a very fine stable, and the young Laycocks were taught to ride almost as soon as they could walk. Once they could swing a mallet, they were all, boys and girls alike, encouraged to play polo, but the main interest was in hunting. The nearest hunts to Wiseton were the Grove and the Rufford, since amalgamated, but their countries had largely been given over to the plough and were heavy going in some weathers. Although the family turned out on occasion with one or other of these, their preference was for the largely grass and woodland countries of the Belvoir, the Quorn and the Pytchley, some way to the south. For that reason Joe bought a house in Melton Mowbray, Newport Lodge, which had its own stables and was in constant use during the season.

Life at Wiseton sometimes verged on the chaotic, as the children, notwithstanding their closeness to their parents, tended to be wild and unruly. Numerous games were indulged in, some of which verged on the foolhardy. On one occasion they made a raft which was floated on the nearby Chesterfield Canal with the youngest, Michael, tied to it. On another, they fired a starting cannon down the drive of Newport Lodge; the wadding, which had been left in the barrel, narrowly missed a lady walking past the gates. Bicycle polo was particularly popular, in spite of the inevitable crashes. There was a menagerie of animals, including a goat, whilst Kitty even kept a monkey. Much of each summer was spent in the north-west Highlands of Scotland, where Joe rented a deer forest, initially at Letterewe and later at Arisaig, for stalking, shooting and fishing. The children were taught to use sporting guns at the earliest possible age.

In August 1914 the carefree life came to an end, at least for the adults, with the outbreak of war. Joe had kept up his close association with the Army, initially as an officer in the Sherwood Rangers Yeomanry. His friendship with John French had endured, as a result of which he became known to many other senior regular officers, and every year he managed to attach himself to the staff of some general during the annual manoeuvres. In 1908 the yeomanry regiments were grouped into fourteen brigades, each of which was to have its own battery of Royal Horse Artillery. The Sherwood Rangers Yeomanry was brigaded with the South Nottinghamshire Hussars and the Derbyshire Yeomanry, and it was decided that a new RHA battery should be raised locally, with the command given to Joe, who was promoted from captain to major. Notwithstanding considerable scepticism in the Army about creating horse artillerymen out of amateur soldiers, Joe set about the task with great vigour, recruiting a battery sergeant major who had served previously as a sergeant in the regular RHA and two other former RHA sergeants to take charge of the orderly room and the riding school. Captain Wilfred Jelf was appointed as Adjutant, an office was acquired in Nottingham and general recruiting began, with a significant excess of applications over places. The officers were all personally known to Joe, many of them hunting friends. He allowed no expense to be spared in achieving his goal, using his own money where necessary to compensate for War Office parsimony. Twelve-pounder guns arrived shortly afterwards, the first camp was held at Wiseton during the following summer and in 1910 the battery impressed with its shooting at camp on Salisbury Plain.

On war being declared the battery moved initially to Norfolk with the Nottinghamshire Mounted Brigade. Joe himself was asked by French to join the staff of the British Expeditionary Force at Montreuil. The C-in-C was keen to retain him there, but Joe pressed constantly to rejoin his battery and to get it into action. It was not to France that it was sent, however, but to Egypt in the spring of 1915, and Joe went too, carrying a piece of paper confirming that he could return to the General Staff at any time.

Sent initially to Ismailia on the Suez Canal, the battery endured six months of boredom before being ordered to join the Western Frontier Force, formed to repel an attack by the Senussi, a religious sect in Libya which had been persuaded by the Ottoman Empire to declare *jihad* against the British. The Senussi had already taken the frontier port of Sollum and were advancing towards Sidi Barrani when a scratch force, consisting of the 15th Sikh Regiment, a Composite Yeomanry Regiment, the Nottinghamshire RHA Battery and some armoured cars was despatched to confront them. A series of engagements took place between mid-December 1915 and 14 March 1916, when Sollum was finally re-taken. Joe's battery distinguished itself in a number of these, as did the Rolls Royce armoured cars of the Cheshire Yeomanry, commanded by his great friend, the Duke of Westminster. As well as participating in the decisive operation at Agagia, in which the Senussi commander and his staff were captured, Westminster led a daring and successful raid to liberate the crews of two Royal Navy ships who had been captured by the Senussi, inviting Joe along for the ride.

Having spent a brief leave in England, Joe returned to Egypt in May 1916 to be appointed Commander Royal Artillery of the Australian and New Zealand Mounted Division, which was then in the Sinai Desert under Major General Harry Chauvel. The division comprised two cavalry and one mounted infantry brigade, supported by the Inverness-shire, Ayrshire and Somerset Batteries of 18 RHA Brigade. Joe tried to persuade Chauvel to include his own battery in the brigade, but although it was fully engaged in the Palestine campaign, it was as part of another division. The Anzac Mounted Division fought in the victorious battles of Magdaba and Rafa and the first and second battles of Gaza, following which the successful Turkish defence resulted in the replacement of Lieutenant General Sir Archibald Murray as Commander of the Egyptian Expeditionary Force by Joe's old friend from the Boer War, Lieutenant General Sir Edmund Allenby.

Joe, however, was not to serve under Allenby. Instead, whilst on leave in England in May 1917, he was appointed CRA Coastal Defences. Pressing to go to France, he eventually achieved his wish in February 1918. He was given no fixed appointment at first but spent a brief period as understudy to his former Adjutant, Wilfred Jelf, as the CRA of 33 Division. Douglas Haig, French's successor and another old friend with whom Joe had remained on excellent terms, used him temporarily as a senior liaison officer to General Pershing. In July 1918, now promoted to brigadier general, Joe was appointed CRA of

59 Division, which participated in the great Allied offensive leading to the Armistice on 11 November. After a 'good' war, his service was recognized by his appointment as a KCMG[3] in the Birthday Honours of 1919.

Bob's life, too, had had been subject to great change, but in his case it had nothing to do with the war and everything to do with his education. In September 1916, at the age of nine, he was sent to board at Lockers Park School in Hemel Hempstead. No explanation exists of why the school was chosen, but it was probably on the recommendation of friends. It was certainly a long way from Wiseton, but this was not unusual in an age when parents were not expected to visit their children very often, if at all, during term time.

The school had been founded in 1874 specifically to prepare boys for entry to Rugby, but by the time Bob arrived it was sending its pupils to a number of the leading public schools. Each of the houses was named after a naval or military commander and Bob was placed in Jellicoe (an admiral then at the height of his fame), possibly because at the time he entertained ideas of joining the Royal Navy. His academic progress up the school was slow at first. In the Summer Term of 1918, after two years at the school, he came first out of a form of twelve in one week and eighth in the next and in the subsequent exams. He was particularly good at arithmetic but, given his lifelong enthusiasm for books, surprisingly weak at English, his good use of grammar offset by poor spelling. In his last year, however, his academic performance was suddenly transformed, and in his final term in the top form he won the form prize.

He also excelled at sport, playing for the 1st XIs at football in the Autumn Term of 1919 and cricket (as wicket-keeper) in the Summer Terms of both 1919 and 1920. He was a member of a particularly strong cricket side, his contemporaries including Bryan Valentine, who went on to play for Cambridge, Kent and England, and Kenneth Carlisle, who later played for Oxford and Sussex.

There appears to have been no question but that Bob would follow his father to Eton, where he arrived for the Michaelmas Half in September 1920, being placed in A. E. Conybeare's House. His academic progress was comfortably above the average for his year, but by no means spectacular at first. He started specializing in Science, with a focus on Physics, at the beginning of his fourth year and in his last year moved to the Army Class, in which the curriculum omitted Classics altogether and concentrated on Maths, English, History and French as well as Science, which would become an abiding interest. Admission to the Army Class was by performance, and the very brightest boys could achieve this from the Removes, a year or more earlier than Bob; but his entry to it was still evidence of good academic achievement.

The Army Class was designed specifically for those destined for regular commissions via the Royal Military College, Sandhurst or the Royal Military Academy, Woolwich, its members sitting the Army Entrance Exam rather than the Higher School Certificate. Most if not all of those in the class were also in the Officers Training Corps, membership of which was not compulsory, even during the Great War. Bob had a very good career in the OTC, becoming in due course the company sergeant major of C Company, where he demonstrated qualities of 'efficiency, energy, reliability and patience'.[4] The Adjutant during his time was Oliver Leese, an Old Etonian on secondment from the Coldstream Guards, who would achieve considerable distinction in the Second World War, during which his path would cross Bob's.

Bob continued to show prowess at both football and cricket, appearing frequently in house teams at every level, without ever graduating to the school sides. In football his stature was an issue, the House Football Book in his first term describing him as 'A wonderful dribbler without much pace. He only came this half and picked up the game very quickly. He is very small.' Even two years later, when he was already playing for Conybeare's 1st XI, it was reported that he 'has wonderful control of the ball, but is very slow and small. He will be very good if he grows.' Similar comments were repeated until his last year, when the house lost narrowly in the semi-final of the knock-out competition and the post-season comment yet again was that he was a very good dribbler. He did not play really well until the House Ties, when he was brilliant.'

His stature may have been a handicap for another sport, boxing, but he reached the finals of the school competition as a lightweight. The report in the *Eton Chronicle* paid testament to his physical bravery. Having won the first round on points, he found himself cornered in the second and was badly shaken by a blow which nearly put him down. Notwithstanding that he was still very shaky, he came out for the third and final round, but was so badly punished that the fight had to be stopped.

It looked at one time as if he might have an excellent cricket career, not only for the house, having been a member of the Junior side in 1922 which won 13 games out of 14, but also potentially for the school. However, this was not to be. Robert Henriques, who was not himself at Eton but who had been a near contemporary at Lockers Park and knew him very well, wrote an article many years later which places an interesting slant on Bob's character:

> If he took the game seriously, said his housemaster at Eton, and if he would practise assiduously, he might play for the School at an earlier age than had ever been recorded in its annals. When he heard this, Laycock gave up cricket and took to rowing and he was careful not to excel at this new sport. Why did he behave like this? Because cricket was a game to be enjoyed, not turned into a business to make one's career.[5]

If Bob failed to make the top flight at school sport, he succeeded socially. The two most prestigious groups in each house were the House Debating Society, with some ten to fourteen members, and the House Library, with no more than six. Both were subject to election by the existing members, so provide good evidence of popularity. Bob was elected to the House Debating Society in the Michaelmas Half of 1923, speaking on a number of occasions, including on a motion proposed in February 1924 on 'Whether it is better to have a large army and navy or a large air force'. He came down decidedly in favour of the first.

No record of the membership of Conybeare's House Library has survived for the years when Bob was there. However, it is highly probably that he was a member, as he would otherwise have been unlikely to have achieved election to the Eton Society, or 'Pop' as it is more commonly known, a self-perpetuating oligarchy, whose members themselves choose who will fill any vacant places. There are no prefects, as such, at Eton, but members of Pop, distinguished by their coloured waistcoats and checked trousers, amount to much the same thing. The rules for election involve the use of white and black balls, contenders for the limited number of places being elected according to the number of white balls, with four or more black balls resulting in absolute rejection. Bob was proposed by the Earl of Feversham in March 1925, but blackballed. He was proposed again by T. A. Pilkington two months later and duly elected.

Of the thirty members of Pop during Bob's time, two were to be lifelong friends, Peter Cazalet and Peter Fleming, whilst another, Quintin Hogg, would later become Lord Chancellor. Many of his other contemporaries who were not in Pop would also remain part of Bob's life or re-enter it at a later date, all of them members of an Old Etonian network whose effectiveness has no equal.

Bob's penultimate term at Eton was disrupted by appendicitis. On 28 February he woke up to a terrible pain and was whisked off to Princess Christian's Nursing Home in Windsor to have the offending organ removed, remaining there for over two weeks. He was visited by a constant stream of friends and remarked in a handwritten diary that 'I had a case of port and a box of cigars sent to me',[6] so the regime does not appear to have been too rigorous. On 17 March he was picked up by his father's blue Rolls-Royce and driven to the family's London home at 47 Charles Street to continue his convalescence.

Shortly afterwards he was invited to accompany Joe to stay with the Duke of Westminster at Eaton Hall for the Grand National Meeting. During the racing at Aintree, another guest, a Colonel Hound, insisted that Joe should put Bob's name down for a commission in the Royal Horse Guards once he had passed out of Sandhurst.

Bob's name does not appear on the list of successful candidates for the Army Entrance Examination in June 1925, and it seems that he was actually the beneficiary of a procedure whereby the headmasters of certain public schools could nominate exceptional candidates for Sandhurst and Woolwich, who were then approved or otherwise by the Army Council. In any event, after attending the Eton OTC camp in August, Bob was admitted to the Junior Division of the Royal Military College on 4 September 1925 as a Gentleman Cadet in No 1 Company.

Chapter 3

Blues

The Commandant and the Adjutant at Sandhurst when Bob arrived were, respectively, Major General Charles Corkran and Captain Frederick 'Boy' Browning, the former late of and the latter seconded from the Grenadier Guards, and they demanded from the gentlemen cadets the high standards expected by that regiment. Browning in particular was a stickler for discipline and came down very hard on any cadet whom he felt showed less than full devotion to his work, although on one occasion when a battalion parade for the whole RMC went badly wrong, Bob expressed surprise in his diary at the Adjutant's lack of concern. This was, however, the exception rather than the rule. The Commissioning Parade on 14 July 1926, at the end of Bob's Intermediate Term, was notable for being the occasion on which Browning initiated the tradition of the Adjutant riding up the steps and into the Old College behind the Senior Term of cadets.

The course was a tough one, with a great deal of emphasis on drill under the instruction of NCOs from the Foot Guards, who would pick up on the slightest lack of attention to dress or inability to perform increasingly complex manoeuvres on the parade ground, with the offending cadets being punished accordingly. Physical Training also played a prominent role, particularly in the early months. There was a great deal of classroom work on all manner of subjects, as well as more practical training in marksmanship, map reading and signalling, accompanied by route marches in full battle order, staff rides and platoon and company exercises, some of which were at night, including one which required Bob's company to construct rafts to cross the Basingstoke Canal.

The commander of No. 1 Company was Major Richard O'Connor of the Cameronians, a highly respected officer who would go on to have an outstanding career. The same could also be said of another of the company officers, Captain Miles Dempsey of the Royal Berkshire Regiment, whom Bob would get to know a great deal better during the war. A third, Captain Alec Gatehouse of the Royal Tank Regiment, would also become a divisional commander. With this galaxy of talent one might have expected No. 1 Company to do very well, whereas in fact its performance was only average compared to No. 4 Company, which took all the honours during Bob's three terms at the RMC. He himself must have impressed his superiors, however, as he was promoted to corporal for the Intermediate Term. Given that he had got into serious trouble in the

Junior Term after drinking too much champagne one night, this showed both tolerance and remarkable insight on the part of his company commander. O'Connor's judgement was vindicated when Bob's leadership qualities resulted in his further promotion to senior under-officer, the top cadet in the company, for the Senior Term.

At Sandhurst there was a wider social mixture than Bob had previously encountered, partly because of a scheme in operation whereby promising non-commissioned officers could be nominated by their regiments to attend the RMC. There were eighteen of them in Bob's term, and the order of merit on passing out some fifteen months later showed all but two of these cadets in the top half of the list, among them the first three. It seems likely that they felt that they had more to prove than the direct entry cadets and worked harder as a result. There was also a great disparity in disposable income between them and their better-heeled contemporaries, which meant that they were less able to indulge in expensive pursuits in their spare time.

These constraints did not apply to Bob and his immediate friends, who led very full sporting and social lives in addition to their work. Bob kept a car at the RMC, but London was easily accessible by train and he took every opportunity to go there. The Laycock house at 47 Charles Street, in the heart of Mayfair, was constantly manned by servants and acted as a hotel for the whole family, at least one of whom seemed to be there whenever Bob visited. There was a strong pull back to Eton, even closer at hand to Sandhurst, as many of Bob's close friends were still at the college, whilst his brother Peter was now also there. Bob was even persuaded to represent the RMC against the college in the Field Game, a peculiarly Etonian sport which he had not played to any great extent whilst a pupil. The result was an inevitable defeat. He was more at home with polo, stabling his own ponies nearby.

In the summer vacation of 1926, Bob was invited by his friend John Crichton, Earl of Erne,[1] a fellow cadet and Old Etonian, to stay at his home in Northern Ireland, Crom Castle. After five days of sailing, shooting and riding, Bob left to catch the ferry from Larne to Stranraer and then travelled up to the far North-West of Scotland, where Joe and other members of the family were guests of the Duke of Westminster at Rosehall, his estate in Sutherland, staying aboard his newly acquired steam yacht *Cutty Sark*. Nothing to do with the sailing clipper of the same name, the vessel was even so of substantial size, 263ft in length and lavishly fitted out. Leaving the Duke behind, two days later the Laycocks sailed in the *Cutty Sark* down to London.

Having spent the rest of the holiday at Wiseton, Bob returned to Sandhurst for the Senior Term in early September and on 18 December he led No. 1 Company in the Commissioning Parade. The results for his term were announced just over a month later, showing that Bob had passed out 15th of the 108 cadets in his term. On 29 January 1927 he was commissioned into the Royal Horse Guards as a cornet,[2] joining the regiment on the following day.

The Royal Horse Guards (The Blues) was second only to the Life Guards[3] as the most senior regiment of the British Army. Raised originally in the Parliamentary cause by Sir Arthur Haselrig in 1650, it was called the Blues from the beginning after the colour of the coats worn by the men. Having served in Scotland initially, it played a significant role in the elevation of Oliver Cromwell as Lord Protector. The command then passed to Colonel Unton Croke and, as Unton Croke's Regiment of Horse, it was one of the three regiments which accompanied General George Monck, later Duke of Albemarle, on his march from Scotland in 1660 in support of the Restoration. After temporary disbandment it was re-raised by Charles II in 1661 as the Royal Regiment of Horse Guards. Its battle honours in the eighteenth and nineteenth centuries included Dettingen and Waterloo, and one squadron formed part of a composite regiment of Household Cavalry in the Cavalry Division under John French in South Africa, when Joe had met many of its officers. During the Great War it suffered from the difficulties experienced by the cavalry as a whole in finding a role for itself in trench warfare. After providing one squadron at a time as infantry, in 1918 the then two regiments of Life Guards and the Royal Horse Guards were converted to machine gun battalions, in which role they accompanied the final advance of the Allied armies. Having suffered considerable losses during the war, in 1919 the Household Cavalry reverted to its peacetime role, which was very largely ceremonial.

The Blues had been proposed by Joe's mother as a suitable regiment for him to join when he left school, only for Joe to reject the suggestion of a regular commission. It is not known what prompted her choice, but she presumably had contacts in the regiment. Joe himself knew it well from South Africa, and his friend, the Duke of Westminster, had served there with the regiment, before resigning his regular commission and joining the Cheshire Yeomanry. Moreover, when the time came to choose a regiment for Bob, the Colonel of the Blues, Field Marshal Earl Haig, happened to be another good friend of Joe's. During his Intermediate Term at Sandhurst Bob was vetted by the Commanding Officer, Lord Alastair Innes-Ker, who evidently approved of him.

There was a decidedly patrician feel to the Blues. During the late 1920s and early 1930s its officers would include the Dukes of Norfolk and Roxburghe, the Marquess of Waterford, the Earls of Erne (Bob's friend, John Crichton), Normanton and Sefton, Viscount Molyneux and Lords Forester, Stavordale and Sudeley, together with a smattering of baronets. The majority of the officers, however, came from the untitled landed gentry, who possessed the two main requirements for membership: they had to be at least competent horsemen and they needed independent means to keep them in the manner expected of them, which could not remotely have been achieved on their army pay. Bob met the specification and soon found that he fitted into this milieu very comfortably, helped initially by having another close and enduring friend, Richard Cotterell, a contemporary at Eton and Sandhurst, join the regiment on the same day.

The duties of an officer of the Blues were not particularly onerous. The subalterns were on a rota to be the Orderly Officer, although this duty was often swapped with a colleague to allow attendance at some social or sporting function. Acting as Orderly Officer was regarded as very tedious, the typical tasks involving attending the riding school, inspecting stables and barracks, sitting in on Educational Certificate exams, attending church parades, inspecting the Barracks Guard and turning it out after dinner.

The ceremonial duties of the two Household Cavalry regiments involved mounting the King's Life Guard at Horse Guards and providing escorts to the Sovereign for specific events, such as the State Opening of Parliament and Trooping the Colour, as well as escorting visiting royalty and occasionally more junior members of the Royal Family, for instance on the occasion of their wedding. The King's Life Guard came in two forms.[4] When the King was out of London, a Short Guard was mounted of a junior NCO and ten troopers commanded by a Corporal of Horse. When the King was in residence, the regiment on duty provided a Long Guard, commanded by an officer with the addition of a Corporal Major and a trumpeter. The guard was changed daily at 11.00 a.m. and the relief had to ride from the London barracks. The officer was thus required to stay overnight, but was allowed to entertain friends to lunch, tea and dinner in his rooms, so this was not necessarily an irksome duty. Moreover, on occasion he received an invitation himself to dine with the equivalent Foot Guards officer responsible for the Guard at St James's Palace.

Most of the ceremonial duties, and invariably the King's Life Guard, were carried out by the regiment which was based in London. When Bob joined the regiment, the London base was Regent's Park Barracks, but this was judged to be too small and in 1932 it was switched to Knightsbridge Barracks. The other regiment was at Combermere Barracks in Windsor, where it supposedly did field training, which Bob later said 'consisted of riding our horses about in the morning in Windsor and either attacking or defending the hill on which stood an equestrian statue of King George known as the Copper Horse.'[5] The two regiments exchanged places once a year. They also decamped at different times to Pirbright for part of the summer, where they took part in training and exercises, the latter often in conjunction with a battalion from the Foot Guards.

None of these moves interfered to a great extent with the officers' social activities, which were extensive, helped by the fact that most regimental duty was carried out in the mornings, leaving the afternoons and evenings free. It was, in fact, uncommon for a large number of officers to dine in the mess, other than on guest nights, and on a number of occasions, usually when acting as Orderly Officer, Bob found himself dining there completely alone. In such circumstances it was the tradition that the lone officer should be entitled to a bottle of champagne! More often Bob dined out in London, and very often lunched there as well, whether based at the time in London, Windsor or Pirbright. If he needed to be back in either of the last two in time for some form of duty or other activity on the following morning, he would catch the last train or, on the many occasions on which he missed it, summon a car from Daimler Hire. If he was not specifically required, he would usually stay at the family London home at 47 Charles Street, or at one of the number of London clubs at which he was a member, including the Turf, the Guards, Buck's, White's and Pratt's.

Much of Bob's social and sporting life involved other officers of the regiment. The Blues observed a very relaxed attitude to seniority, and Bob was often to be found in a social context in the company of officers of many years standing. When they were in the mess or off duty, all officers up to and including the rank of major addressed each other by their first names or nicknames, of which there were many – Peekaboo, Little Man, Fish, the Boob, the Hen and Whisky being some examples – whilst the commanding officer was called simply 'Colonel'. Formal mess etiquette was otherwise traditionally almost non-existent in the Household Cavalry and the Foot Guards, unlike in many more junior regiments.

Whilst the NCOs and other ranks enjoyed football, the sporting interests of most of the officers centred on horses. The Blues held its own annual Mounted Sports Day, and London District, the military area in which both the Foot Guards and the Household Cavalry served, ran a Bronze Medal Tournament in which Bob acquitted himself well in the Officers' Sword, Lance and Revolver Competition. He came second in the same discipline in the Royal Tournament of 1927. Both the Household Brigade and the Blues alone held their own race meetings or point-to-points, in which Bob occasionally distinguished himself, although the best rider over fences in the regiment at this time was Peter Grant-Lawson, who in 1932 won the Grand Military Gold Cup at Sandown Park, the premier race for amateur military jockeys, and came a very creditable fifth in the Grand National a week later.

Bob was also a very capable polo player and began playing very early in his career, representing the regiment or its B Team on frequent occasions. This was not a period of notable success for the Blues in the sport, early elimination from the two main competitions, the Subalterns Cup and the Inter Regimental Cup, being commonplace, but there were still a number of satisfying wins. Bob also played for a number of other teams at Hurlingham, Roehampton and Ranelagh. In 1929, in the knowledge that he was to be away from London for much of the summer, he sold all his ponies and did not play at all, but he returned to the sport the following year.

The late autumn and winter were devoted to hunting. All the cavalry regiments encouraged their officers to hunt as frequently as possible at weekends and granted special 'hunting leave', lasting weeks in some cases, on the grounds that this was a more useful way of occupying them than having them either hanging around the barracks or spending too much time on their social lives. Bob's favourite hunts were the Quorn and the Belvoir. Although his father no longer owned Newport Lodge in Melton Mowbray, the meets were easily accessible by car from Wiseton and the horses were stabled locally with friends. Very often other members of the family would participate. However, Bob also stayed at a succession of country houses owned by his various friends for both hunting and shooting, as well as for out-of-town social events such as hunt balls.

If purely military activity did not appear to take up a great deal of a subaltern's life, it was not entirely forgotten. The annual visits to Pirbright were complemented by the bi-annual camp for manoeuvres on Salisbury Plain, in which selected squadrons of the Life Guards and the Blues were merged into the Household Cavalry Composite Regiment – something which, it was understood, would happen in the event of a war. Although the accommodation was in tents, the usual standards were upheld and, as London was too far away, the evenings were largely devoted to drinking large quantities of champagne and playing chemin-de-fer.

In May 1928 Bob and some of his fellow officers went down to Larkhill for machine gun training, together with officers from the Life Guards, King's Dragoon Guards and 17th/21st Lancers. He must have shown some aptitude, as three months later he was sent on an eight-week course in machine gunnery at the Small Arms School at Netheravon. Regular trips to London were made difficult by the fact that the work was time-consuming and difficult; indeed, Bob thought that much of it was above his head and those of the other attendees. Weekends were free, but staying at Wiseton necessitated a very long journey, although he managed to go twice by dint of the fact that there was no work on Friday afternoons. However, Bob's half-sister, Kathleen, and her husband, Bill Rollo, had a house at Oare, near Marlborough, where he was made welcome, whilst another friend had taken a cottage near Lymington, so he was able to get away whenever his duties permitted.

The course, which he passed successfully, did at least provide him with one practical modern military skill, in which he was otherwise seriously lacking. His reward was to take command of the regiment's machine gunners. In the following summer of 1929 he was appointed as instructor in machine gunnery at the annual camp of the Cheshire Yeomanry, staying at Eaton Hall, the seat of the Duke of Westminster, which was rather more comfortable than a tent. He much enjoyed the company and at the end of the camp a large ball was given by the Duke, so from Bob's point of view it was a thoroughly satisfactory experience. Not long afterwards he was appointed to command the Household Cavalry Machine Gun Troop and in the following year he returned again to instruct the Cheshire Yeomanry, their annual camp on this occasion being near Scarborough.

His military education continued with a battlefield tour of Northern France. He later wrote in his diary: 'As an amusing trip the thing was a great success but as an instruction tour it was a complete failure.' On the first day, the senior officer, Major A. C. 'Fish' Turnor, who was leading the tour, never knew where he was; on the second, they failed to find General Sir Horace Smith-Dorrien,[6] who had been brought in specially to conduct the party over the battlefield of Le Cateau, where he had commanded; and on the third, the guide was a French officer who neither spoke nor understood English. In the end Turnor was persuaded to call off the rest of the tour, and Bob and a number of others spent the remaining day at Le Touquet, where they lost a lot of money at the casino.

By the early 1930s Bob had begun to wonder about his future in the Army. It was common, particularly in the Household and Line Cavalry Regiments, for young officers to join as subalterns, only to leave after a few years to manage their family estates.[7] This happened in the case of a number of Bob's contemporaries, notably Richard Cotterell and Harry Stavordale, to both of whom Bob had acted as best man at their weddings. Joe was dead set against his son resigning and could not understand why he was not more enthusiastic about the Army as a profession. In the peacetime army, however, promotion was exceptionally slow. Bob had been promoted to lieutenant in early 1930, but was unlikely to achieve his captaincy for several more years, and it might be another decade before he was a major. Moreover, he was getting bored. Like many others in the same situation he needed a fresh challenge, and in his case he chose to go to sea.

Chapter 4

Barque

In his love of boats and the sea Bob took after Joe. Indeed, his original career preference had been for the Royal Navy, but it seems that he was firmly overruled by his father. Although Joe himself no longer owned a vessel, he continued to sail and was a member of the Royal Yacht Squadron. In June 1930 he was a guest on the King's yacht *Britannia*, which was competing in a big race in the Solent, when Bob passed in a very similar yacht, *Brynhild*, as a guest of the owner on a cruise from Southampton to Torquay and back. This was the first occasion on which Bob had been sailing, other than in small boats, since he had joined the Army.

Bob was clearly much taken with this pastime and that summer returned to sea on a number of other occasions, on either friends' or chartered boats, usually from the Beaulieu River or the Hamble. His principal companion on most of these occasions was Antony Head, a subaltern in the Life Guards, whom Bob had known at both Eton and Sandhurst, albeit in a higher term in each case. Head was now to become one of his closest friends and one whose path he would frequently cross professionally as well as socially. He had been commissioned five months before Bob into the 15th/19th Hussars, but had transferred to the Life Guards in 1928. The two men had renewed their acquaintance several months before his transfer, whilst Bob was at Larkhill and Head was also there learning how to train horses. They got on very well and, once Head had joined the Household Cavalry, found many opportunities to socialise together.

Bob and Head had one particular leisure activity in common other than yachting, which was burglary! This sport, for so it was treated by the participants, was all the rage in the upper classes of the time, possibly inspired by the film 'Raffles', based on the books by E. W. Hornung, which was released in 1930 starring Ronald Colman as the 'Amateur Cracksman'.[1] The objective was to break into a house of a friend, remove a valuable item which would certainly be missed, and return it again two or three nights later. Bob, as it happened, already had form: his Old Etonian friend, Lord Feversham, when staying at Wiseton had boasted that he had made his house burglar-proof. Bob immediately bet him £50 that he would be burgled within the next three months, with Rosemary and Peter each weighing in for same amount. Six weeks later, there was a burglary!

The qualities required for success were stealth and nerve, which would certainly be useful to Bob in later years, and, for the most part, the perpetrators went undetected. Not always, however! On one occasion, whilst the Household Cavalry Composite Regiment was at Tidworth and Head was there on other business, the two men broke into Beaulieu Abbey, where a friend of theirs was staying, and purloined a statue, which was then put on display in the mess. Three nights later they returned to reinstate it, only to be disturbed as they were doing so. They fled, concealing their identities by the skin of their teeth, and drove to Southampton, only to find that all the hotels were full so they had to sleep on the floor of a rather dirty boarding house, a suitable punishment for their crime!

Most of their sailing was for a day at a time, but in early October 1930 Bob, Head and two others chartered the yacht *Baroque* for an expedition across the English Channel to Le Havre, from where they visited Amiens and Rouen. Over the winter months Bob's reading list included Claud Worth's *Yacht Navigation and Voyaging*, six volumes by Captain O. M. Watts on coastal navigation and, most tellingly, *By Way of Cape Horn* by A. J. Villiers, the account of a voyage in a fully rigged ship from Australia to Ireland in 1929.

Bob and Head returned to the water in the early summer of 1931, spending a number of weekends yachting and also looking at boats, including a Bristol cutter, with a possible view to purchase. By this time, however, Bob was planning a far more ambitious project, in which he hoped to emulate the exploits of his father in sailing to Australia in the *Pericles* in 1894. It was unlikely that he would be allowed enough time to undertake such a long voyage and return again to England, but he applied for six months leave, which would at least enable him to cover a considerable part of the route. There was no objection from his regiment, but the War Office proved to be very difficult. After considerable wrangling, Bob was eventually granted permission for up to six months leave, on condition that only the first two months would be paid leave and that the rest of the time spent away would count for neither pay nor increase of pay nor time towards promotion. It was pointed out to him that the lost months might make a big difference to his military career in a peacetime army in which the promotion of junior officers was awarded strictly by seniority; but he remained determined to go ahead.

The next step was to choose the ship. Bob's enquiries revealed that a number of shipping companies accepted passengers on sailing vessels. He approached some agencies in the City of London and had a reply in early May from Clarksons, advising him that they had chartered the *Herzogin Cecilie* to carry a cargo of timber from South Finland to Lourenço Marques and Beira in Portuguese East Africa and expected it to sail from Kotka in Finland in the second week of August. Clarksons estimated the length of the voyage at 80 to 90 days, which would allow Bob to sail out and return comfortably within the period allowed for his leave. A few days later he was able to look over the *Archibald Russell*, a very similar barque owned by the same company, which was berthed at the

Victoria Docks, and he liked what he saw. He asked Clarksons to contact the owner of the *Herzogin Cecilie* and received a reply in early July to say that the passenger accommodation had recently been renovated and that there were now four cabins available, three of which had already been reserved. The fourth was still free, the terms being ten shillings per day, £45 being payable in advance for a 90-day voyage, any difference either way to be adjusted prior to disembarking. He immediately cabled Clarksons with instructions to reserve the last cabin.

The *Herzogin Cecilie* was a four-masted barque, with no auxiliary propulsion, built specifically for the Norddeutsche Lloyd Bremen line and launched in 1902. She operated in both the Chilean nitrate and Australian wheat trades and was one of the fastest of her type, on one occasion achieving a time of 106 days from Portland, Oregon to the Lizard around Cape Horn. Interned by Chile during the Great War, she was handed over to France as part of the post-war reparations and sold to Gustaf Erikson, a ship owner based in Mariehamn in the Åland Islands off the south-east of Finland. At over 3,000 tons, with a length of 334ft and a sail area of 30,000 square feet, she nevertheless only required a permanent crew of thirty-one. She had no licence to carry passengers and Bob thus had to sign on as a temporary crew member.

The timing of the voyage was far from precise, but Clarksons recommended that Bob should join the vessel at Copenhagen, where she would have to call in order to take on stores and where Bob could obtain precise details of signing on and boarding from the local agents. Having obtained a letter of credit from his bank and armed with two bottles of champagne from his brother Peter and a bottle of vintage brandy from Antony Head, on the evening of 4 August he took a train from Liverpool Street to Harwich, boarded an overnight ferry to Esbjerg and travelled on by train to Copenhagen, where he stayed in the Hotel Angleterre.

The initial news from the agents was that the *Herzogin Cecilie* was unlikely to arrive for a few days, but walking around the city on the following day, Bob spotted her entering the roads and dropping anchor. He immediately hired a launch out to the ship to look around and later met the captain, Sven Erikson, who was only twenty-eight years old and spoke good English. On the following day he signed on as a member of the crew, bought a case of whisky for the voyage and took some of his luggage out to the ship, in which he had been allocated a spacious double cabin. However, due to the wind being contrary, she did not sail until 14 August, so Bob spent much of the time in the company of Peter Kasberg, a young Dane working in London whom he had met on the journey to Copenhagen and who showed him the city and introduced him to his family.

Once under way, Bob was able to take stock of the crew and his fellow passengers. Of the former he would be closest during the voyage to the captain and the three mates, as they would all eat together in the saloon. There were three other passengers, two of whom were a German called Selle, a man of about thirty-five, and a very fat Dane called Knudsen. The third was an American heiress and divorcee, Miss Rickson, who had met the captain and the second mate ashore and decided to come on the voyage, much to their delight.

From the start Bob was determined to join the crew in their work and spent much of the first few days climbing the masts and familiarizing himself with the rigging: by ten days out he was able to go aloft with some confidence to help setting and taking sail. He did not have to stand watch, but he frequently volunteered to help in any task. He also began to take lessons in navigation from the captain, finding before long that he was able to work out the ship's position by himself. Initially the weather was fair, indeed the ship was becalmed for a time off Fair Isle, but six days out the wind freshened from the north-east, driving her into the North Atlantic. However, as Bob soon realized, it was highly capricious as to both strength and direction, one moment too light, the next blowing a gale; indeed, by twelve days out from Copenhagen the weather was the worst that the captain had seen in that part of the Atlantic, and several sails were shredded before they could be taken in. The captain blamed the crew, of whose members he held a low opinion except for the donkeyman[2] and the sailmaker, who was now kept very busy converting canvas into new sails. Both Selle and Knudsen retired to their bunks for the duration of the storm, but Miss Rickson was in her element, as was Bob.

The officers turned out to be most hospitable, and large quantities of alcohol were consumed in the saloon, the most popular form being schnapps, although other drinks were available, including Bob's own supply of Scotch. Miss Rickson, unfortunately, was incapable of realizing when she had had enough and had frequently to be carried off to bed. When not working with the crew or learning how to navigate, Bob spent a lot of time reading, having brought with him a plentiful supply of books, including several on sailing themes. In calm weather he discovered that the place where he stood the greatest chance of being undisturbed was up on the mizzen top.

By 5 September, twenty-two days out, the ship was off the Cape Verde Islands and making satisfactory progress. When the wind was light, especially in the Doldrums, it became intolerably hot in Bob's cabin and he took to carrying some of his bedding on deck and sleeping on the after hatch.

On 18 September, thirty-five days out, the *Herzogin Cecilie* crossed the Equator, and on the following day the traditional ceremonies were conducted, which Bob considered somewhat barbarous. All those who had not previously crossed the line were compelled to undergo ritual humiliation by members of the crew playing the Doctor, the Barber, the Policeman and Neptune. Much of their hair was cut or shaved off and they were daubed alternately with soft soap worked up into a lather, tar and red paint, before being dunked in a tarpaulin bath full of sea water. Most, including Bob, took it in good heart, but the cook objected and tried to escape, only to be recaptured and subjected to even more drastic treatment.

This was, however, as nothing to the events which took place later. It was traditional to entertain the crew to drinks and cakes after the ceremony, but, unbeknown to the captain, Miss Rickson became very drunk and insisted on taking even more alcohol to the fo'c'sle, where the crew's quarters were located. Knudsen in the meantime obtained the captain's permission to do the same thing. The result was a high state of inebriation for all, during which Miss Rickson claimed that the first mate had accused her of sleeping with one of the crew, became hysterical and had to be forcibly removed. Selle tried to defend her, attacked the captain and was knocked down for his pains, then handcuffed and locked in his cabin. Miss Rickson, in the meantime, threw the key of her cabin through the porthole in anticipation of being locked in herself. It was 1.30 the next morning before things had quietened down sufficiently for Bob to retire to bed, leaving the first mate to finish mopping up the blood.

Relations between some of the occupants of the saloon were understandably somewhat frosty the next day, but gradually improved thereafter. The ship was now far closer to Brazil than to Africa, her course determined by the north-easterly trade winds, and it was not until 4 October, fifty-one days out of Copenhagen, that she picked up the westerlies, which were followed a few days later by a northerly gale. This enabled her to re-cross the Atlantic, passing 80 miles south of Tristan da Cunha. Bob, to his dismay, was bitten by the captain's Alsatian dog, leaving a large wound in his hand which should really have been stitched and made it impossible for him to carry out some of the seamen's jobs, especially those aloft.

The *Herzogin Cecilie* was now well to the south of the Cape of Good Hope and on a poor course for her destination, hampered by encountering the worst storm of the voyage, with all canvas taken in other than three storm-sails. The captain brought the ship up into the wind so that she was almost stationary. Moreover, it was very cold, and Bob resorted to spending a lot of time in the galley, the warmest part of the ship. A pig which the cook had been feeding up died in mysterious circumstances and had to be buried at sea; as the ship had by now also run out of potatoes, the cook was reduced to serving salt meat and stockfish, which Bob found distinctly unpleasant, whereas previously the food had been good.

At last the wind turned into the south, driving the vessel towards her destination. Two days later it changed direction, blowing the vessel on absolutely the opposite course. Shortly afterwards, however, the wind swung round yet again and three days later land was sighted for the first time since the vessel had lain off Fair Isle. The landfall was excellent, just off the mouth of the Limpopo River and not far north of Lourenço Marques. After going aground briefly in

Delagoa Bay, the *Herzogin Cecilie* was taken in tow by the pilot boat and dropped anchor at 17.42 on 1 November, seventy-nine days out of Copenhagen.

The next two and a half weeks were spent at Lourenço Marques, where Bob bought a sun helmet and two cotton suits and generally amused himself, either alone, with his fellow passengers or some of the officers or, on a few occasions, with an attractive German girl. A number of letters from England were waiting for him there, including from his father, who was in a nursing home suffering from rheumatoid arthritis, his mother, his sisters, Head and Cotterell; he was able to cable news of his arrival and send off his replies. There was a good hotel and some reasonable cafés, and on one occasion he, the captain and the first mate went to a bull fight.

On 19 November the *Herzogin Cecilie* weighed anchor bound for Beira, a mere four days sailing. There Bob was taken in hand by a British expatriate, a Mr Golding, and given temporary membership of the club. On 30 November he bade his farewells to Captain Erikson and his officers and crew and boarded the SS *Calgary*, a relatively modern small cargo ship of the Elder Dempster Line with accommodation for a number of passengers, although on this occasion Bob was the only one. It was clean and comfortable, the officers were very agreeable and the food was good. Bob took lessons in navigation from the third mate, which made him realize that what he had been taught aboard the *Herzogin Cecilie* had been somewhat rough and ready. The ship arrived in Durban on 3 December.

Bob's stay in Durban was disrupted by a bout of food poisoning, but he was well enough to arrange a passage back to England on the SS *Guildford Castle*, an 8,000 ton passenger ship of the Union Castle Line, on which he was allocated a very small cabin, about half the size of the one he had occupied on the *Herzogin Cecilie*. She sailed early on the morning of 6 December and by lunchtime he was thoroughly bored. The other passengers were dull, and he felt idle and unfit after all the activity he had been used to. He received the permission of the captain to go up to the bridge and indulge his new enthusiasm for navigation, but other than a brief call at Tenerife, there was nothing much else to amuse him and he was very pleased when the ship docked at Southampton very early on the last day of 1931.

It would be an exaggeration to say that the voyage was the making of Bob, but he had clearly derived a great deal of benefit from the experience. He understood the sea very much better, he had acquired a new skill in navigation, he had learnt to work as part of a team under pressure in extreme conditions and he had obtained a new qualification, that of registered Finnish able seaman, which might have seemed at the time unlikely to advance his chosen career, but which was to do so in circumstances which he could never have foreseen. As far as his character was concerned, he had demonstrated qualities of courage, determination and tolerance and learned how to fit in with people whose background was far removed from his own.

He was not yet quite done with the *Herzogin Cecilie*. In June 1932 the ship put in to Liverpool for dry docking on her return voyage to the Baltic and Bob went up to see her, entertaining Erikson and the first mate to dinner at the Adelphi, before returning with them to stay the night in his old cabin. He had arranged for his father, now recovered from his illness, two brothers and sister Rosemary, together with some other friends, to take passage on the barque for the short voyage to Copenhagen, so that they could get some idea of what he had experienced. Moreover, later that summer Antony Head embarked in the ship to undertake the same voyage as Bob.

Chapter 5

Angie

The rhythm of Bob's life returned to normal immediately. The Blues were in London, so acting as Orderly Officer and standing Guard did not preclude a full social programme. As Bob had not taken the full six months leave allowed by the War Office, he was also able to get in his fair share of hunting. The only disruption came when he was operated on for a longstanding sinus problem.

Bob's family continued to play a large part in his life, and he paid frequent visits to Wiseton and to the homes of his two sisters. Rosemary and Joyce had both married in 1927, Rosemary to the Hon. Arthur Baillie, who had served in the Life Guards in the Great War, and Joyce to the Hon. Edward Greenall, always known to family and friends as Toby, who had also served briefly in the Life Guards and was on the Reserve of Officers. Greenall came from a well-known brewing family and was a keen huntsman who was to be Joint Master of the Belvoir between 1934 and 1937. Joyce herself had a thirst for excitement, manifested not only in hunting, in which she emulated her mother in her fearlessness, but also in her participation in ladies' polo. Furthermore, she developed an enthusiasm for flying and acquired her own aeroplane, a De Havilland 60M Moth, in which she took Bob for a ride soon after his return from Africa. Some months later she had a bad accident in the plane, but emerged relatively unscathed.

Given, or perhaps because of, Bob's recent experience, there was surprisingly little sailing that summer, other than a weekend on the Norfolk Broads, as different from the South Atlantic as it was possible to be. By contrast, Bob committed a great deal of his time to polo, playing for the Blues in a team which reached the semi-final of the Subaltern's Cup, which they lost narrowly 5-3 to the Life Guards, and for a number of other teams as well.

Bob's military career was also showing signs of progress. In March 1932 he took over the Signals Troop of the regiment and later that year attended a signalling course at Catterick, earning an Instructor's Certificate. In June 1933 he succeeded 'Piggy' Grant-Lawson as Adjutant of the Blues, a significant appointment. He should strictly have attended one other course usually expected of cavalry adjutants, at the Army School of Equitation, but he was already a first-class horseman and this doubtless counted in his favour. It seems likely that by this time he had shown himself to be a more thoughtful soldier than many of his contemporaries, and certainly his reading list of this period provides evidence of both a catholic taste and an enquiring mind. In early 1932 he wrote an essay on 'Discipline', which he submitted to his Commanding Officer, who thought it very good and forwarded it to HQ London District, whose comment was 'most interesting'. In this he drew on his experiences both in the army and at sea, noting that 'The well disciplined man will, in cases of extreme emergency, danger or fatigue, perform certain automatic actions with surprising reliability', but also pointing out that 'Discipline must never be driven to its ultimate conclusion when all initiative is destroyed.'[1] This balance would certainly be reflected in his approach to discipline less than a decade later.

The Commanding Officer of the Royal Horse Guards by now was Lieutenant Colonel D. C. Boles, who had succeeded 'Fish' Turnor in June 1930 after the latter's unexpected death in a road accident. Boles had only transferred from the 17th/21st Lancers to the Blues in 1929, as a brevet lieutenant colonel and second-in-command, due to the lack of majors of sufficient seniority. He came with a record of achievement both at Eton, where he had been President of 'Pop' and scored 183 runs at Lord's against Harrow, a record which still stands, and at polo, in an era in which the 17th Lancers and, after its merger in 1922, the 17th/21st Lancers, had dominated the Inter-Regimental Cup, winning in every year bar one from 1920 to 1930. Boles himself had been selected to play for the British Army against the United States Army in 1925. He was thus most acceptable to his new regiment.

The Adjutant was the only officer in the regiment, other than the Quartermaster, expected to make a significant day-to-day commitment to his work. The Quartermaster, who was responsible for stores, supplies and transport, was traditionally a lieutenant or captain who had been promoted from the ranks, and although he was a member of the officer's mess, he would expect no further promotion. The Adjutant, by contrast, was an officer with excellent career prospects, who dealt with all other aspects of organization and administration and was effectively the chief of staff to the Commanding Officer. He was also responsible, together with the Regimental Corporal Major, for general discipline and for the appearance of the regiment at parades and inspections and on formal occasions, which were significantly greater in number for the Household Cavalry than for any other cavalry regiment. His additional duties meant that he received higher pay than others of his rank.

Whilst the regiment was on duty in London, the Adjutant also held a ceremonial appointment in the Royal Household, that of Silver Stick Adjutant-in-Waiting, supporting the Commanding Officer, who acted as Silver Stick-in-Waiting. This required Bob to ride in the procession for the annual Trooping the Colour and to attend levées and investitures at Buckingham Palace. There were also other formal occasions, the most notable of which during Bob's tenure was the funeral of King George V on 28 January 1936 at which he walked behind the Dominion High Commissioners, together with his equivalent in the Foot Guards, the Adjutant-in-Brigade-Waiting, and the Crown Equerry. During the preceding week Bob, with three other officers from the Blues, had taken his turn to stand guard in full dress uniform around the late King's coffin at the lying-in-state in Westminster Hall.

Bob was still a lieutenant when he began his new job, but passed his exams for captain and was promoted on 2 June 1934. At about the same time Boles was succeeded as CO by Lieutenant Colonel F. B. de Klee, who was the last serving officer to have been in the regiment at the outbreak of the Great War.

With his considerable additional responsibilities, Bob's social and sporting activities were necessarily somewhat curtailed. However, in the winter of 1933/34 he fell head over heels in love, and most of his energy outside the regiment was now to be devoted to securing the hand in marriage of the party in question. This was not the first time that he had been smitten, but his previous experiences had not followed a conventional path and matrimony had certainly not been seriously considered by either party.

Shortly before his eighteenth birthday, Bob had been at Aintree for the Grand National, where he met Katie Crichton, 'who was perfectly charming'.[2] He saw her again the following day, when he sat in Lord Sefton's box with her, and again the day after that. Quite how the relationship developed is not clear, but by the summer of 1926, when Bob was in his Intermediate Term at Sandhurst, he was seeing her on most of his visits to London, but almost always in the company of others. In the summer vacation, as he was about to go to Wiseton and she was off elsewhere, he wrote in his diary: 'Fear that I will not see her again for ages'.

Katie Crichton was born Katherine Trefusis in June 1881 and was thus forty-five when Bob met her at Aintree. She married the Hon. Arthur Crichton, the third son of the 4th Earl of Erne, in the year before Bob was born and they had two children, Michael, who was the same age as Bob and a contemporary at Eton, and Jean, who was born in 1911. Her nephew by marriage was Bob's close friend John Crichton, who succeeded his grandfather as Earl of Erne in 1914. She and Arthur lived in London at 8 Southwick Crescent,[3] but she spent much time with her sister Margaret, who lived with her husband, Lieutenant Colonel Edgar Brassey, at Dauntsey Park in Wiltshire.

No diary exists from July 1926 to 6 October 1927, by which time Bob and Katie were carrying on a full-blown affair. She was still living with her husband, but it is clear that they led significantly separate lives, as they were almost never mentioned in each other's company in the society columns of the period. Although Arthur had served in the Gordon Highlanders in both the Boer War and the Great War, he was no professional soldier. He had gained a degree at Oxford and then gone into the City, where he had a distinguished career in the insurance and investment trust industries. He almost certainly had little time for society gatherings and was frequently away on business, on at least one occasion in America, whilst his wife was a prominent hostess. It is even possible that he condoned what was going on, sometimes under his own roof, as a harmless dalliance.

To Bob, however, it was anything but that. His affair with Katie was made much easier by the fact that she was completely *persona grata* with his own family, staying at Wiseton on a number of occasions, lunching or dining regularly at 47 Charles Street and even joining the family party in Paris on the occasion of the wedding of Bob's half-brother, Lord Francis Hill. The opportunities for intimacy were necessarily somewhat constrained, but he and Katie took them when they could.

This state of affairs continued until December 1928, when Bob recorded that 'Katie and I had a long, serious and dreadful talk'.[4] Thereafter the relationship changed. The couple do not appear to have continued as lovers, but a strong friendship remained, with the later introduction of a third party, Katie's daughter Jean, who was by then seventeen and about to come out into society. Katie and Jean used to go out together with Bob and were often joined by a fourth, usually either Bob's brother Peter, or Antony Head. They were often away from London, visiting cathedrals all over the country or sailing together. In February 1931 Bob, Katie, Jean and Peter spent a week in the Netherlands, seeing the sights in Delft, Leiden, the Hague and Amsterdam, and similar gatherings resumed after Bob's return from his sea voyage.

In the summer of 1929, in the light of the changed relationship with Katie, Bob began an affair with a woman known in his diary only as Doris. He saw her quite frequently during that autumn, but a 'fateful weekend' in Paris was the beginning of the end of their affair, which petered out early in the next year. Since then he had had no regular girlfriend, although he certainly became closer to Jean Crichton. If there was more to this, it came to nothing, as Jean married Eion Merry, a fellow officer of Bob's in the Blues, in May 1933.

Bob's life then changed. At a meet during the 1933/34 hunting season, he was introduced to Angela Dudley Ward. She did not ride, but he was nevertheless strongly attracted to her and by April 1934 was making it quite clear that he wanted to take their relationship further, possibly even to make it permanent.

Angie, as she was known to all, was born on 25 May 1916, the daughter of William Dudley Ward and his wife, Freda. Ward was the great-grandson of the 10th Lord Ward and his mother was the daughter of the 1st Viscount Esher. He was an outstanding oarsman at Eton and Cambridge and had also succeeded as a yachtsman, notably as a member of the British 8-metre crew which won the bronze medal in the 1908 Olympic Games. He was elected to the House of Commons as the Liberal member for Southampton in 1906, serving as a senior whip under Herbert Asquith and later under David Lloyd George, who was Angie's godfather.

Freda Dudley Ward was the daughter of Colonel Charles Birkin and his American wife Claire, and the granddaughter of Sir Thomas Birkin, who had made his fortune in the Nottingham lace industry. She was famous for having become the mistress of the Prince of Wales, later King Edward VIII, in 1918. Their affair lasted five years, but she remained his close confidante until 1934, when the relationship was abruptly broken off by the Prince following his new attachment to Wallis Simpson. Freda and Ward had long lived separate lives, but it was only in 1931 that that they were divorced. This was handled in a civilized way and, although they lived apart (indeed, Ward moved later to Canada) he and Freda continued to see each other and even on occasion to go on holiday together.

The Wards had two daughters, Penelope, born in 1914, and Angie. If Angie was unquestionably attractive, her sister, always called Pempie, was a real beauty, appearing in a number of films in the 1930s and '40s. The two sisters were always close to each other and to their mother.

Bob's pursuit of Angie was by no means smooth. She did not entirely approve of his profession and was, moreover, nine years younger, on one occasion taunting him as a 'cradle-snatcher'. He countered the accusation by telling her that she was a spoilt little girl and accusing her of being cold and beautiful, for which he subsequently had to apologize. Not long after they met, she went to the United States to visit her mother's relatives, and Bob's mood was not improved by her aunt, Vera Seely, telling him that she thought Angie was having far too good a time there and might not return.

Bob had already agreed to accompany Katie Crichton on a cruise in the Mediterranean in August 1934, sailing in a Yugoslav ship, the SS *Kraljica Maria*, from Venice to the Greek Islands and Constantinople. He wrote to Angie to say that he would have loved the trip if he had not been missing her so badly and that he was proving poor company for Katie. He spent as much time as he could on the bridge so that he could avoid the other passengers, although he did concede that there were some who were not too bad. Not long after his return he was away again, for a week's shooting on Islay, during which a distinct chill entered the relationship, one letter being addressed to 'Dear Angela' and signed 'Yours sincerely, Robert Laycock';[5] but within days of his return he received 'the sweetest and most divine letter'[6] from her and all was well again. He finally proposed to her at Doncaster Racecourse, and they announced their engagement on 17 November 1934.

The wedding took place at St Margaret's, Westminster, on 24 January 1935. The best man was Antony Head and the eight pages were dressed in copies of Life Guards uniforms of a century earlier. Warrant officers, NCOs and troopers of the Blues formed a guard of honour, their swords raised in an arch as the bride and groom emerged after the ceremony, and a bouquet from the regiment was presented to Angie by a squadron corporal major. The reception was held in Lady Cunard's house at 7 Grosvenor Square, following which Bob and Angie left for their honeymoon on Cyprus.

That July Bob was able to return the compliment to Antony Head by acting as best man at his wedding to Lady Dorothea Ashley-Cooper. Head had been appointed Adjutant of the Life Guards a week after Bob's wedding, which was highly convenient as the two men had to liaise on all manner of business, including the annual exchange of barracks between Windsor and Hyde Park and the activities of the Composite Regiment. The Laycocks and the Heads became very close friends, often sailing together. They never purchased a boat, but chartered them, very often vessels of quite substantial size, for longer or shorter periods as appropriate.

At the time of Bob and Angie's wedding the Blues were at Windsor, so the couple bought a house in Ascot called Heron's Brook. The regiment returned to London later that year, with Bob's term as Adjutant expiring in the following summer, giving him more time to devote to his family, which grew with the birth on 2 September 1936 of Edwina Ottillie Jane Laycock, always called Tilly, in the very nursing home in which Bob had had the operation on his sinuses. Bob was now second-in-command of a squadron, in which capacity he sometimes commanded a Captain's Escort on state occasions. The most notable of these came in May 1937, when King George VI and Queen Elizabeth, with the young princesses, drove in a carriage through Eton and Windsor a few days after their Coronation, in which Bob had acted as one of the marshals of the procession.

At that time Bob had not long returned from an anti-gas course at Winterbourne Gummer. One day in the early spring of 1937 he happened to walk into the Orderly Room to find his successor as Adjutant, Jackie Ward, seriously worried about getting on the wrong side of one of the officers by nominating him to this rather obscure course, on which a place had been allocated to the regiment by the War Office. Bob, however, had always been interested in chemistry and it suited his book to be away for a few weeks because, as he wrote later:

> An Adjutant, if he has been efficient, has almost certainly made himself fairly unpleasant from time to time, not so much with the N.C.O.s and other ranks, but with his own brother officers both junior and, as the Colonel's mouthpiece, to a certain extent to the Squadron Leaders and their seconds-in-command who are, of course, his seniors.[7]

He found when he arrived at the course that he was regarded with some suspicion as a member of the Household Brigade. Bob, however, had never been a snob and possessed an extraordinary ability to make friends with all sorts and conditions of men, as had been demonstrated aboard the *Herzogin Cecilie*, so he got on well with his fellow students. His interest in chemistry allowed him to grasp the subject matter better than most and, in spite of the fact that the instructors kept gassing the students, on one occasion knocking Bob out cold for two hours, he enjoyed it very much. At its conclusion, to the surprise of many, he was one of only two to be graded 'Distinguished' and was awarded an Instructor's Certificate.

Angie took the opportunity of Bob's three-week absence to sail to New York, leaving the six-month old Tilly in the care of a nanny at Heron's Brook, where Bob visited her at weekends.

One officer on the course, Major George Pennycook, was considerably senior to his fellow students, which puzzled Bob and the others. At the dinner to mark the end of the course, Pennycook asked if Bob was genuinely interested in chemical warfare and, on receiving a reply in the affirmative, enquired how he might respond if he was invited to become an instructor at a new gas school being set up by the War Office in Chatham. Bob replied that he would be flattered but surprised. Some months later, he heard that the school was indeed being established to provide advanced instruction and he asked Bertie de Klee if he might attend a course there. De Klee was happy to recommend him, only to receive a reply from the War Office that Bob was not sufficiently well qualified. To the surprise of both men, a further communication was then received to ask if he was available, not as a student, but as an instructor. De Klee replied that if Bob was not sufficiently qualified to be a student, he could hardly be qualified as an instructor. The War Office responded rather tartly that they would be the best judge of that! It subsequently turned out that Pennycook had attended the course at Winterbourne Gummer in preparation for his imminent appointment as the Chief Instructor there and that he had strongly recommended Bob.

Accordingly, on 3 January 1938, Bob reported for duty at the School of Military Engineering at Chatham.

Chapter 6

Gas

When Bob read the joining instructions for his attachment to the School of Military Engineering, he found to his dismay that the term of his appointment was for three years.[1] This did not go down at all well with Angie, who had assumed that his postings would be confined to Central London and Windsor, on which grounds they had purchased Heron's Brook. The house was now put up for sale, and they decided that Bob should start by living in the Royal Engineers officers' mess. Angie then arrived to begin looking for a house to rent and they moved temporarily to a hotel near Maidstone, before taking the Friary, near Aylesford, a former Carmelite house, which Bob described as 'strangely beautiful but unbelievably uncomfortable'.[2]

Bob's role at the school was primarily to instruct War Office civilians, who worked not only in Whitehall but also at a number of establishments around the country, on how best to take precautions against bombing attacks, both chemical and high explosive. However, he was also expected to instruct Royal Engineer officers how to retaliate in kind in the event of such attacks. He found that he got on very well with the Chief Instructor, Lieutenant Colonel K. N. Crawford, and the other two instructors. He did, however, cause some consternation on his first morning when, crossing the parade ground in shiny field boots and a Royal Horse Guards' cap, he was mistaken by the Guard Commander for the Engineer-in-Chief, who was expected imminently on an inspection tour. The Guard was turned out and arms were presented, only for the Guard Commander to discover his mistake. In the confusion which followed, the arrival of the distinguished inspecting officer only minutes later was completely missed!

Bob quickly settled down to his work, cheerfully gassing his students much as he had been gassed himself. Angie, on the other hand, was initially somewhat at sea in a garrison town, an environment she had not experienced before. In particular, it was traditional to drop calling cards on all the other married officers and their wives, a custom completely unknown in the Household Brigade. Before long, however, they had become part of the local military community and also invited friends to stay for weekends, notwithstanding the fact that Angie was pregnant again. Their first son, Joseph William Peter Laycock, was born in London on 7 July 1938.

This was the summer of the Sudeten Crisis and the subsequent Munich Agreement, during which the War Office was rather belatedly gearing up for what was seen by some, and certainly by Bob, as an inevitable war. At just this time a Colonel Douglas from the War Office rang to say that he would like to visit the school to see what was going on. Bob had been warned about the possibility of this visit by a fellow instructor who was just going off on holiday but who asked that he should be contacted in the event that Douglas called, as he wished to escort him personally. All Bob's attempts to locate this officer failed and Douglas refused to delay his visit, so Bob had to accompany him, arranging for good measure a demonstration of how to extinguish an incendiary bomb. Douglas was highly impressed, said that he was looking for a GSO3 in his branch at the War Office and asked if Bob was interested. By now somewhat bored with giving the same lectures and demonstrations over and over again, Bob said that he would welcome the move, on which Douglas applied for his transfer. On the return of Bob's fellow instructor from holiday, it turned out that he knew all about the War Office job and was hoping for it himself. Bob tried to get his posting changed, but Douglas was immoveable, and Bob was ordered to report to Whitehall forthwith. The lease on the Friary was surrendered and Bob, Angie and the children took up temporary residence at 86 Chester Square, which was owned by the same landlord, before moving to a larger house at 56 Rutland Gate, which belonged to their friend Ralph Cobbold.

In the War Office Bob found himself in sub-department TO3, which was one of three in the Department of Training and Organization (TO) and specifically responsible for defence against gas. TO was headed by Brigadier Kenneth Loch, and TO3 consisted of Colonel Douglas, a single GSO2 and Bob, the three of whom sat in a large room with four other officers, creating bedlam when all were on the phone at the same time, as happened only too often. However, part of the job was to advise the War Department contractors' factories on their arrangements in the event of bombing, and Bob was delighted when he was ordered to tour as many of them as possible. His social connections meant that he had friends scattered throughout the country, so he would ring and ask if he could stay, by day visiting factories, in which he had always been interested, and by night enjoying his friends' hospitality. One of the factories, which he visited whilst staying with his brother-in-law Toby Greenall, who had just succeeded his father as Lord Daresbury, was manufacturing a product which was so highly secret that supposedly not even its employees were aware of what it was. However, when Bob, dressed in civilian clothes to maintain the deception, asked a taxi driver to take him there, the response was, 'Oh, you want the place where they make that stinking mustard gas, do you?'[3]

Back in London in the early months of 1939, Bob's workload increased significantly, so much so that he was unable to get away with Angie for winter sports in Gstaad. The prospect of remaining for too long in Whitehall started to become distinctly unappealing.

Bob was delighted when Antony Head was also posted to the War Office, in his case as Secretary to the War Office Selection Board, vetting applications for emergency commissions. However, whilst Head was kept very busy in the summer of 1939 as events in Europe began to look serious, for the first time since he had arrived at the War Office Bob found that he had very little work to do and was thus delighted to be able to go on leave to Scotland with the whole family in mid-August. His parents had taken an estate at Loch Torridon for stalking, shooting and fishing, and Rosemary was also there. This idyllic interlude was all too short, as on 24 August, the day after the signing of the German-Soviet Non-Aggression Pact, Bob received a telegram for the War Office requiring his immediate return. He caught the train that afternoon and Angie also returned to London the following day, leaving the children with Bob's parents.

Bob was at the War Office on 3 September, when Neville Chamberlain announced to the British people that the country was again at war with Germany. Shortly afterwards there was an air raid warning and, in accordance with instructions, all the staff took to the shelter below the War Office building. After the 'All Clear' Bob returned to his office to find the telephone ringing. On the line was an officer from Aldershot Command, who said he had heard that London had been subjected to a bombing raid and asked how extensive the damage was. Bob replied that, if the scene from his window was anything to go by, then the much vaunted destructive capabilities of the Luftwaffe had been much exaggerated!

Bob now feared that he would be doomed to office work for the foreseeable future, when what he craved was active service. A day or so later, however, whilst his colleagues were out to lunch, an officer from the Staff Duties branch appeared, looking very flustered. He had been charged with staffing up the GHQ of the British Expeditionary Force, which was then forming at Camberley prior to going to France, and was short of a GSO3 who specialized in chemical warfare. Bob told him that he knew of just such a man, a certain Captain Laycock of the Blues. The officer said that he doubted if the commanding officer of the Blues would be prepared to release one of his officers for such a job, but Bob assured him that he knew the CO and would speak to him personally. Thanking him profusely, the officer then dashed off to the Military Secretary's office to arrange the transfer, without ever enquiring about the identity of the man who had solved his problem. Colonel Douglas, when he found out, was predictably furious, but by that time the cogs had been set in motion and GHQ BEF had priority for staff, which he was unable to have overruled.

The First Echelon of GHQ BEF formed at the Staff College, with officers messing in the Royal Military College. Extraordinarily, the C-in-C had only been chosen on the very day that war was declared. General the Viscount Gort had been serving as Chief of the Imperial General Staff, but had fallen out with Leslie Hore-Belisha, the Secretary of State for War, who was keen to see him go elsewhere. Most had expected Lieutenant General Sir John Dill, the GOC-in-C of Aldershot Command, to be given the job, but he was instead subordinated to Gort as one of the two corps commanders, the other being Lieutenant General Alan Brooke, whilst General Sir Edmund Ironside, although completely unsuited to the role, was appointed CIGS. As the BEF's Chief of the General Staff, Lieutenant General Henry Pownall, was only appointed on the same day as Gort, and as most of the officers were strangers to each other, it was remarkable that the First Echelon was in a fit state to leave for France, but it duly entrained at Farnborough for Southampton on 12 September.

Bob was still a very junior cog in the organization, as a GSO3 Chemical Warfare within the Operations branch of GHQ. The GSO1 was his old friend from Winterbourne Gunner, Lieutenant Colonel Pennycook, described by Bob as 'tall, thin, reticent, gentle and sensitive',[4] whilst the GSO2, Major Davis, was 'short, fat, jovial, and as tough as they come'.[5] They were to make an effective and happy team. They sailed from Southampton in one of a small fleet of cross-Channel steamers and landed the following day at a port whose name was supposedly secret, but which Bob instantly recognized from yachting trips as Cherbourg. That night they boarded a train for an undisclosed destination, whose identity became clear when French railway officials chalked the words 'Le Mans' on each of the carriages. GHQ and Dill's I Corps HQ both established themselves there temporarily until a more permanent location could be found closer to the Belgian frontier. A few days later Bob was ordered to accompany Colonel Hubert Rance, the Chief Signals Office, on a reconnaissance to find suitable premises in the area of Arras. The emphasis was on dispersal, this being thought likely to mitigate the impact of any bombing campaign, with the result that GHQ was scattered over an area of about 20 square miles in at least fifteen different villages, making inter-branch communication exceptionally difficult, especially initially, when nobody knew where anybody else was.

Bob was initially located in Noyelle-Vion, about ten miles west of Arras, alongside Q Maintenance, the Military Secretary and his staff and the Camp Commandant's department. He was reluctant to leave as an excellent mess with a French cook had been set up, but he was required to join Pennycook and Davis at Wanquetin, a few miles closer to Arras, where he was billeted in a farm just outside the village. The farmer, his wife, attractive daughter and young son were very welcoming, and the accommodation was reasonably comfortable, other than the sanitary arrangements, which were distinctly primitive. Bob bought a tin bath and amazed his hosts by performing his daily ablutions in it, but there was nothing he could do about the earth closet in a wooden shed at the end of the garden!

Bob had two concerns of an even more personal nature than his accommodation, the first being the emergency Budget introduced by the Government, which had included a significant rise in income tax. One of the conclusions he reached was that he could no longer afford the subscriptions to his many clubs and he resigned from all of them other than the Turf Club and the Royal Yacht Squadron, provoking 'furious letters'[6] from White's and the Hurlingham. Angie had moved into a small cottage which they had bought in Hawthorn Hill, between Bracknell and Maidenhead, but they could not afford a gardener. His other worry was the lack of letters from Angie. The postal arrangements of the BEF were totally chaotic at first and it was not until 14 October, over a month after he had arrived in France, that he received seventeen letters in one delivery; but even then, the first six which Angie had written did not appear for another ten days.

The arrival of the Second Echelon produced not only a competent driver – his first had only driven tractors before and had some difficulty in distinguishing between the accelerator and brake pedals – but also a soldier servant. The RASC driver, Private Birks, was a fervent socialist, but once he realized that Bob was not only prepared to listen to his views but even sympathized with some of them, they got on very well during the long drives around the BEF which they had to undertake. The soldier servant was a Cameron Highlander called Kavanagh, a former miner whose accent Bob found close to unintelligible, but who managed mysteriously to make himself understood to the French family. He was particularly good with their young son, the two of them playing with a clockwork train bought by Bob. Pressing or cleaning Bob's uniform remained beyond him, but Bob wrote to Angie that 'he manages to produce comforts for me in a wholly miraculous way and always refuses to tell me how he procured them.'[7]

Bob's role as GSO3 Chemical Warfare was to go round the BEF to advise its formations and units on the precautions which should be taken against gas attacks. One such visit was to Gort's own chateau, during which he inspected the cellar and pronounced it suitable, only to be told by the C-in-C that he had absolutely no intention of using it! His duties also included some flying, in order to judge how the British lines might be affected by a gas attack from the air. On one occasion he was aloft in a De Havilland Tiger Moth when the aircraft was fired upon by the AA batteries below. There had been some high level reconnaissance by the Germans, but the aircraft should have been easily identifiable. Roundly cursing the gunners below, Bob and the pilot frantically fired Very flares until the shooting stopped.

The French liaison officer attached to the Operations branch was a charming soldier who had fought in the Great War and with whom Bob became very friendly. The pair enjoyed drinking brandy late into the night and, on one of these occasions, Bob was dismayed to hear the Frenchman say that he believed that the French Army was rotten to the core and that, if nothing happened before the following summer, it would desert in large numbers to get in the harvest or, if the Germans attacked, would prove to be no match for them. He had an opportunity to find out more when he was ordered to go to the French GQG (*Grand Quartier General*) to find out how Britain's ally was approaching the question of gas, staying during his visit with the Senior British Liaison Officer, Major General Sir Richard Howard-Vyse, a former officer and future Colonel of the Blues. Bob was impressed by the seeming efficiency of GQG, which had not seen the same need for dispersal as the British. On the other hand, he was appalled by an encounter with a large contingent of French troops on his return journey, finding them 'slovenly, dirty, disconsolate, ill turned out, ill equipped and lethargic'[8] and with very poor transport.

Having conveyed these impressions to his brother officers in the mess, Bob found himself summoned by the senior Royal Engineer officer at GHQ, Colonel C. G. Woolner, to receive a severe dressing down. Woolner had overheard what he had said and told Bob that, although the French had looked scruffy in the Great War they had always fought with great determination, and that Bob's views would be highly damaging to morale. In short, he was minded to have him returned ignominiously to England. Bob apologized, saying the he believed that the GHQ officers were capable of making up their own minds and that he had been careful only to voice his opinion once the mess waiters had left the room. Woolner said that he was prepared to forget the incident, but that if he heard such defeatist talk again he would have Bob sent home with an adverse report. As it happened, he was indeed shortly to be posted back, but in quite different circumstances.

A report written by Bob had found its way to the GSO1 Staff Duties at GHQ, Lieutenant Colonel Viscount Bridgeman, who was very complimentary about it. Some days later he summoned Bob to see him, telling him that he thought he was wasted in his current job. Bridgeman then asked whether Bob had been to Staff College, as he had been asked by the Army Council to nominate a limited number of GHQ officers to attend the next course at Camberley, which would begin in January 1940. Bob replied that he had not, but would be delighted to do so, and Bridgeman submitted his name as one of about forty from the BEF.

At thirty-two, Bob was actually getting close to the age limit for peacetime attendance at the Staff College, and there is no evidence that he had ever been considered as a potential candidate. This might have been because it was not generally considered part of the career path of an officer in the Household Cavalry, due to its focus on ceremonial. There had been examples of Staff College attendance in the Blues, of which Howard-Vyse was one, but they were the exception rather than the rule. Bob himself had been unusual in seeking an outside attachment, most of his brother officers remaining in regimental service until their early resignation or retirement due to age.

He was thus delighted to have the opportunity, recognizing that the magic letters '*psc*' after his name could be a key to further advancement. Not having taken the exam, as he wrote to Angie, he believed that nomination was a feather in his cap. This might well have been true at that time, but before long all wartime attendees at the three staff colleges, at Camberley, Quetta and Haifa, would enter solely on the basis of a nomination.

His posting came through in late November. However, as Bob and the other attendees from the BEF were not required at Camberley until early January, the War Office decided that they should be taken on a conducted tour of all the services which supported a field army, and this began at the end of the month. Bob found it very interesting, albeit extremely hectic. The group, under the guidance of Lieutenant Colonel Milford, an instructor from Camberley, started at the Base Port and then moved forward along the lines of communication through the various formations until it arrived at the front line units. Milford told the would-be students that they were 'about as idle, inefficient, conceited, empty headed and useless a collection of officers as one could expect to meet in a century'[9] and that, unless they mended their ways, he doubted that many would complete the Staff College course. The dislike engendered by this harangue gradually turned, however, to respect, and the tour turned out to be of real benefit.

Bob returned to GHQ to find that it had at last decided to ignore the strictures on dispersal and had moved virtually all its offices into Arras itself. In any other place this would have caused great concern about bombing, but the town was honeycombed with cellars, tunnels and sewers, which made excellent and inter-communicating air raid shelters, whose construction Bob now supervised.

Shortly after Christmas he left for England, as he had been given a fortnight's leave before starting at Camberley. This was spent substantially at Wiseton with Angie and the family. His brothers Peter and Michael were both subalterns in the Sherwood Rangers Yeomanry, which was stationed close by, enabling him to see a lot of them. Their regiment was part of 5 Cavalry Brigade, itself a component of 1 Cavalry Division, which was concentrating in the area prior to its departure for the Middle East. The Household Cavalry Composite Regiment was also nearby in 4 Cavalry Brigade of the same division, and Antony Head was temporarily acting as brigade major. He and his wife, Dot, had taken a house at Southwell, and Bob was delighted to find that Head would be on the same course at the Staff College. The Heads' own house was at Winkworth, near Camberley, and Bob and Angie were invited to stay until they found a place of their own.

The Second War Course at Camberley opened on 11 January 1940. It was quite different in scope and objective from the pre-war course, which had lasted two years and which, many said, was intended to develop future generals rather than staff officers. The new and truncated course was designed to produce, in the shortest possible time, Grade 2 General Staff Officers and their equivalents in the logistics and personnel branches, Deputy Assistant Quartermasters General and Adjutants General. The First War Course had been largely populated with Territorial Army officers, but its successor was substantially for pre-war regulars who were either already serving or had rejoined from the Reserve of Officers.

The Commandant was Major General R. J. Collins, who had retired from the Army in 1938, only to be brought back again. Bob found him most uninspiring, locked in the mindset of the previous war. The opposite was true of the Chief Instructor, Brian Horrocks, and of two of Bob's three syndicate leaders, Charles Loewen and Charles Keightley, all of whom impressed him greatly and went on to have highly distinguished careers. Bob found many friends amongst the students, including a number of other Old Etonians. His fellow officers from the BEF included Tom Churchill, who had been a near contemporary at Sandhurst and who was to serve under him later in the War, whilst Bob made a new friend in Bernard Fergusson, who was to achieve great distinction with the Chindits before he, too, served under Bob.

As the course was only fourteen and a half weeks long[10] and a great deal of information was compressed into it, it was extremely demanding, with homework in the evenings and the only time off lasting from midday Saturday until first thing Monday morning. Bob and Angie had rented 'a nasty little villa' nearby, in which entertaining was difficult, particularly as the cook turned out to be hopeless and then contracted pneumonia. However, it was at least close enough to the Staff College for Bob to be able to bicycle in every day, with all his paraphernalia in the front basket, although there was one unfortunate incident when the brakes failed on an icy road and he crashed into an old lady, who was sent flying; happily no serious harm was done. From a professional perspective, Bob enjoyed the course, but he felt that he had actually learned relatively little apart from basic staff duties. There was not a great deal of instruction on how to fight a battle and next to nothing at all on combined operations, at the time an almost unknown science.

At the end of the course the outstanding students, who were to find immediate employment, were sent for by the Commandant. One of these was Antony Head, who was posted as Brigade Major of 1 Guards Brigade, a plum appointment.[11] Bob was told by Horrocks that he was to become GSO2 (Chemical Warfare) of the Norwegian Expeditionary Force, then being put together in the light of the German invasion of Denmark and Norway. However, he was not to take up his appointment until the force was securely established in Norway itself and, in the meantime, he was to attend an advanced gas course at Winterbourne Gummer. He and Angie left their villa with great relief and moved into a hotel in Amesbury.

The preconditions for Bob's posting to the Norwegian Expeditionary Force were never satisfied. Indeed, not only were the British and French forced to withdraw from Norway, but the Germans then invaded Belgium and the BEF was evacuated from Dunkirk. Instead, prior to the conclusion of the course at Winterbourne Gummer, Bob was informed that he was still to become a GSO2 (Chemical Warfare), but that this would now be at GHQ Middle East in Cairo.

Chapter 7

Commando

Bob was ordered to report to the Household Cavalry Training Regiment at Windsor and await instructions regarding his passage to the Middle East. He was very low on the priority list and on several occasions was asked to stand by, only to have the movement order cancelled, which was deeply frustrating. The Commanding Officer of the HCTR was Lieutenant Colonel Lord Forester, whom Bob had known since he joined the Blues and who was delighted to have a staff trained officer, assigning him to instruct the newly joined subalterns. Bob spent most of his time preparing and umpiring TEWTS (Tactical Exercises Without Troops).

Bob and Angie moved into the Bridge House Hotel in Eton, but not long afterwards they decided that she should take the two children to stay with her father in Canada. He was deeply concerned about the dangers of the Atlantic crossing and relieved when he heard that they had arrived safely, later asking her to promise that she would not return until he sent for her.

Leaving the hotel one day, Bob met a fellow officer who told him of a letter which had been circulated to all units calling for volunteers for a special force to be used for raiding the coast of Occupied Europe. In the Orderly Room he read a copy of the letter and liked what he saw. Forrester, who would be losing him anyway, was perfectly happy to nominate Bob, and his name was duly submitted to London District.

The genesis of the letter – War Office No.20/Misc./1786 (A.G.I.a.) dated 9 June 1940 to Northern and Southern Commands and 17 June to Eastern and Western Commands and London District – lay with none other than the Prime Minister. Churchill, in office for less than a month, during which time the Germans had overwhelmingly defeated the Allies, was already thinking of ways to hit back. In a minute to the Chiefs of Staff on 3 June he wrote:

> The completely defensive habit of mind, which has ruined the French, must not be allowed to ruin all our initiative. It is of the highest consequence to keep the largest numbers of German forces all along the coasts of the countries that have been conquered, and we should immediately set out to organise raiding forces on these coasts where the populations are friendly. Such forces might be composed by self-contained, thoroughly equipped units of say 1,000 up to not less than 10,000 when combined.[1]

Two days later he wrote again in much the same vein:

> Enterprises must be prepared with specially trained troops of the hunter class, who can develop a reign of terror first of all on the 'butcher and bolt' policy.
>
> I look to the Chiefs of Staff to propose me measures for a vigorous, enterprising and ceaseless offensive against the whole German occupied coastline.[2]

John Dill had replaced 'Tiny' Ironside as CIGS on 27 May and, following Churchill's first minute, he instructed his Military Secretary, Lieutenant Colonel Dudley Clarke, to produce some ideas on how this might work. On 30 May Clarke had already aired the possibility of raising a force to engage in guerrilla warfare on the Continent, and now he jotted down an outline plan on a single sheet of paper. He had been born in the Transvaal just before the beginning of the South African War, to a father who had ridden on the Jameson Raid, and his thoughts turned instinctively to the Boer Commandos, hand-picked men who had lived off the land and caused the British considerable trouble long after the war was thought to have been won. He later wrote: 'There seemed no reason why we could not adapt the principle of the leader with his loose-knit band of followers, why specially trained British soldiers should not learn to throw off heavy equipment and echelons of supply, and go stripped into a quick action ready to "live off the land" for the short time it lasted.'[3]

The CIGS was attracted to the idea and put it to Churchill, who gave his approval. Clarke enlisted the support of the Deputy Director of Military Operations, Major General Otto Lund, and the two officers set up Section MO9 at the War Office to assume responsibility for all kinds of raiding operations. A small staff was assembled, one of whom was the actor David Niven, who had served in the Army in the 1930s and rejoined when war was declared.

There were two priorities: to raise the force and to start raiding as soon as practicable. As Lund pointed out, there was one ready-made source for the first, in the shape of the Independent Companies, ten of which had been formed in April 1940 to fight in Norway, although in the event only five had been committed there. Clarke immediately set off for Scotland to visit them before they could be disbanded and to select a number of men to form what became 11 Independent Company for the first raid.

Clarke also enlisted the support of the Royal Navy, which seconded Captain G. A. Garnons-Williams to help with assembling the necessary vessels. A few days later he was somewhat disconcerted to hear from Garnons-Williams that the Adjutant-General Royal Marines, Lieutenant General Alan Bourne, had been appointed as Advisor, Combined Operations, to the Chiefs of Staff, with overall responsibility for raiding. Whilst this was evidence of a tri-service approach, which was welcome, it also complicated the command structure. Nevertheless, Clarke was able to mount the first raid, which he accompanied himself. Operation COLLAR took place on the night of 24/25 June, when a small number of men were landed a few miles south of Boulogne. Some contact was made with the Germans, two of whom were killed in an exchange of fire, and the only British casualty was Clarke himself, wounded in the ear. The results were otherwise negligible, but an official communiqué was released, playing up the operation for public consumption.

Clarke could now get on with the process of raising the commandos. Major General R. H. Dewing, the Director of Military Operations and Plans, set out in a memorandum of 13 June how this would happen:

> The procedure proposed for raising and maintaining commandos is as follows. One or two officers in each Command will be selected as Leaders. They will each be instructed to select from their own Commands a number of Troop Leaders to serve under them. The Troop Leaders will in turn select the officers and men to form their own Troop. Whilst no strengths have yet been decided upon I have in mind commandos of a strength of something like 10 troops of roughly 50 men each. Each troop will have a commander and one or possibly two other officers.[4]

At the time Bob read the War Office letter and decided to apply, he had no idea that someone he knew well was to become involved in his potential selection. This was Niven, whom he had met on a number of occasions and who later took the credit for Bob's eventual appointment and rise to prominence:

> I did something for which, in my opinion, the military has never adequately rewarded me. I suggested to my new uncle by marriage, Robert Laycock, that he should join the Commandos.
>
> He was then a captain in the Royal Horse Guards and had just received a posting to India to become gas officer of a division and was due to embark in a few days' time. He came to the War Office and I introduced him to Dudley Clarke who immediately decided that this was just the man he wanted.
>
> Bob and I paced the stone corridors of that dreary old building while Clarke dashed about, pulling strings as a result of which someone else went to India and Bob formed No. 8 Commando.[5]

Typically of Niven, this brief passage is not entirely accurate and was subject to some embellishment. He did not marry Primmie Rollo, the daughter of Bill Rollo and Bob's half-sister, Kathleen, until three months later and, at the time of his application to join the Commandos, Bob had no idea that Niven even knew her. Perhaps more importantly, the idea of Bob joining the Commandos did not emanate from Niven, although he undoubtedly made a significant contribution towards securing the desired result.

The true story was rather more complex. It began with Forrester forwarding his nomination of Bob to the GOC London District, Lieutenant General Sir Bertram Sergison-Brooke.[6] 'Boy' Brooke and Bob had previous history, and it was distinctly mixed. The first incident had occurred when Bob, as Silver Stick Adjutant-in-Waiting, was standing next to Brooke, then in his first term as GOC London District, on the steps of St George's Chapel, Windsor during the funeral of King George V. Throwing a salute to the coffin, Bob's fingers had caught the back of Brooke's cocked hat which, whilst it remained on his head, became tilted at a rakish angle, which he was forced to endure until the coffin had passed. Brooke was not amused. The second incident had arisen on the occasion of a dispute between Bob and the Regimental Veterinary Officer, in which the former had used strong language to the latter, his senior by many years, in front of the Commanding Officer of the Blues. The matter was referred to Brooke who, perhaps surprisingly, came down in favour of Bob.

Even so, Bob was somewhat apprehensive when summoned by Brooke for an interview. The GOC began by saying that he disapproved of his units being deprived of good men, but as the War Office had issued the letter, he had no alternative but to comply. He then astonished Bob by saying that he would be recommending not that Bob should be given command of one of the troops in the Commando to be formed out of London District, but that he should be its overall commander, an appointment which would see his accelerated promotion to lieutenant colonel. Bob was overjoyed, only to be dismayed moments later when Brooke told him that he was fairly sure that he would find it impossible to be relieved of his staff job. Nevertheless, the recommendation went forward to MO9.

Arriving at the War Office for his next interview, Bob was delighted to find that the staff officer handling the applications was Niven. His spirits fell, however, when he discovered how many officers were there, all after the same position, all filling in questionnaires detailing their relevant experience. They rose again when he read the questionnaire, which seemed to have been designed for him:

> 'Do you like the sea?' 'Yes.' 'Have you ever been yachting?' 'I am a member of the Royal Yacht Squadron and several other yacht clubs.' 'Can you ride a horse?' (incongruously enough, I thought.) 'Yes. I have hunted since I was five years old and am in a cavalry regiment.' 'Have you ever been deer-stalking or big game hunting?' 'Yes. I shot a "royal" before I went to Eton and was on a stalking holiday just before the outbreak of war.' 'Have you ever taken leave to carry out an expedition not connected with the

> Army?' 'Yes. I sailed half way round the word in the four-masted barque *Herzogin Cecilie* and worked for a fortnight as a stevedore in the port of Beira in Portuguese East Africa.'[7] 'Have you ever boxed?' 'Yes. I boxed for my public school.' 'Have you ever been on a machine gun course?' 'Yes.' 'A signal course?' 'Yes.' Do you suffer from sea-sickness?' 'I have never been sea-sick in my life: etc., etc.'[8]

The only question on which he was forced to dissemble was about his language skills: he claimed to be able to get by in French, whereas his vocabulary was in practice largely confined to gastronomy.

The interview with Clarke went very well, and Clarke told him that he had been in two minds about the leadership of the Commando in question but had come down in Bob's favour because of his experience at sea. His qualification as a Finnish Able Seaman had more than proved its worth and, when Clarke told Bob that he would apply to the Military Secretary for his posting as a Commando Leader, he left a happy man.

A few days later, Bob was summoned back to see Clarke, who delivered bad news. The Military Secretary had flatly turned down the transfer on the grounds that Bob had been expensively trained as a staff officer and should thus fill a staff job for which he was one of only a tiny number with the requisite qualifications. Shortly afterwards came another shock, when the Movements branch at the War Office advised him that his passage had now been fixed on a ship leaving in three days' time. Clarke immediately appealed to the DCIGS and the Deputy Military Secretary, and Bob went across to the latter's department to see what might be arranged, all to no avail.

Bob then sought an interview with the CIGS himself, which as he later admitted was highly presumptuous. However, he had met Dill on a pre-war cruise in the Mediterranean, on which the latter had been lecturing, and had found him very friendly. To his surprise Dill agreed to see him and listened sympathetically, saying that he would discuss the matter with the Military Secretary. Shortly afterwards he delivered a ruling, which was that Bob would be able to transfer but only he if could produce an officer with identical qualifications who was willing and able to travel immediately.

This seemed highly unlikely, but Niven persuaded Clarke to give Bob a chance and Bob himself returned to the Military Secretary's department, where he talked to the officer whose responsibility it was to come up with the names of officers possessing a certain combination of qualifications. The system rapidly produced three names: the first was Bob, the second had already been posted to a GSO2 job and the third was Captain Geoffrey Marnham of the Royal Artillery, who was serving as a GSO3 (Chemical Warfare) with a division in Western Command. As it happened, Bob knew him well as a member of his syndicate on the staff college course.

Bob was now staying temporarily in Wells Rise, north of Regents Park, with Angie's mother Freda, who immediately put her phone at his disposal. Persuading telephone operators to divulge numbers was far from easy, but by sheer persistence Bob managed to get through to the duty officer at the divisional HQ concerned, who refused to tell him where Marnham was. Bob then said that he was calling from the War Office and insisted on speaking to the divisional commander, who was reluctantly summoned from dinner to the phone. Bob explained that Marnham was urgently required for another job and was both surprised and delighted to hear from the general that he had no time for Chemical Warfare, that Marnham was a complete nuisance and that the sooner he got rid of him, the happier he would be. The duty officer was instructed to contact Marnham and get him to ring Bob.

When Marnham rang later that night, Bob immediately asked him if he would like to leave his job and take on another, with promotion to major. Marnham said that he would be delighted. Bob then told him that there was a potential snag: he needed to be on a ship to Egypt less than forty-eight hours later. Far from protesting, Marnham was highly enthusiastic, saying that any posting which would get him out of his current job would be welcome and, moreover, that his wife was in Africa and he had been desperate to get closer to her; this was, in fact, manna from Heaven as far as he was concerned! On the following day Marnham appeared in Clarke's office and the problem had been solved.

Bob was later to question the element of luck in his career, but if it ever played a role it was at this time. The delay in his posting to the Middle East, which caused him to be with his regiment when the appeal for volunteers arrived, the fact that Sergison-Brooke already regarded him highly enough to support his application, the presence of Niven as Clarke's GSO2 and, most of all, the availability and willingness of Marnham to take his place at short notice, were the factors which combined to see him through. However, the result would not have been achieved without Bob's refusal to accept defeat when the odds seemed to be stacked against him.

On 7 July 1940 Bob was duly appointed to raise and command No. 8 Commando and promoted to acting lieutenant colonel. He immediately set about choosing his officers, who would in turn select their men. The Commando was to consist of a headquarters, with himself, a major as second-in-command, an adjutant, an administrative officer, a medical officer and three liaison officers. There would then be ten troops of fifty men, each commanded by a captain, who was himself assisted by a Troop Sergeant, and divided into two sections, comprising one subaltern and twenty-three other ranks.

Bob's first move was to appoint his second-in-command and, after consulting Clarke, he turned to the officer who had been rejected in his favour, Major Walter Curtis of the Somerset Light Infantry. Eight years older than Bob, Curtis was a highly experienced regimental officer, who was to do an excellent job before leaving to command a battalion six months later. Bob had not known him previously, but with many of his other officers he worked on the principle that if he had to go to war, he might as well do it amongst friends, and this was very evident in the process which now took place.

Bob and Curtis needed a location at which to conduct their interviews. A myth has grown up that the officers were all recruited in the bar of White's, the club from which Bob had resigned in late 1939, only to join again in 1940.[9] Whilst he is likely to have met some would-be officers there during the process, and whilst the club network probably spread the word amongst the so-called 'smart set', the formal interviews were in fact all conducted on the ground floor of 32 Cadogan Square over the week following his own appointment. This was the residence of the sister of Richard, Lord Sudeley, always known as 'Bones', whom Bob had managed to get released from the Blues as a Troop Leader against the initial opposition of Forester. His first recruit for the HQ other than Curtis was Harry Stavordale as Adjutant, a job for which he turned out to be poorly equipped, although he was excellent in his other role, which was to keep everyone at HQ happy. Yet another member of the Blues, Philip Dunne, became the senior liaison officer. Robin Campbell, the son of Sir Ronald Campbell, who had been British Ambassador to France until that country's capitulation, after which he was posted to Portugal, and Bill Barkworth were recruited as the other two liaison officers, both of them fluent German speakers. James Gilroy became the Medical Officer and a Major Gardner the Administrative Officer. The latter had established something of a reputation as the Town Major of Brest during the evacuation from France of the remnants of the BEF and was the only officer to be selected by the War Office. He was inclined to drink too much and did not get on well with Curtis. Many weeks later, Bob wrote to Angie: 'All here greatly amused by a battle between my very GS Line Infantry 2 i/c and my fat and drunken Administration Officer who has chosen to be wilfully incompetent!'[10]

Last, but in Bob's view not least on his HQ staff, was his soldier servant and runner, Trooper Cook. Cook had served in Bob's machine gun troop in the early 1930s, before leaving the Blues at the end of his term of service. He had rejoined from the reserves at the beginning of the War and was quick to volunteer for the Commandos. When he arrived, Cook informed Bob that it would be unseemly for his batman to be a mere trooper and had himself promoted to corporal!

By mid-July Bob had selected most of his officers, who now had to choose their men. He had decided very early on that each troop should be recruited from a single regiment serving in Eastern Command or London District, the intention being to promote a healthy rivalry between them, but this turned out to be much more difficult than he had expected. It was pointed out to him that the Royal Horse Guards and the Life Guards could hardly be expected to find fifty men each, and he was compelled to form a Household Cavalry troop from both, commanded by Sudeley, with two scions of newspaper publishing empires, Gavin Astor from the Life Guards and Julian Berry from the Blues,[11] as his subalterns. The Foot Guards turned out to be even more troublesome. The commanding officers of each of the battalions concerned had been instructed to submit returns of volunteers by 20 July, but Bob encountered serious resistance from them and most actively discouraged their best men from volunteering whilst allowing applications from those they wished to be rid of, who rarely proved to be suitable.

In desperation, Bob appealed to Sergison-Brooke. He discovered that the GOC's views had not changed, but Brooke conceded that since he had personally recommended Bob, it was only reasonable that he should have some soldiers. He suggested that Bob should see the Regimental Lieutenant Colonels of the five regiments, to which Bob replied that he had met two of them and been sent away with a flea in his ear. Brooke promised to speak to all of them and suggested that Bob should try again two days later. This time they were much more cooperative, as a result of which Bob was able to form one troop each from the Grenadier, Coldstream and Scots Guards and a combined one from the Irish and Welsh Guards, which had fewer peacetime battalions.

By the end of the first week of August, 8 Commando was substantially up to strength, with No. 1 Troop (Household Cavalry) under Captain Lord Sudeley, No. 2 Troop (Grenadier Guards) under Captain Kenneth Tufnell, No. 3 Troop (Coldstream Guards) under Captain Mervyn Griffith-Jones,[12] No. 4 Troop (Scots Guards) under Captain Dermot Daly, succeeded in January 1941 by Captain Frank Usher, No. 5 Troop (Irish and Welsh Guards) under Captain Eddie Fitzclarence, No. 6 Troop (other units in London District and Eastern Command and known as 'the Buffaloes') under Captain Toby Milbanke, succeeded in December 1940 by Captain the Viscount Milton, No. 7 Troop (Somerset Light Infantry) under Captain Geoffrey Lance, No. 8 Troop (Line Cavalry) under Captain Godfrey Nicholson and No. 10 Troop (Royal Artillery, Royal Engineers and Royal Marines) under Captain George Smyth-Osbourne. No. 9 Troop was formed much later as another composite troop under Captain Pat Ness.

The presence of Royal Marines in No. 10 Troop was the result of an initiative on Bob's part whose outcome was far less successful than he hoped. He recalled that, following his appointment:

> I immediately asked if I could have a high percentage of Royal Marines contending that at least half the unit should come from the Corps whose tradition so obviously fitted them for the business of sea-borne raiding. Dudley said that he thought I might find some difficulty in getting agreement to this but suggested that I should go and plead my case with the Admiralty. At the Royal Marines Office I had little success. For reasons which I shall never understand, the Commandant General – or Adjutant

> General as he was called in those days – set his face against Commandos. Logically the Royal Marines should have taken over the whole Commando organisation on its conception. They should have scrapped the Royal Marine Division and never allowed the Army to usurp their traditional role.
>
> After considerable argument I was eventually allowed to recruit one officer and twelve Royal Marines, the first and only from the Corps to join the Special Service Brigade until the formation, later on, first of No. 40 and then of No. 41 Royal Marine Commandos. Later still in 1943, in conformity with my original ideas, the R.M. Division was disbanded and Nos. 42–48 Commandos were formed from it.[13]

This disappointment aside, Bob was immensely proud of the unit which he had raised. He had certainly attracted a number of officers who would go on to have remarkable wartime careers. Many would be decorated for leadership or bravery, the most notable amongst them being a tall, gangling and seemingly rather idle subaltern in No. 4 Troop, David Stirling, who had already built up a reputation as a mountaineer. He would in due course go on to form the Special Air Service Regiment, together with Jock Lewes, an Australian in No. 5 Troop, who was emphatically not one of the 'smart set', but who had led Oxford to victory in the 1937 Boat Race. Carol Mather, Stirling's fellow subaltern, was also to join the SAS, as was George Jellicoe of No. 3 Troop, the former later becoming one of Field Marshal Montgomery's longest serving personal liaison officers, the latter better known as the daring leader of the Special Boat Squadron. A fifth member of 8 Commando to join the SAS in its early days was Gordon Alston, a young gunner subaltern in No. 6. Troop. In contrast to all these warriors, No. 8 Troop's Randolph Churchill, the son of the Prime Minister, was never really cut out to be a soldier and was distinctly poor at commanding others, but he was certainly a most entertaining companion and, in his way, a brave man. He would also spend a short time with the SAS, which at least had the considerable benefit of raising the Regiment's profile with his father.

Recruiting ceased on 22 August, by which time 8 Commando had concentrated at Burnham-on-Crouch in Essex.

Chapter 8

Training

The Conditions of Service of those joining the newly formed Commandos were quite different from those of the rest of the British Army. Since all the men were volunteers, they were free to apply to return to their units, whose cap badges they continued to wear, after any operation. However, they could also be returned to their units at any time at the absolute discretion of their Commanding Officer, without any reason being given and without any right of appeal. In practice, being RTU'd was regarded as shameful, and this had a beneficial impact on both discipline and professional expertise.

The officers and men did not live in barracks or camps, but were instead required to find their own accommodation and make their own arrangements for food and drink. They also paid their travelling expenses, other than when they were posted to a new station. For all such expenses the other ranks received a special allowance of 6/8d per day and the officers 13/4d, the latter also covering the costs of their soldier servants. The purpose was to encourage self-reliance and initiative, in accordance with Dudley Clarke's vision. Thus, as the troops of 8 Commando arrived one by one at Burnham during August 1940, the first task of everyone was to find lodgings for themselves and to make arrangements with their hosts to be fed and watered. This did not prove to be a problem, as most of the town's landladies were only too pleased to have another source of income.

The officers were billeted out like the men, but they decided to mess together and were delighted to be offered facilities at the Royal Burnham Yacht Club, whose members were keen to show appreciation for their services. A private sitting room and dining room were made available, as well as the club bar, and one of the members lent the Commando a 30-ton ketch, which was used for sail training up and down the Crouch and out to sea as far as the boom defences. In the words of Carol Mather, 'The mess bore a resemblance to the effortless ease and nonchalance of a London Club.'[1]

If any of the members of 8 Commando thought that their essentially informal living arrangements, far removed from the rigid Army procedures to which they had been accustomed, would be reflected in their training, they were to be in for a surprise. In the Training Instructions which Bob issued on 12 August, the immediate emphasis was on discipline. Not only that, but discipline in the first instance meant drill, with at least two drill parades per week required of each troop. However, he also laid down:

> It cannot be too firmly impressed upon all ranks that drill is merely a means to an end and that the movement of men in formed bodies or in regular formation will NEVER be employed by personnel of No. 8 Commando EXCEPT on drill parades which will be regarded as completely separate and distinct from all other forms of training.[2]

For a unit which comprised to a substantial extent members of the Household Brigade, drill was never likely to be a problem, but the next essential of training, the development of what Bob called 'A Special Technique', was quite another matter. Bob defined the characteristics of this as:

> Physical fitness.
>
> Mental alertness.
>
> The offensive spirit.
>
> Complete disregard of danger.
>
> The instinct of the hunter.
>
> The lightning, destructive and ruthless methods of the gangster.
>
> Absolute self-reliance.
>
> A knowledge of various tricks, ruses and devices.
>
> And, above all, the ability to move and act at night fearlessly and noiselessly and to regard the blackest darkness as an aid rather than as a hindrance to the attainment of a difficult and hazardous objective.[3]

Bob also emphasised *esprit de corps*, not only in the individual troops with their regimental traditions, but in the Commando as a whole, and security, which he insisted must become a fetish with every man.

Weapons training focused on personal weapons, which would be the tools of the trade. Most of these – rifles, pistols, sub-machine guns, grenades, even the 2″ mortar – were familiar to every man, but few would have contemplated also being taught to use knives in hand-to-hand combat or to improvise bombs. A number of the general training subjects were also unfamiliar, notably boat handling, climbing, demolitions, sabotage and even 'thuggery'! It was quickly evident to all that this was to be a different type of soldiering from that to which they had previously been accustomed. After three very hard weeks, each troop had a week off; there were few, if any, drop-outs.

In addition to the training at Burnham, small parties of officers and senior NCOs were sent up to complete a course at the Special Training Centre at Lochailort in north-west Scotland, not only to develop their skills, but also so that they could become instructors themselves. The STC pre-dated the founding of the Commandos, having been set up in May 1940 on the initiative of Bill Stirling, David's brother, and Brian Mayfield, who with four others had formed part of a team established to go to Norway, only to be frustrated by the collapse of the campaign there. They persuaded the War Office to let them start up a school for special forces, teaching fieldcraft, climbing, weapons training, demolitions and close-quarter fighting, with Mayfield as Commandant and Stirling as Chief Instructor.

Stirling recruited his cousin, Lord Lovat,[4] as Fieldcraft Instructor, and the other instructors included 'Mad Mike' Calvert, who subsequently found fame with the Chindits, Freddy Spencer Chapman, who formed a 'stay behind party' after the Japanese conquest of Malaya and was later in Force 136, and two rather elderly former Shanghai police officers, Captains Fairbairn and Sykes, who taught every known method of killing or disabling an enemy at close quarters. They also designed the eponymous knife, which was later issued to all in the Commandos and incorporated into the design of their shoulder badges. Bob's old school friend Peter Fleming ran the Signals wing for a time, and students from outside the Commandos included David Niven and Fitzroy Maclean. Some of the officers, including David Stirling and Robin Campbell, had already completed the course prior to joining 8 Commando, and most of the others did so during August and September, but Randolph Churchill was ignominiously returned after only a few days, following an acrimonious argument with a sergeant instructor.

Back at Burnham, personal training was complemented by collective training, which escalated from sub-section to section to troop and then to the Commando as a whole. Schemes and exercises were mounted, in one of which the nearest Home Forces formation, 46 Brigade, played the role of the enemy. The brigade was deployed in Harwich against what was seen to be the likelihood of an imminent German invasion, and the exercise was designed to determine how it would react to being attacked not from the obvious direction, the sea, but from the landward side by a force of parachutists. Having been warned of this possibility, the brigade established positions on the outskirts of the town facing inland, as well as on the waterfront. In mid-morning 8 Commando suddenly manifested itself in the town itself, taking 46 Brigade completely by surprise. It had achieved this by stopping a train to Harwich some miles away from its destination, the men concealing themselves on the floor amongst the initially startled, but later highly amused passengers, and then alighting with alacrity in the middle of the town in order to overcome all the defences from behind. The brigade commander was delighted, writing later to Bob: 'The tonic, which your trained and unorthodox methods provide, is just what my units need to smarten them up and develop initiative and quickness.'[5]

On 17 July Admiral of the Fleet Sir Roger Keyes had succeeded Bourne as Director of Combined Operations. He was a hero of the Great War, in which he had led the Zeebrugge Raid, which was still regarded as a model of amphibious warfare in spite of being only partially successful. Once Keyes had set up Combined Operations Headquarters ('COHQ') in Richmond Terrace, he assumed responsibility for all the Commandos, of which there were initially ten.[6] Bob had met him socially before the War and greatly admired his aggressive spirit.

Unbeknown to anyone except Bob, the first five weeks of 8 Commando's stay at Burnham was a period of great uncertainty, reflected in the fact that recruitment had stopped abruptly on 22 August, before 9 Troop could be raised. At just that time Bob heard confidentially from the War Office that there was even a possibility that the Commandos would be completely disbanded, and the uncertainty continued into early September, causing him considerable concern about his own future. He wrote to Angie: 'I shall be furious if I have to go back onto the Gilded Staff as a Capt.'[7]

The problem lay with a growing movement of opposition to the Commandos among conservatives in the Army. With invasion believed to be all too likely, a number of officers, including some who were very senior, argued that it made no sense to post good officers and men to units which were the antithesis of the traditional battalions in their structure and training and which were not committed to Home Forces for the defence of the British Isles. Although Dill and others remained supportive of the Commandos, these sentiments were widely voiced, both at the War Office and in Home Forces, as a result of which there was a hiatus whilst the whole project was reconsidered. The situation was saved by the Prime Minister, who was deeply unhappy with the failure to satisfy his demands. He later wrote:

> The idea that large bands of favoured 'irregulars' with their unconventional attire and free-and-easy bearing should throw an implied slur on the efficiency and courage of the Regular battalions was odious to men who had given all their lives to the organised discipline of permanent units … It was easy to understand their feelings without sharing them. The War Office responded to their complaints. But I pressed hard.[8]

The Secretary of State for War, Anthony Eden, who was himself generally sympathetic to the Commandos, was on the receiving end of the opposition. Churchill made it quite clear to him in a series of minutes that he was not going to be swayed in his determination to see his directive to Dill fully enacted and, by the end of the second week in September, the threat had been lifted, although the War Office tried later to have the special allowance stopped. After a considerable battle, Keyes managed to have this proposal abandoned, but he was less successful in obtaining permission for the men to wear a distinctive headdress. The Commandos had been saved from disbandment, but antagonism towards them would continue in the War Office and some other parts of the Army right up to and beyond the end of the War.

Keyes paid his first visit to 8 Commando on 13 September, accompanied by the ACIGS, Major General Laurence Carr, one of the leading sceptics at the War Office. Bob had arranged for the two senior officers to be greeted by an immaculately dressed and expertly drilled guard. Carr, expecting a scruffy band of licensed killers, was somewhat taken aback and accused Bob of borrowing regular troops from elsewhere; Bob replied that these were men from his own Grenadier troop, who were according to an Admiral of the Fleet the honours due to his rank.

Carr and Keyes went first to look at a demonstration of folbots, folding canoes which would become one of the most useful pieces of equipment, not only of the Commandos, but of all special forces. The Folbot Section, independent of the ten troops, had been formed under the leadership of Roger Courtney, who before the War had paddled one of these frail craft along the length of the White Nile from Lake Victoria to Egypt and who would be largely responsible for its widespread adoption.

For the next demonstration, in the knowledge that Carr was particularly keen on weapons training, Bob had prepared a surprise. The ACIGS was taken to see instruction being given on an unfamiliar machine gun. On being asked what it was and how it had been acquired, Bob replied that it was a German MG15, going on to explain that the Commando, which had not even been equipped with Bren guns at this stage, had collected many such weapons, together with a good supply of ammunition, from German bombers shot down in the vicinity, of which there was no shortage. After later seeing a demonstration of a raid from the sea, which was executed to a very tight timetable, Keyes and Carr departed, the latter grudgingly impressed.

The acquisition of the machine guns was a consequence of the Battle of Britain, which was at its height during 8 Commando's stay in Burnham. The town lay on the route from Belgium to the RAF airfields at North Weald and Hornchurch and later to London during the Blitz. Bob instructed that a watch be kept for downed German bombers and that any surviving crew should be taken prisoner, also that any RAF pilots who had baled out should be returned to their squadrons as quickly as possible.

On the night of 21 September Burnham itself was hit by a land mine dropped by a returning German bomber. Six civilians were killed and twenty-seven injured. There were no casualties in the Commando, which was called out to rescue people buried under houses and subsequently to provide guards against looting; this was, for most of the men, their first real taste of war.

With invasion believed to be imminent, in mid-September 8 Commando was temporarily placed under the operational control of Eastern Command, which allocated to it a number of localities to defend, mostly on high ground overlooking possible landing beaches. It was ordered not to man these until the receipt of the code word CROMWELL, whereupon vehicles from a neighbouring battalion would provide the necessary transport. One evening Bob received a call from the local divisional HQ with the code word, and the Commando was duly deployed, only to be stood down on the next day.

As autumn set in, however, the threat of invasion receded and 8 Commando was ordered north for more advanced training. On 10 October it boarded a special train, which left Burnham at 05.00 and arrived in Greenock at 00.30 on the following morning, to be met by Bob, who had driven up with Harry Stavordale, staying a night at Wiseton on the way. At Greenock the Commando boarded MV *Ulster Monarch*, formerly a passenger ferry on the Liverpool to Belfast route. The ship's officers were expecting only personal packs, whereas baggage for a whole month had been brought, together with operational stores. All this had just been stowed away when another train, with No 3 Commando aboard, arrived at the quayside for embarkation in the same ship.

Later that night the *Ulster Monarch* set sail for the short journey to Inverary on Loch Fyne, where the Combined Training Centre had recently been established. It was commanded by a naval officer, Vice Admiral Sir Theodore Hallett, who had retired in 1933 but had then been recalled, initially to serve as a beachmaster in Norway and at Dunkirk, and then to form the CTC.

The only raids carried out until then, near Boulogne in Operation COLLAR and subsequently on Guernsey in Operation AMBASSADOR, had been damp squibs, with very little accomplished. Little or no opposition had been encountered, but it was abundantly clear to those who had participated in them that landing even a small force on hostile beaches would require a great deal of specialized training. Whereas the early operations had been mounted in RAF Air-Sea Rescue boats, borrowed from the Air Ministry, the first effective assault landing craft, the LCA, capable of carrying forty men, including a crew of four, was now being delivered and would be used for all future landings. Inverary was ideal for training on these craft. It was so remote that there was little likelihood of being interrupted by the enemy, as was all too possible at Burnham and other East and South Coast locations, whilst Loch Fyne was endowed with both good beaches and deep water for the new class of Landing Ship Infantry ('LSI'), which would carry the men and the LCAs. The training took the form of frequent exercises, by day and by night, involving embarking in the LCAs from the LSIs, landing on a variety of beaches and then moving inland, sometimes to a distance of several miles over mountainous country, with times recorded at each stage. This process was then repeated until it became second nature. It was very exhausting, but also exhilarating, and the competition between the troops of 8 Commando to get furthest quickest was intense. The training continued until 30 October, when 8 Commando embarked in one of the LSIs,

HMS *Glengyle*,[9] for Gourock, before travelling on to its new base at Largs by bus and train.

On the day on which 8 Commando moved up to Scotland, the first part of a major reorganization took place. The Commandos, which had until then been only loosely associated with each other under the umbrella of COHQ, were now formally grouped into the Special Service Brigade. This was inevitably abbreviated as 'SS Brigade', a name which had sinister connotations and was universally disliked by all who served in it, although it was not changed until four years later. The newly appointed Brigadier was Charles Haydon, who had commanded the 2nd Battalion Irish Guards in the defence of Boulogne in May, for which he had won a DSO. Bob knew him slightly from their service together at the War Office, where Haydon had been Military Assistant to the Secretary of State for War. Haydon would be closely associated with the Commandos for the next three years and would become a good friend of Bob's, who respected him greatly, writing later that Haydon 'combined stern discipline with great sympathy for our problems. He grew to be inordinately proud of the Commandos and championed us with unshakeable loyalty against the machinations of Whitehall and the antagonism of Home Forces.'[10]

The machinations of Whitehall were responsible for the second part of the reorganization, in which each Commando became a company within one of five Special Service Battalions, 3 Commando as A Company and 8 Commando as B Company of 4 Special Service Battalion. Bob was appointed to command the battalion, which had a small HQ separate from the two companies, whilst B Company was now commanded by Walter Curtis, with Daly as his second-in-command, himself succeeded at No. 4 Troop by Frank Usher. The two companies each retained their ten troops. In Bob's own words, 'a more impracticable and unwieldy an organization it would be difficult to conceive'.[11] Bob's new appointment upset the CO of 3 Commando, John Durnford-Slater, who had actually formed it earlier than 8 Commando and, moreover, had some active experience from Operation AMBASSADOR. Durnford-Slater continued to reply to all War Office communications as 'CO 3 Commando', notwithstanding that they had been addressed to him as 'OC A Company, 4 Special Service Battalion'.

The association of the two former Commandos within a single unit was not a happy one. Durnford-Slater had formed his Commando out of volunteers from Southern Command who came from very diverse backgrounds. The officers were as different from their distinctly patrician 8 Commando counterparts as it was possible to be. As one of them, Peter Young, later wrote, 'The officers of 3 Commando seemed practically like Roundheads – horrid thought – by comparison with this glittering band.'[12] Whilst the officers of each company kept to themselves, the men were very inclined to fight whenever they met each other in the public houses of Largs, even though their billeting areas were kept separate, A Company to the north of the town and B Company to the south. The sole compensation for Bob was that he only needed only one Administration Officer, and he acceded readily to Durnford-Slater's urging that this should be Captain J. E. 'Slinger' Martin of 3 Commando, who had served as a trooper in the 9th Lancers in the Great War and stood no nonsense from anyone, rather than the inefficient and occasionally drunken Major Gardner.

Bob announced the reorganization to 8 Commando on 13 November, when the officers and men were given the opportunity to return to their original units, an offer which very few accepted. On the same day, Lieutenant Evelyn Waugh reported for duty. On arrival at Largs from Inverary, Bob had received a letter from Brendan Bracken, then Minister of Information, asking him to give sympathetic consideration to Waugh's application to join. Bob, who had met Waugh on a couple of occasions at country house parties before the War and had read *Decline & Fall*, *Vile Bodies* and *Scoop*, agreed, on the grounds that 'often even funnier in fact than in fiction, (he) could not fail to be an asset in the dreary business of war.'[13] Waugh, at the suggestion of Bracken, had already been in touch with Bob towards the end of August, but in the meantime had participated, as an officer in a battalion of Royal Marines, in the abortive expedition to oust the French from Dakar. He was dismayed by the expedition's failure and yearned for a more glorious role in the War, which he felt the Commandos might provide. He was to be seriously disappointed.

Waugh's immediate impression of his new unit was far from entirely favourable. In *Memorandum on Layforce*, written by him privately at the end of 1941, he commented on what he found:

> When formed they had been exceptionally zealous: discipline was already deteriorating when I joined. After RM Brigade the indolence and ignorance of the officers seemed remarkable, but I have since realized that they were slightly above normal Army standards. Great freedom was allowed in costume; no one even pretended to work outside working hours. Troop leaders never sent in returns required by the orderly room at the proper time or in the proper form. Officers took their leave when the troops were not allowed it. The special lodging allowance did little to cover the high expenditure in No. 8. Two night operations in which I acted as umpire showed great incapacity in the simplest tactical ideas. One troop leader was unable to read a compass. The troops, however, had a smart appearance on inspection parades, arms drill was good, the officers were clearly liked and respected.[14]

These are serious criticisms, although it must be said that they were written by someone who was highly disgruntled at the time he wrote them. Jellicoe was to say later that Waugh never really fitted in.[15] In spite of his fame as a writer, he was essentially a middle class intellectual, quite different in background from the landowning 'smart set' who formed much of 8 Commando's officer group. Moreover, whilst most of them were flush with money, which they splashed out on visits to Glasgow and gambling in the mess, Waugh was far from wealthy and had to be very careful in his expenditure. He had been an outsider in the Royal Marines for entirely different reasons and now he was an outsider again. The fact that Bob failed to recognize him when he reported for duty also rankled.

Officer discipline was almost certainly adversely affected by the presence of a number of wives, notably those of Dunne, Stavordale, Nicholson, Churchill and Campbell, who had arrived in Largs to stay at the Marine Hotel. Waugh had not been able to bring up his own wife, Laura, who was in the last stages of pregnancy. The child, a girl, was born on 1 December, but died twenty-four hours later, just before Waugh arrived to see her. In such circumstances the presence of the other ladies in Largs was unlikely to be conducive to good humour.

The hopes of Bob and his officers for action were raised by the prospect of their first operation. Operation WORKSHOP, the capture of the Italian island of Pantelleria, was the brainchild of Keyes, proposed to the Chiefs of Staff at the end of October. The plan involved three of the new Special Service Battalions, including No. 4, with Keyes himself leading the expedition and Haydon as the military force commander. Bob and Dudley Lister, the CO of 3 Special Service Battalion (4 & 7 Commandos), were summoned down to London for an initial briefing. They were met by Haydon, who told them that he was not permitted to divulge the identity of the target and produced some Admiralty charts from which all the names had been expunged. Shortly afterwards Keyes himself entered, saying that he proposed in the case of the two Commando officers to disregard the Chiefs of Staff's strictures regarding the identity of Pantelleria. An outline plan was agreed and Bob and Lister returned north to carry on with the detailed work and begin the rehearsals. These were carried out on the Isle of Arran, to which 4 Special Service Battalion was relocated, Bob setting up his HQ in the Brodick Bay Hotel.[16] Lister also brought his battalion over to the island, as did Lieutenant Colonel Saegert of 2 Special Service Battalion (9 & 11 Commandos), with whom Bob was less than favourably impressed.

Two days later a package arrived, containing aerial photographs of the target. Bob and Robin Campbell spent hours poring over them, but experienced considerable difficulty in correlating some of the beach defences with the latest intelligence summaries. After hours of frustration Bob asked Haydon if he might invite Tom Churchill, who after leaving staff college had specialized in the interpretation of aerial photography, to come up to help. Haydon agreed, and Churchill was located and summoned to COHQ, where he was shown the photos. From the characteristic lake in the middle of the island, he immediately recognized it as Pantelleria, which he had been asked to study by the Air

Ministry before the War. Enjoined to complete secrecy, he set off for Arran, where his impressions over four days were very different from those of Waugh:

> This was long enough for me to become profoundly impressed with the organization and system of the commandos; I liked their realistic approach to the work that lay ahead of them, their absence of red tape, and their terrific enthusiasm and keenness; every officer and man was a volunteer and their physical fitness, self-reliance and specialist training made them a *corps d'élite*. In an England hardly recovered from the Dunkirk retreat and hourly expecting invasion from the French coast, it was a tonic to meet troops who had the prospect of offensive operations, and were so eager to undertake them.[17]

In the meantime, Bob had been joined by a new recruit in the shape of Peter Beatty, like George Jellicoe the son of one of the two foremost naval commanders of the Great War and himself a sub-lieutenant in the RNVR. Beatty, whom Bob had only met relatively recently, but who was an old friend of Angie's, arrived unannounced and asked to be taken on in 8 Commando. Bob told him that he was not allowed naval officers on his establishment and that, moreover, Beatty would be unsuitable because of his very poor eyesight. Undeterred, Beatty went straight off to see Keyes, who was a friend of his father, and persuaded him to create the new post of Naval Liaison Officer.

This provided the excuse for another, much more senior naval officer to join 11 Commando as an NLO. Admiral Sir Walter Cowan had commanded a battlecruiser at Jutland and led a light cruiser squadron with great distinction in the Baltic shortly after the Great War, eventually becoming C-in-C Americas and West Indies. Still eager for action at the age of sixty-nine, he was delighted with the new job to which he was appointed by his old friend Keyes, accepting with alacrity the reduced rank of commander. Bob was to see much of him before the War was over.

Keyes and Haydon set up their own HQ at Lamlash Bay, whereupon the rehearsals began in earnest for WORKSHOP. On the back of Tom Churchill's advice, Bob had selected for his battalion the beaches on Arran which bore the closest topographical resemblance to those on Pantelleria. Most of the rehearsals went very well, but there was one exception and it was highly unfortunate that, in this case, Keyes had invited some members of the Board of Admiralty to be present as observers. The landing, by 3 Commando from HMS *Glenroy*, was due to take place at first light, and Durnford-Slater gave instructions for the men to be called in plenty of time to assemble and board the LCAs. However, the officer charged with this duty delegated it to another, who for some reason then failed to take the required action. Three quarters of an hour after the designated time, Durnford-Slater himself woke up, realized to his horror what had happened and roused as many men as he could. This result was a fiasco as the LCAs arrived late and with far less than their full complement of men. Keyes was predictably furious, although when Durnford-Slater came to apologize, he told him that he should have learnt a lesson which would not now be repeated in a real operation.

For his part, Bob was convinced that the Officer of the Watch on *Glenroy* had realized that the reveille had not been sounded at the right time but had been content to sit back and watch the Army making a fool of itself. This was symptomatic of the relationship between the two services, which was not good, at least aboard the LSIs. Part of the problem was that the boat handling and navigation skills of the mostly RNVR crews of the LCAs was particularly poor, arousing a lot of criticism from those in the Commandos, like Bob, who were experienced sailors. Bob believed strongly that the Royal Navy should only have responsibility up until the 'Lowering Position' had been reached, when the LSI stopped to allow the LCAs to be launched. Thereafter, the Commandos should be responsible for the run-in to the beach. This was never to happen and, although boat handling improved greatly over the next few years, in the immediate future the landing craft as often as not either ran aground on some obstruction or landed on the wrong beaches.

A greater immediate problem was the atmosphere on board the LSIs. Each of them was captained by a retired officer returned to service, including Captain Sir James Paget of the *Glenroy*, described by Waugh as 'a man of irritable disposition and poor judgement'.[18] The two sets of officers never hit it off. Waugh encapsulated this neatly: 'No 8 Commando was boisterous, xenophobic, extravagant, witty, with a proportion of noblemen which the navy found disconcerting; while the navy was jejune, dull, poor, self-conscious, sensitive of fancied insults, with the underdog's aptitude to harbour grievances.'[19] This was highly unfortunate as they were before long to be thrown together for a long voyage, although it would not be to Pantelleria.

In early January 1941, WORKSHOP was cancelled, to the bitter disappointment of Bob and his men. Bob wrote later:

> Despondency was the order of the day. The confidence of the junior officers and their men in the leaders … was shaken and they began to wonder whether their chances of action would have been better if they had stayed with their Regiments, many of which had been sent to the Middle East, where the battle was in full swing.[20]

Keyes spoke to all the men, but it was Haydon who came up with a more practical response, which was to send everyone who had trained for WORKSHOP on a fortnight's leave. Just before they left, the welcome news was received that the

Special Service Battalions were to be scrapped and the Commandos restored. In Haydon's words:

> There is no doubt that the Commandos, each raised by an individual officer and each filled with his individual enthusiasm, had a most marked spirit and pride of their own.
>
> This characteristic was to some extent drowned out and lost when the Commandos were amalgamated into Special Service Battalions. It was, however, my hope that it would be replaced by an equally beneficial battalion spirit. I do not think that I can say that this proved to be the case.[21]

At the same time, Keyes announced that, on their return from leave, three of the Commandos, including No 8, were to be sent overseas, where an operation of some importance awaited them.

Bob was about to go on leave himself when a telegram arrived from Angie to say that she had just arrived back from Canada via Lisbon and was on her way to Arran. The two of them stayed for a few days on the island, now devoid of Commandos, before spending the rest of his leave in London.

Chapter 9

Layforce

It had been decided that an overall commander would be appointed to Force Z, the umbrella formation for the three Commandos being sent overseas, Nos. 7, 8 and 11. Bob surmised correctly that the choice would lie between him and Dudley Lister and, immediately after the announcement, had sought an interview with Haydon, who told him that he had guessed what Bob was coming about and that he was not to worry about it. Haydon had gone on to suggest that he should leave by the tradesman's entrance as he could see Lister coming up the path!

Bob arrived back from his leave on 25 January 1941 in order to begin supervising the arrangements for the embarkation of the three Commandos. Walter Curtis had elected to return to his regiment but provided invaluable assistance, and Dermot Daly stepped up to lead 8 Commando, which had undergone one significant change. No. 8 Troop had been disbanded, Godfrey Nicholson calling a parade to tell his men that they had not come up to the standard required in training. According to James Sherwood, one of their NCOs, this provoked an extremely angry reaction, but the decision was irrevocable. For most it meant being RTU'd, but Sherwood himself heard that Courtney was recruiting for the Folbot Section, which in future was to operate separately from 8 Commando; he applied for a transfer and was accepted.[1] A few others, notably Randolph Churchill, were transferred to other troops. In order to make up the numbers, A Troop from 3 Commando, under Captain Mike Kealy, was transferred to become the new No. 8 Troop.

Of the two other Commandos, No. 7 was the better known to Bob. Raised by Lister from Eastern Command, it had been stationed in Felixstowe, where it was a near neighbour of No. 8 at Burnham. It had been decided that Lister was to remain in the UK to lead 4 Commando, and the command passed to Major F. B. Colvin. Bob was not familiar with 11 Commando, in which the only officer he knew at all well was Keyes's son Geoffrey, the second-in-command. The Commando had recruited almost exclusively from Scottish regiments and was not only informally styled 'the Scottish Commando' but emphasized its national affiliation in every way it could, notably by requiring all its officers and men to wear Balmoral bonnets, with black hackles rather than regimental badges. The commanding officer was Major R. R. N. Pedder.

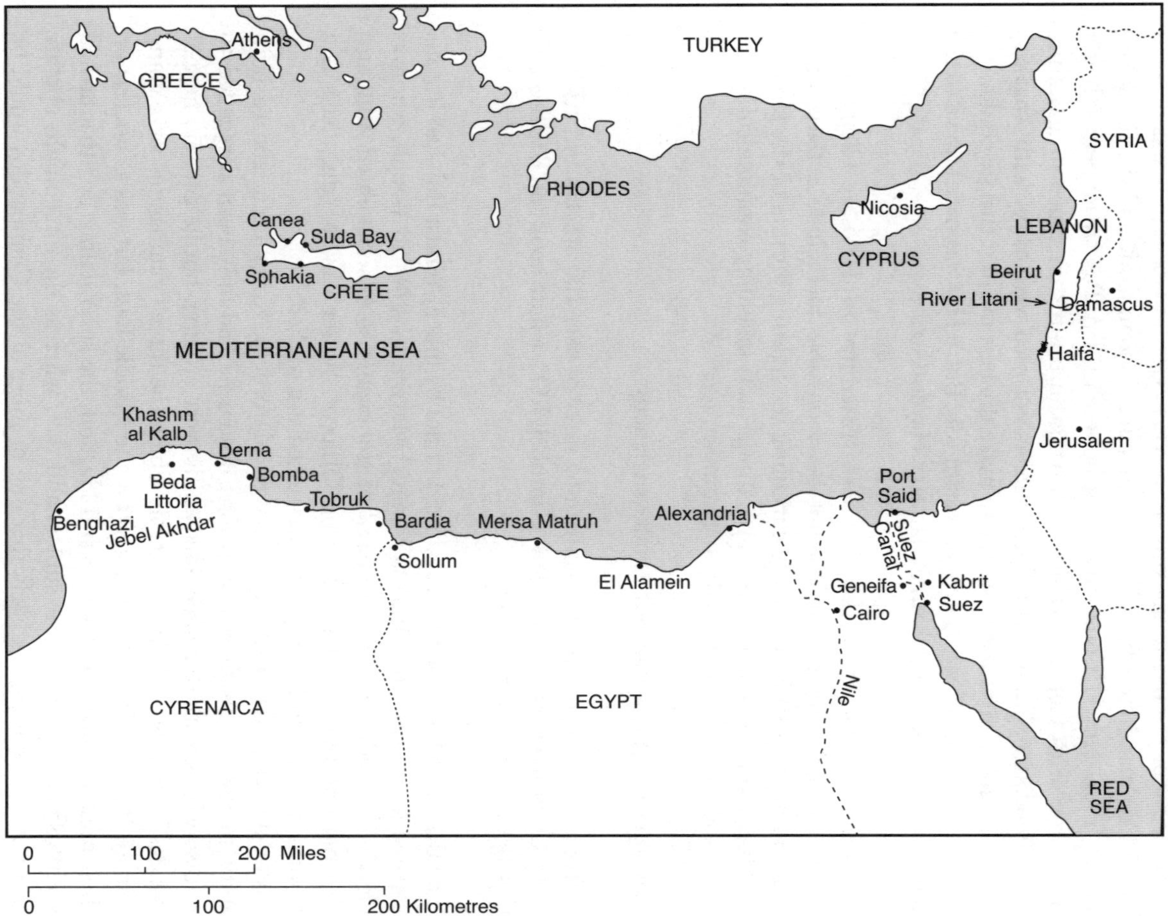

The Eastern Mediterranean.

All three Glen ships were sailing to the Middle East, but *Glenearn* was required to carry other troops, including the personnel of a Mobile Naval Base Defence Organization (MNBDO), leaving the three Commandos to be crammed into the remaining two ships, *Glengyle* and *Glenroy*. It was decided that 7 Commando would go in the former and 8 Commando and the Force HQ in the latter, with 11 Commando split between them. Pedder immediately got into a row with Curtis, accusing him of favouring his own men in allocating accommodation; but in fact neither officers nor men were happy with what was provided, and Curtis was only able to make the best job of it that he could.

The lack of space was the main reason why Bob's HQ was pared down to the bone. In his orders to Bob on 31 January Haydon wrote:

> Within the limits of the numbers travelling on H.M.S. 'Glengyle' and H.M.S 'Glenroy' it has not been possible to include a Battalion Headquarters without unduly curtailing the fighting portion of the force. Thus you must select a small operational staff including communications personnel and train them during your voyage.[2]

Haydon's Brigade Major put it more succinctly:

> You appear to be going to command a force of over 100 officers and 1,500 O.R.s with one staff officer (Lt. Campbell I.O.), a note book and 8 wireless sets which nobody can work.[3]

The Brigade Major was exaggerating, but not by much. Whilst Bob had lost his capable Administration Officer, 'Slinger' Martin, he still had Waugh, who was clearly unsuitable for the command of troops and so was appointed Adjutant, and not one but two Naval Liaison Officers, Walter Cowan, 'disguised as a Commander',[4] and Peter Beatty, 'disguised as a soldier'.[5]

On the same day that Bob received his orders, Keyes came aboard both ships to address his departing troops, whom he had only been persuaded to release with great reluctance. His words were stirring, but he gave no hint of the destination or, indeed, of the role which the three Commandos were going to play. Bob knew they were bound for the Middle East, but was as unclear on their military objective as Keyes and Haydon, the latter telling Bob that he had no information at all on the subject and that, whereas the force might operate as a whole, it was just as likely that one or more of the Commandos would be ordered to take independent action.

On 1 February the convoy, joined by the Cunard liner SS *Georgic* with reinforcements for the Middle East and escorted by the light cruiser HMS *Devonshire* and some destroyers, sailed from the Firth of Clyde, almost immediately encountering a strong gale. Conditions in the Glen ships were appalling. Although three officers were required to share cabins originally designed for two, they were in a state of great comfort compared to the men, who were packed like sardines into recently constructed mess decks, where they slept in hammocks. In spite of their recent experiences in boats of many sizes, seasickness was rife for the next three days whilst the gale lasted. Bob insisted on as many men as possible getting into the fresh air on deck, but this was only really practicable for large numbers when the rough weather subsided. Thereafter, PT and weapons training, which included instruction on the ship's armament of 4-inch guns, 2-pounder pom-poms and 20mm cannon, were the order of most days, although a small canvas swimming pool was rigged up in the tropics.

Officers were required to prepare and give lectures, and Bob, who had prudently brought along a large number of maps and charts, ran TEWTs based on these. By far the most comprehensive TEWT, which took several mornings to complete, was a plan for the capture of the island of Rhodes, with the support of both tanks and artillery. Bob was able to comment with authority on the solutions produced by the various syndicates as he had visited the island before the War

Relations between the Army and the Royal Navy in the *Glenroy*'s wardroom remained poor, and the fault lay almost entirely with the former. 'I was beginning to wonder,' Bob wrote later, 'whether I would not have been wiser to have recruited a lot of stodgy, plodding, patient beings rather than the high-spirited, aggressive, devil-may-care individualists whom I had originally been convinced were the right type for the Commandos.'[6] Many of the officers had travelled in luxury liners before the War and expected much the same treatment now. The wardroom had been re-arranged with small tables, but even so there had to be two sittings for each meal. On one occasion Philip Dunne, having been asked to make way at the first sitting for the Chief Engineer and the Paymaster Lieutenant Commander, caused great offence by comparing his treatment with being refused a seat in a restaurant car on a train so that the engine driver and the ticket collector could be served first. On the following morning Eddie FitzClarence, standing just aft of the bridge, compounded the affront when approached by a naval officer determined to be friendly, who asked him the time. FitzClarence replied that he had not got a clue but suggested, pointing up to Captain Paget, that he should ask 'that silly looking booby on the roof'.[7]

That evening Bob assembled all the Army officers in the wardroom, where he read them the Riot Act, telling them that they were guests of the Navy and that, if there was any repetition of such behaviour, the officer concerned would be returned to his unit from the next port. Peter Beatty volunteered, as NLO, to make amends with the captain. Bob replied that it would be far more appropriate for him to do this himself, but found when he met Paget that not only had Beatty, in his enthusiasm, got there first, but that he had made matters much worse by explaining to the captain that the Army officers had expected to find themselves with the 'real Navy' and not with a collection of amateurs!

Cowan shared the Army's view of their ship's officers, although he tried not to let it show. Notwithstanding his reduction in rank to Commander, he was in practice immeasurably senior to all others on board and thus, whilst his criticisms were never voiced openly, Paget was only too aware that the beady eye of a former Naval Commander-in-Chief was on him at all times, which made him distinctly tetchy. It might have been expected that he would ask Cowan to mess with him, but the arrangement would probably have been embarrassing to both. The solution to this problem of protocol was for Cowan and Bob to use a small compartment next to the wardroom, in which a table was laid for their exclusive use. Cowan had a badly fitting set of false teeth, which meant that he ate very slowly, but Bob was invariably fascinated by the tales from his long career and thus not disposed to hurry him up.

By way of entertainment after dinner, the wardroom was turned into a casino. There was a table each for roulette, chemin-de-fer and baccarat, and two for poker, one high stakes for the rich or the good players, the other low stakes, run by Waugh for beginners. He would only allow his pupils to graduate to the other table when he thought they were ready, and many returned for a refresher course having lost a great deal of money in the meantime. David Stirling was one of the gamblers, but disliked any other form of organized activity. Instead he spent more and more of his time asleep in his cabin, gaining the nickname 'the giant sloth'.

On 10 February the convoy anchored off Freetown in Sierra Leone for twenty-four hours. Nobody was allowed ashore, but the troops were just happy to have something new to look at, both by day and by night, as there was no blackout. The exception was Bob, who was summoned to report to the Area Commander, taking Campbell with him. The general turned out to be none other than Christopher Woolner, the officer who had ticked off Bob in the BEF for allegedly lowering morale with his description of the poor state of the French Army. Woolner was perfectly pleasant, however, and not a little intrigued by the Commandos. Whilst ashore, Bob met for the first time Bill Stirling, David's brother, who was travelling in the *Glenearn* and had also been ordered to report to Woolner.

The next leg of the voyage was through the tropics and the ship became increasingly unpleasant in the heat. Tropical kit was issued, including shirts with collar pads and pith helmets, to which the members of 11 Commando attached their black hackles. Bob, mindful of his experiences on the *Herzogin Cecilie* and against the advice of the doctors, thought that it would be preferable for the men to shed most of their clothing. They found this far more comfortable, and there were no cases of sunstroke. Sleeping conditions, on the other hand, were atrocious. Even the officers, three to a small cabin, were suffering, not least

Randolph Churchill, who was sharing a cabin, known to all as 'the pigsty', with Stavordale, whose huge frame overflowed his bunk, and Waugh, who insisted on smoking evil-smelling cheroots. In desperation he elected to sleep on an inflatable mattress outside, only to receive the full force of two fire hoses early in the morning when the wooden deck was swabbed down.

The only excitement on this leg of the voyage came when a signal was received that the German battlecruisers *Scharnhorst* and *Gneisenau* were believed to be in the general vicinity. The convoy was clearly no match for them and the captains agreed that their only chance if attacked was to try to get away under cover of smoke. Cowan was horrified at any thought of retreat and insisted that he should be lowered over the side in a motor torpedo boat which was slung in *Glenroy*'s davits, so that he could engage the enemy. Happily, another signal was then received that the Germans were elsewhere.

On 19 February the convoy arrived at Cape Town, where at last its passengers were allowed to disembark. Pedder showed what 11 Commando was made of by marching it to the top of Table Mountain and back in record time, accompanied by Cowan, who in spite of his age of seventy and his height of 5 feet 4 inches, matched the soldiers step for step, going off afterwards to dine with his old friend, the South African Prime Minister Field Marshal Smuts. Route marches of a less arduous nature were undertaken by the other two Commandos. The hospitality extended to all ranks by the South Africans was outstanding, as every wartime convoy found, but the ships were only there for forty-eight hours.

The final leg of the journey was uneventful, although the new escorts, HMS *Dorsetshire* and HMS *Glasgow*, were briefly despatched to hunt for a German commerce raider which failed to materialize. A scheduled call at Durban was cancelled and the convoy sailed without stopping until it arrived at Suez on 7 March. The troops were told to stay on board, but Bob was ordered to proceed by car to Cairo. Accompanied by Cowan, he arrived in the Egyptian capital and booked into Shepheard's Hotel. On the following morning, he reported to Major General John Evetts, the GOC of 6 Division, under whose command Layforce, as Z Force was now renamed, would initially come. Evetts was highly enthusiastic about the Commandos, telling Bob that he had an operation lined up which would suit them very well:

> He said that he had permission to divulge the objective to me but that it was for my ears and my ears only. One breath out of me on that subject would result in an immediate Court Martial. Rather dramatically he said: 'I shall mention one word to you now, but neither of us will ever use it again until a certain date unless we are behind closed doors.' Needless to say, that word was Rhodes.[8]

When Bob explained that he and his officers had spent some days planning an assault on the very island, Evetts nearly had a fit. When he recovered, he said that there was no point in crying over spilt milk, but that Bob should instead leave a map of Sicily, marked 'Most Secret', lying about in his HQ tent to put anyone off the scent. Bob had to explain that his officers and men had been taught to put tight security above any other consideration and would quickly realize that this was a ruse.

Whilst Bob was away, the Glen ships had moved up the Suez Canal to Kabrit, where the troops disembarked before moving to their camp at Geneifa on the Great Bitter Lake. Evetts arrived there two days later to address the assembled officers on the change of name of the force and on a more general reorganization. Each of the Commandos was now to become a battalion, No.7 as A Battalion, No. 8 as B Battalion and No. 11 as C Battalion. Colvin, Daly and Pedder were all promoted to lieutenant colonel and the seconds-in-command, respectively Ken Wylie, Sudeley and Keyes, were made up to major.

Another unit, to be known as D Battalion was also to be created out of 50 and 52 Commandos, which had been raised in the Middle East. The CO was to be Lieutenant Colonel George Young, who had formed 50 Commando in the summer of 1940, at much the time that the same process was taking place in the UK, out of volunteers from within Middle East Command. In addition, it accepted into its ranks a number of Spaniards who had served on the losing side in the Spanish Civil War. The Commando had initially been based on Crete. It had conducted one operation, the seizure of the Italian island of Castelorizzo, which lay off the Turkish coast some 80 miles to the east of Rhodes. Successful at first, the Commandos were subjected to a counter-attack by the Italians and had to be evacuated, an outcome which had gone down particularly badly with Churchill, but was more the result of a lack of appropriate action by the Royal Navy than any failing by Young's men. No. 52 Commando had been raised at the same time as 50 and had served briefly against the Italians in Ethiopia, along with 51 Commando, formed largely of Palestinians, both Arab and Jewish, which remained in East Africa. The two Middle East Commandos which were to join Layforce each numbered little more than half the men of their UK-raised equivalents, so the new combined battalion was of similar size. Its traditions were somewhat different from its fellow battalions – the private soldiers, for instance, had been called 'Raiders' and had never practised self-billeting – but it was now subject to an identical training regime.

As the Layforce establishment would be not much less than that of an infantry brigade, Evetts recommended that Bob should be promoted to the rank of acting brigadier, but the Military Secretary's department baulked at this, due to his youth and lack of seniority. The compromise was that he should instead become a full colonel. He was, however, allowed to increase the size of his staff. Campbell returned to B Battalion, with Waugh taking over his role as Intelligence Officer. No officers with the requisite staff qualifications or experience existed in Layforce to take on the role of Brigade Major, so the job went to Major Freddy Graham, a regular soldier serving in Egypt. Captain Brian Franks, a yeomanry officer, became the Signals Officer and Captain E. L. Francis from 11 Commando was transferred to be Staff Captain Q in charge of administration. The HQ establishment now consisted of five officers and twenty-four other ranks, together with the Folbot Section of two officers – Courtney and Lieutenant 'Tug' Wilson – and seventeen other ranks. In addition, there was a signals section.

Not long after arriving at Geneifa, Layforce was visited by the C-in-C Middle East, General Sir Archibald Wavell, together with John Dill, the CIGS, and Anthony Eden, the Foreign Secretary, who were in the theatre primarily to visit Greece, to which country it had been decided to render military assistance. Bob asked if they would like to look over one of the Glen ships, and they readily agreed. No boats were immediately available, so Bob signalled to *Glengyle* to send one to pick them up. Although a landing craft arrived to carry the party to the ship, somehow the message was not received in its entirety and there was no one to greet them. Captain Petrie, when he heard, was horrified that the three distinguished visitors had not been given the reception due to them and bent over backwards to make amends.

For the rest of March and in early April training was carried out for Operation CORDITE,[9] the capture of Rhodes. An outline of the town of Rhodes and the coast on either side of it was scratched out to scale in the desert, although other lines were also made just in case enemy reconnaissance planes were able to take photos of it. For this purpose, 6 Division was to consist of 16 Infantry Brigade, 22 Guards Brigade, Layforce and a regiment of tanks, with Layforce tasked to make the initial assault on the town itself. Bob attended numerous conferences in Cairo, and pre-operation leave was granted in batches to all ranks. Bob always stayed at Shepheard's but frequently enjoyed the hospitality of David Stirling's brother Peter, who was serving in the British Embassy. He had hoped to see something of his own two brothers, Peter and Michael, but they were with the Sherwood Rangers in Tobruk, where, having lost their horses, they were temporarily acting as gunners.

With CORDITE scheduled for the end of the first week of April, Courtney and Sherwood from the Folbot Section were embarked in HM Submarine *Triumph* for a reconnaissance mission. On the nights of 30 and 31 March Courtney and Lieutenant Commander Nigel Willmott, an RN navigating officer, paddled their frail craft on to the proposed landing beaches, returning with valuable intelligence which would have prevented disaster.[10] Bob attended a final conference for the operation on 1 April and a full scale rehearsal was carried out three days later.

On 6 April CORDITE was postponed and later it was cancelled. The reason was a sudden and significant deterioration in the military situation. In Cyrenaica, where the Italians had been decisively beaten less than two months earlier, a German/Italian force under General Erwin Rommel attacked on 31 March, pushing the occupying divisions into headlong retreat and capturing three British generals, including Bob's Company Commander at Sandhurst, Richard O'Connor. The Germans swept on to the Egyptian frontier, but failed to capture Tobruk, which was invested instead. On 6 April the Germans simultaneously invaded Yugoslavia and Greece, and 22 Guards Brigade was immediately transferred to the Western Desert, leaving 6 Division with insufficient troops to be sure of success.

It was only the first of many disappointments.

Chapter 10

Bardia

The setback to the British strategic position in the Mediterranean theatre had profound implications for Layforce, which was now put into GHQ Reserve. The four battalions were ordered to move to camps near Alexandria, three of them travelling in the Glen ships and D Battalion proceeding there by train. Layforce HQ was set up alongside A Battalion at Sidi Bishr, between Alexandria and Aboukir Bay, whilst the other battalions went into camp further east at Amiriya. In desperation, Bob drove to Cairo to see Lieutenant General Arthur Smith, Wavell's Chief of Staff, to propose that Layforce should be used to attack Rommel's flank on the coast of Cyrenaica, so that the German general could never be sure of the security of his lines of communication. His immediate impression was that the staff at GHQ had adopted a wholly defensive strategy, which they only understood how to implement by fighting stereotyped battles, completely lacking in imagination. Smith, who was disposed to be helpful, made time to come to Amiriya to address the troops, but Bob knew that the only way to assuage their disappointment over the cancellation of CORDITE was a promise of operations in the near future. Encouragingly, two such were now proposed.

On 14 April Bob was summoned to attend a conference chaired by the Naval C-in-C, Admiral Sir Andrew Cunningham, aboard his flagship, HMS *Warspite*. Accompanied only by Freddy Graham, Bob found the three Glen ship captains already there. Cunningham immediately asked why he had not brought with him his old friend, Walter Cowan. Bob replied that he had indeed requested Cowan to be present, but it seemed that he had not been informed when the boat was leaving *Glenroy* for the flagship. The Glen ship captains, who thoroughly disapproved of Cowan, looked smug, only to be discomfited when the old admiral arrived ten minutes later, to be warmly greeted by the C-in-C.[1] A second interruption came fifteen minutes later when Waugh was ushered in, looking distinctly scruffy, wearing a beard which he had been trying to cultivate rather unsuccessfully, a pair of shorts several sizes too large and a solar topee. 'Good God, Evelyn, what brings you here?' asked Bob. 'Merely loyalty, Sir,' came the reply.[2]

Waugh's sudden and unexpected appearance came as the result of a conversation between him and Bob some days beforehand, when Waugh had asked for a precise definition of the duties of the Brigade Liaison Officer, a position he held concurrently with that of Intelligence Officer. Bob told him that these were laid down in Field Service Regulations, where he could read them for himself, but they might be roughly interpreted as being his shadow. On occasions when Waugh was needed he must materialize without Bob having to send for him. On all other occasions he was to bother Bob as little as possible. Waugh had clearly decided that the conference fell into the first category.

The purpose of the conference was to discuss two operations, both of which were to take place on the following day. The first was for four troops of B Battalion under Sudeley to attack the coast road at Bomba, west of Tobruk between Gazala and Derna. However, although the men embarked in the destroyer HMS *Decoy* and sailed initially to Tobruk, whence they departed for Bomba, the sea conditions were unfavourable and at one point the destroyer ran aground, so the operation was cancelled.

The second and much larger operation was a raid by Layforce on the small port of Bardia, which was situated close to the Libyan frontier with Egypt and had been recaptured by the Axis forces during their rapid advance. The objectives were to harass the enemy's lines of communication, inflict the maximum amount of damage and take a number of prisoners for interrogation. The original plan was for two battalions to take part, A in *Glengyle* and C in *Glenearn*. The ships duly sailed, but the operation was called off on 16 April when Captain Petrie of the *Glengyle*, the Senior Naval Officer, decided that the swell at sea and the surf on the beaches were both too high to permit the successful launching, loading and beaching of the LCAs.

With a new forecast of four days of fine weather, GHQ Middle East decided that another attempt should be made, this time by A Battalion alone. *Glengyle* sailed again on 19 April, accompanied by the anti-aircraft cruiser HMS *Coventry* and three Australian destroyers. HM Submarine *Triumph*, carrying Courtney, another member of his section and a folbot, was to provide navigation lights for the approach to the beaches. Bob and two members of his brigade staff, Franks and Waugh, supplemented for the occasion by Cowan and Campbell, accompanied the expedition in order to gain experience of operations. They were not, however, expected to go ashore.

A Battalion was divided into seven detachments of varying sizes, which would be landing on four beaches. Six LCAs and one larger LCM would be carrying four detachments on to Beach A, their tasks being:

No. 1 of 50 men – to secure and hold the beach.

No. 2 of 100 men – to establish a road block, take some prisoners and destroy a bridge

No. 3 of 100 men – to assault and capture a nearby camp

No. 4 of 50 men – to enter Bardia town from the north, destroy all vehicles and take some prisoners

Two LCAs were to land on Beach B, carrying No. 5 Detachment of 70 men, which was to enter Bardia from the south, destroying vehicles and taking prisoners. Two LCAs were to land on Beach C, carrying No. 6 Detachment of 70 men, whose objective was demolish a bridge and a pumping station and to crater the road at two points. A single LCA was to land No. 7 Detachment of 35 men on Beach D, their role being to destroy coast defence and anti-aircraft guns located on a nearby peninsula. Nos. 2, 3, 4 and 6 Detachments were to be accompanied by small parties of men from the Royal Tank Regiment, whose job was to employ and, in due course, to demolish any armoured vehicles which had been captured.

The timetable provided for the first LCA to leave *Glengyle* at 22.15 and the last to depart from the beaches on the return journey at 02.30 on the following morning, allowing the LSI and her escort to get under way for Alexandria in darkness. Bob announced that he would allow no deviation from the latter.

As Bob was to write later, 'The operation was a miserable affair from the word "go".'[3] The first setback occurred as *Glengyle* approached the lowering position, when a green light should have been seen towards the shore. This was to have been placed on a small rocky island off the shore by Courtney. However, his folbot was damaged as he tried to launch it from *Triumph* and, before he could repair it, the submarine was forced to dive by an air attack.

There followed an altercation between Bob and Petrie concerning the weather, the latter suggesting once again that the swell and the surf were too great, the former, strongly supported by Cowan, disputing this by reminding Petrie that they had trained successfully in much worse conditions. Petrie then contended that the lack of a guiding light meant that the landing craft would be unable to locate the correct beaches. This opinion was countered by a remarkable character who had come along as a guide, Lieutenant Alfred 'Pedlar' Palmer, an Australian naval reserve officer who was making his name as the skipper of the schooner *Maria Giovanni*, running supplies into Tobruk under the noses of the Germans and Italians, and who knew the coast well. Insisting that he would be able to find the right beaches from the leading craft, he provided Bob with the ammunition to overrule Petrie.

The LCAs were all launched satisfactorily, except for one which got caught up in its davits, whilst the quick release mechanism for the LCM became temporarily stuck, causing some delay before it was fixed. The LCAs left for the shore no more than fifteen minutes later than the plan demanded. Palmer was as good as his word, and all the LCAs and the LCM bound for Beach A landed their men satisfactorily. One of the two craft destined for Beach B also landed at Beach A, causing some confusion, whilst the other was the one which had failed to be launched. Of the LCAs heading for Beach C, one arrived late and the other very late due to problems with its steering gear. At Beach D, which proved to be narrow and difficult to land on, the LCA was eventually lashed to a rock so that the men could clamber over the side into waist-high water.

The landing was unopposed, the only enemy being some motorcycle combinations which made off speedily in the other direction to raise the alarm. No. 1 Detachment deployed immediately to protect Beach A. Unfortunately, however, an officer from another detachment, trying to make contact, failed to respond to a sentry's challenge with the correct password or to show the recognition signal on his torch and was shot and seriously wounded; although evacuated to the ship he died the next day. No. 2 Detachment set up a roadblock, but no vehicles passed by. No. 3 Detachment reached the camp it was intended to attack, only to find it empty, with no signs of recent occupation other than in one building. The detachment did find a stock of motor tyres, which it set alight with incendiary bombs. No. 4 Detachment found Bardia unoccupied and had to return for lack of time before it could make a detailed search. No. 5 Detachment, having landed at the wrong beach, was unable to reach Bardia from the other direction. No. 6 Detachment sent one party to the pumping station, but the directions were poor and, by the time it arrived there, the party was forced to return in accordance with the timetable before it was able to inflict serious damage. The second party found the road impossible to crater satisfactorily and was only able to make the bridge impassable to motor transport. No. 7 Detachment found no trace of mobile guns, but located four old Italian naval guns once used for coast defence. These were missing their firing mechanisms, but, just to be sure, the breeches were blown apart with gelignite.

Bob himself ignored instructions to remain on the ship and went ashore with the members of his staff. Cowan and Waugh wanted to take an active role in the proceedings, but since they were not supposed to be there at all, Bob insisted that they stay with him. Aiming for high ground, where they hoped to watch the action, the group of officers was startled to come across a *wadi* which was full of dead Italians. Returning later across the *wadi*, Franks and Campbell leant over the edge to pull up one of the other members of the party, who was having difficulty climbing up. Believing him to be Waugh, they decided to pull him on his belly along the side for a few yards before heaving him over the top. To their dismay, they discovered that they had mishandled a highly indignant Cowan!

All the LCAs except two returned safely to the *Glengyle.* One had breached to in the surf and could not be refloated, so was destroyed. The other lost its way but managed to sail along the coast to Tobruk. Its problem appeared to be a faulty compass and, during his return trip, Bob found that the coxswain of his own LCA, trying to keep on the right compass course, was heading towards Tobruk rather than out to sea. It turned out that the compasses on all the landing craft had been affected by the magnetic metal casing around them and were giving totally inaccurate directions. After a certain amount of zigzagging, the ship was reached safely by all the others, but as a result their recovery was completed much later than planned. *Glengyle* and her accompanying escort nevertheless weighed anchor before dawn and arrived back in Alexandria shortly before midnight.

The biggest upset occurred when a large party of 70 men from No. 3 Detachment took a wrong turning and arrived in a small bay between Beaches A and B. It then made its way across a headland to Beach B, where it hoped to be picked up, only to find no landing craft there. It was by now too late to make for Beach A, so a message was sent for the party to make for Sollum in Egypt, but they were in due course taken prisoner.

The Bardia raid was not so much a failure as a fiasco, caused substantially by the very poor intelligence on which it had been based. This had spoken of a garrison of some 2,000 men and a large number of vehicles and pieces of equipment. Apart from the fact that Rommel diverted a brigade-sized formation to protect against further such raids, it had achieved very little.

Not all was lost, however, as Layforce had learnt a number of lessons which were to prove valuable for the future. Among these were that it should be possible to load the LCAs before the LSI had anchored in order to get them away without any delay. Bob also felt that heaving to four miles offshore was too far out for the LSIs, especially when the landing craft were trying to find the ship on their return from the beaches, and recommended that the distance should be reduced to two and a half miles, which he did not believe would compromise safety. He identified a number of unnecessary delays in clearing the beaches following the landing and suggested that parties arriving on the wrong beach should wait there until the others had left to avoid confusion, alternative plans being made in advance for such situations. The close formations adopted for Europe's dark nights were now seen to be unnecessarily vulnerable under the much lighter Mediterranean skies. More attention needed to be given to back bearings during the advance from a landing beach, as some of the returning parties, and not only the one which was lost, found it difficult to remember where they were. The Navy beachmasters were not fully familiar with landing procedures and Bob recommended that they should be accompanied by Army liaison officers. Anti-magnetic casings were clearly to be essential in future for the landing craft compasses.

The experiences of A Battalion at Bardia did nothing to improve the overall morale of Layforce. Bob was starting to become seriously concerned, not least because the six months service for which the men had all signed on would shortly be coming to an end. Whilst there was no appreciable indication of officers and men wanting to return to their units, Bob knew that this would become the case if the prospects for action remained slight. Once again he went to see Arthur Smith in Cairo. Smith invited him to set out his concerns in writing and Bob sent him a long letter on 6 May, the key sentiments of which were as follows:

> Since our arrival here … we have pursued the heart-breaking course of working up to concert pitch for projects which have eventually been cancelled.

> The effect on the troops may be summed up by an inscription written up on a partition in the mess decks of one of the Glen ships (the culprit was never apprehended) which read: 'Never in the history of human endeavour have so few been b-----ed about by so many.' Frivolous as this may seem I cannot but sympathise with the sentiments expressed.
>
> I think that we all feel that if the higher authorities consider our useful employment to be problematical then it would be better to disband the Special Service Brigade now rather than to see it deteriorate.
>
> Although all would feel a disappointment at witnessing the disbandment of a force on which they had set their hearts, to which so much time and money has been devoted, and in which we originally felt so much pride, the time is rapidly approaching when all ranks of the Special Service Brigade are beginning to doubt the justification of our existence.[4]

Disbandment was not to take place yet, however. Instead, Layforce was to be subjected to yet further disappointment and, in the case of two of its battalions, to disaster.

By the time that Bob wrote to Smith, C Battalion had already been removed from Bob's command and sent to reinforce the garrison of Cyprus, which up to then had consisted of a single infantry battalion and which was thought in the new circumstances to be highly vulnerable. Waugh was later to claim that there was some discontent with Pedder, the CO, 'whose peculiarities came very near megalomania',[5] but this was certainly the best trained and most committed of all the battalions and it was disappointed to be assigned to a static role.

B Battalion's morale was particularly low as it had not participated in any actions apart from the abortive raid on Bomba. At the end of April it was decided to send it to Mersa Matruh, from where it would carry out small-scale seaborne operations. These were made much more difficult by all three Glen ships being despatched to Greece to help evacuate the British and Australian troops who had been unable to withstand the German advance through that country. Instead, the battalion was allocated a China river gunboat of Great War vintage, HMS *Aphis*. This vessel, which mounted two 6″ guns and some pom-poms for air defence, had a particularly shallow draught but proved otherwise to be totally unsuitable. She was incapable of carrying landing craft, so the troops had to practise paddling ashore in collapsible pontoon punts, into which they could step directly from the ship's side thanks to her very low freeboard.

On 14 May Bob, with Waugh and the advance party of B Battalion, sailed in *Aphis* from Alexandria to Mersa Matruh, with the rest travelling there by train. Having heard that his old school friend Peter Fleming had been evacuated from Greece, Bob sent Waugh to pick him up in Cairo and bring him to Mersa Matruh to demonstrate new types of bombs and booby traps. Bob stayed there for a pleasant few days, the only unwelcome incident coming when a party of

Australian soldiers fired in his direction whilst he was swimming off the beach, missing him by a few yards. Distinctly irate, he complained to their commanding officer, who brushed it off with 'Well, if you give them rifles and ammunition, you must expect them to want to do a bit of practising!'[6]

The objective of the first raid of B Battalion was the airfield at Gazala, about 40 miles west of Tobruk. Under the overall command of Daly, a party of eleven officers and 99 other ranks was selected from Nos. 1, 3, 4, 8 and 10 Troops and included three future SAS officers, Lieutenants Stirling, Jellicoe and Mather. With this contingent on board, *Aphis* sailed from Mersa Matruh on 20 May. In the words of Mather:

> During the course of this operation we spent seven days on this little vessel (there was no room below) under spasmodic and then continuous attack by enemy dive-bombers. One hundred and seventy-two bombs (according to the ship's log) were aimed at the *Aphis*, not one of which made a direct hit. But the near misses deluged us in spray and played ducks and drakes around the ship, landing on one side of the ship and exploding on the other. We returned a hot fire at the enemy aircraft with our puny weapons, Bredas, pom-poms and anything we could lay out hands on, LMGs, Tommy guns and rifles, downing several aircraft.[7]

Naturally they were accompanied by Cowan, who was in his element, firing at the aircraft with his own tommy gun. However, all hope of surprise was lost and the swell was breaking over the deck, so the captain returned to Mersa Matruh on 22 May. After a second abortive voyage three days later, the ship put to sea once more on 26 May but was spotted almost immediately, and this time a bomb put the steering gear out of action. Early on the following morning *Aphis* made port under a jury steering rig, but this was her last attempt.

Having seen *Aphis* off on her first sortie, Bob returned to Sidi Bishr and then flew to Cairo for a meeting at GHQ on 22 May to discuss the possibility of converting two of his battalions into four Long Range Desert Groups. The LRDG commander, Major Ralph Bagnold, expressed a strong preference for recruiting from existing AFV regiments and motorized units and, although Bob emphasised the adaptability of his men, the matter was referred to a higher authority.

That evening Bob returned to Sidi Bishr, leaving at 20.00 for Mersa Matruh, where he wanted to be brought up to date on the Gazala raid. He arrived at 04.45 the next morning to find that *Aphis* was at sea. His visit proved to be 'an exceedingly brief one, lasting precisely the five minutes it took me to drink a whisky and soda and my driver to refill the car with petrol.'[8] Daly was waiting for him with the news that a telephone message had just been received from GHQ, ordering Bob to return to Alexandria as quickly as possible.

Chapter 11

Crete

The reason for Bob's urgent recall to Alexandria was the sharply deteriorating situation on Crete. Even before the occupation of mainland Greece was complete, Hitler had issued a directive for the seizure of the island for use in air operations in the Eastern Mediterranean, a threat which was confirmed by subsequent ULTRA intercepts. Major General Bernard Freyberg, who had led 2 New Zealand Division in Greece, was placed in overall command of the Allied force defending Crete, which comprised two brigades from his own division, a brigade from 7 Australian Division, a British regular brigade, a number of other unattached British and Australian units, the Mobile Naval Base Defence Organization, comprising about 2,000 Royal Marines, who were mostly gunners serving in coast and air defence batteries, and nine weak regiments from the Greek Army.

Crete is over 150 miles long as the crow flies and its northern coast is very much longer, due to its many indentations. Its defence thus presented a considerable problem for Freyberg, who decided to concentrate his strength around the three airfields at Maleme, Rethymno and Heraklion, the port of Canea and the anchorage at Suda Bay. These were linked by a single road which would be very easy to cut. Freyberg had little in the way of transport and few armoured fighting vehicles, and there was thus no possibility of mutual support by his widely dispersed forces.

Following six days of bombing, the German invasion began on the morning of 20 May, with parachute drops near the three airfields by General Student's XII Fliegerkorps. The assault was extremely costly for the Germans. In spite of their attempts to locate drop zones away from defended areas, they were highly vulnerable before they were able to concentrate and were slaughtered in large numbers. However, one regiment managed to gain control of Maleme airfield by the following morning. The local New Zealand commander withdrew his force precipitately from the airfield and the high ground dominating it, allowing Student's reserve battalion to drop successfully. Later on the same day, the first transport aircraft arrived, carrying reinforcements composed of experienced mountain troops. A counter-attack failed to restore the situation.

The capture of Maleme was the key to the battle. Notwithstanding that the defenders were holding on well elsewhere and that the Royal Navy dominated the seas north of Crete by night and was able to sink many of the ships carrying

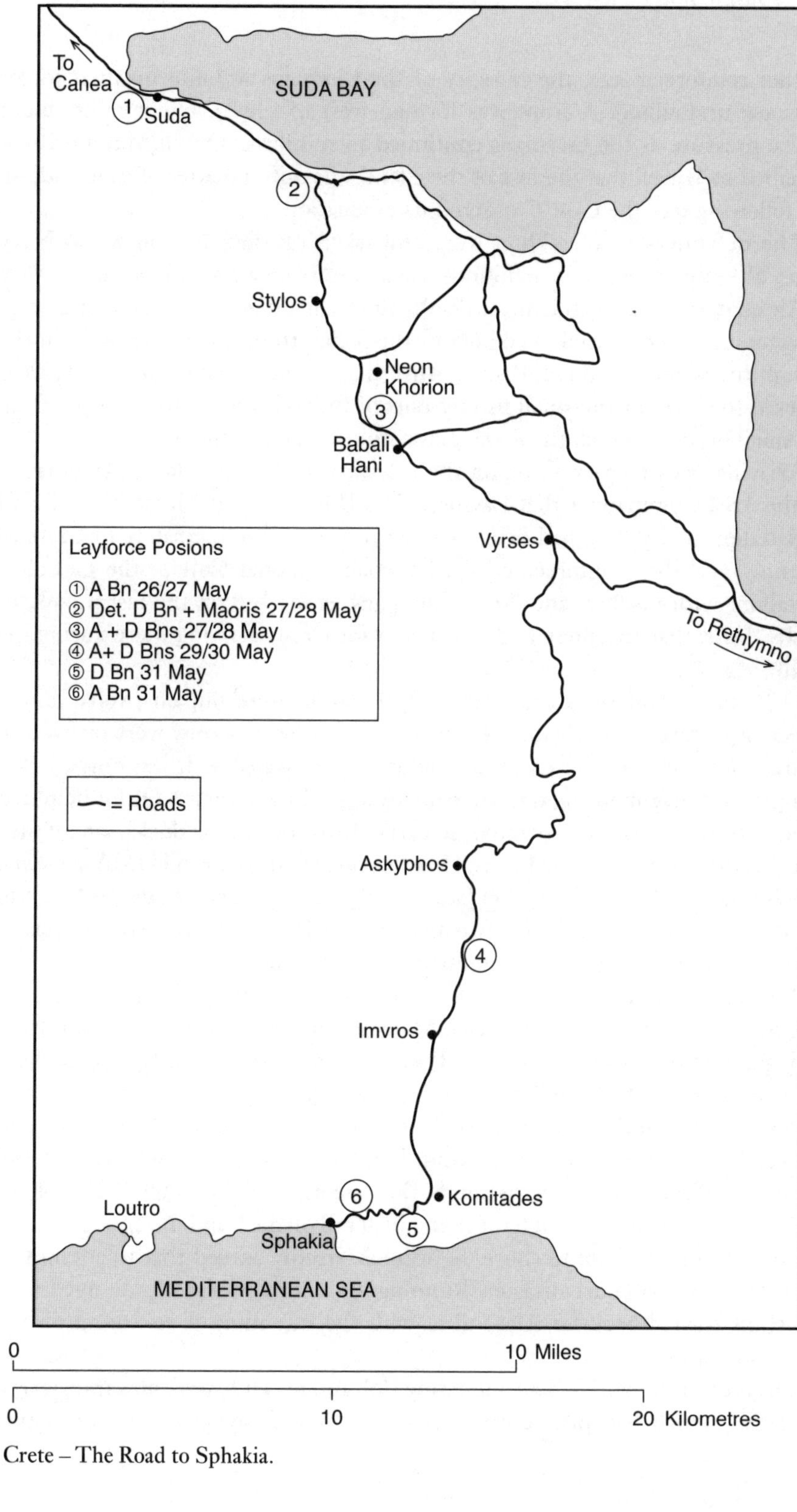
To Canea
SUDA BAY
Suda
Stylos
Neon Khorion
Babali Hani
Vyrses
To Rethymno
Layforce Posions
① A Bn 26/27 May
② Det. D Bn + Maoris 27/28 May
③ A + D Bns 27/28 May
④ A+ D Bns 29/30 May
⑤ D Bn 31 May
⑥ A Bn 31 May
= Roads
Askyphos
Imvros
Komitades
Loutro
Sphakia
MEDITERRANEAN SEA
0
10 Miles
0
10
20 Kilometres

Crete – The Road to Sphakia.

further reinforcements, the capacity of the Germans to build up their forces was now undoubted. A front was formed west of Canea, but it came under severe pressure as the Germans continued to reinforce. On 26 May Freyberg signalled to Wavell that the loss of the island was only a matter of time and, on the following day, the C-in-C ordered its evacuation.

The defenders of Heraklion were embarked satisfactorily on Royal Navy ships, although there were significant casualties from air attacks on the voyage to Alexandria. The Australians at Rethymno, cut off in both directions, were surrounded and captured. The bulk of the Allied troops, however, were in the west of the island and these, British, Australian, New Zealand and Greek, were ordered to make for the small fishing port of Sphakia on the south coast, from the small beach at which the Royal Navy would evacuate them.

Arriving back in Alexandria on the morning of 23 May, Bob was informed by the Area Commander that Layforce, less B Battalion at Mersa Matruh and C Battalion in Cyprus, had been ordered to proceed immediately to Crete as the only available reinforcements. Lieutenant Colonel Colvin, the CO of A Battalion, with his staff and No. 1 Company, embarked on the fast minelayer HMS *Abdiel* that afternoon and sailed later for Crete, arriving there during the night.

D Battalion and the remainder of A Battalion were put on twelve hours' notice of departure. Early on the following day, however, they were ordered to embark by 07.00, but there was no road transport available. It was only by Bob going round neighbouring units personally appealing to their COs for help that enough transport was put together to carry the troops to the docks, where they boarded four destroyers, HMS *Isis*, HMS *Decoy*, HMS *Hero* and HMAS *Nizam*, which sailed at 10.45. What Bob later described as 'a very untidy prelude'[1] to their operations occurred when two men from D Battalion fell overboard just as the ships were leaving harbour and had to be left behind.

The destroyers headed initially for Selino Kastelli on the south-west corner of Crete, in line with a plan to attack Maleme from the south. However, during their passage they were diverted to Porto Loutro, just west of Sphakia, where the troops were to be landed in the ships' boats and met by motor transport and mules, which would take them over the mountains towards the fighting around Canea. As they approached the island, however, the weather deteriorated and the sea conditions became very rough. Bob spent the night on the bridge of *Isis* with the captain, but although the men mustered on deck and the crew appeared to be keen to row them to shore, he wholeheartedly agreed that to attempt to land would be to court disaster. Running short of fuel for a prolonged stay, the ships turned back for Alexandria with the intention of returning on the following night.

The men on *Isis* and *Nizam*, including Bob and his HQ, were now transferred to *Abdiel*, which had just returned from her first foray, and the little flotilla sailed again at 23.00 on 25 May, having also taken on board the two men who had fallen into the sea on their previous departure. *Abdiel* was commanded by Captain Edward Pleydell-Bouverie, the brother of a friend of Bob's, who told him in confidence that the news from Crete was far worse that Bob had been led to believe, that Maleme had been taken and that the Allied forces were being pushed back. The new destination was Suda Bay, which meant that the flotilla had to run the gauntlet of German bombers in daylight around the eastern end of the island and along the north coast. *Abdiel* was one of a class reputed to be the fastest in the Royal Navy and, with the two destroyers, made good time, arriving at Suda Bay twenty-four hours later without being spotted. Pleydell-Bouverie told Bob that he would have to engineer a very quick disembarkation into two LCMs which would come out to meet them, in order to allow the ship time to avoid the dangerous waters before daylight; Bob was able to reassure him that his men were the best trained in the Army at doing just that.

Unfortunately, it did not turn out as they had hoped. The LCMs arrived full of wounded, who had to be lifted on to the ship, which took a great deal of time. Moreover, after they had taken the first parties from Layforce ashore, they returned with even more wounded. The situation was compounded by the naval officer in charge being badly shell-shocked, which not only affected his judgement in carrying out the operation, but also spread great concern when he described in graphic terms the state of affairs on land, which he assured everyone he met was close to disaster, strongly recommending a return to Alexandria. Bob told him very curtly that he did not require his advice, and Pleydell-Bouverie threatened to put him under arrest if he did not pipe down.

In the very small hours of 27 May the last men were taken ashore, but because of the need for the ships to sail well before daylight, a great deal of equipment was left behind, including most of the radio sets. The situation in and around Suda was chaotic, with fires and other bomb damage everywhere and parties of soldiers, seemingly detached from their units and with little semblance of discipline, moving in the wrong direction, away from the fighting. Bob was met by a liaison officer from A Battalion, which had established a line just west of Suda, and one from Major General Weston, the Royal Marine officer who had commanded the MNBDO prior to the invasion and who had recently been given responsibility for all those formations and units which had defended Canea, Suda Bay and Maleme. These, it was now confirmed, were in full retreat. Having consulted a small-scale map by torchlight, Bob ordered George Young to move D Battalion to an area east of Suda where, after establishing a defensive position, the men should try to get some much needed sleep; he also ordered Freddy Graham to set up the HQ nearby. He then set off with Waugh to find Weston.

It took about an hour and a half to locate Weston's HQ, and when Bob arrived he found the general fast asleep in a state of exhaustion. His GSO1 begged

Bob and Waugh not to wake him, but Weston did open one eye and, on being informed that Layforce had landed, murmured, 'Thank God' and went back to sleep. The GSO1 explained the situation, which was dire. The counter-attack on Maleme had failed, all the Allied fighter aircraft had been destroyed and the Germans now had complete air superiority, on which they were capitalizing by using dive bombers on the retreating troops. He warned that movement by day was highly dangerous. Layforce's orders were to form a rearguard with the Marines of the MNBDO, covering the withdrawal eastwards to the point where a small secondary road branched off the coast road towards Sphakia.

Bob instantly realized that this was a role for which his men were supremely ill-equipped. Carrying only sub-machine guns, pistols, knives, a limited number of rifles and a handful of Bren guns, with no heavy machine guns, mortars or mines, let alone artillery support, this was the antithesis of the kind of operation for which they had prepared for so many months. Bob determined to take the matter up directly with Freyberg, but before he did so he visited Colvin, who appeared to be greatly relieved to see him. A Battalion had been bombed but had thus far suffered no casualties since landing. Bob gave orders for it to hold a defensive position astride the coast road until D Battalion had moved into position just south of the road junction, upon which it would leapfrog back to another position which it should select itself.

Bob and Waugh, having somehow appropriated for themselves a truck and a Marine driver, then drove on to Freyberg's HQ. As Bob wrote subsequently:

> Later in the morning I found General Freyberg. He confirmed that the battle of Crete was lost, that our own forces in the island were utterly exhausted and that it now only remained to evacuate as many of them as possible. Since Layforce was composed of comparatively fresh troops it was to be used to take the brunt of the rearguard fighting necessary to cover this withdrawal. When I suggested that we might be more effective if, for example, we were landed in the rear of the enemy to harass his lines of communication and thus throw his advance into confusion, I was told in no uncertain terms to get on with the job allotted to me without further argument.[2]

The only comfort was that this was not to be a defence to the last man; the Layforce battalions were to withdraw once they were put under extreme pressure. Bob was later to say that withdrawal was made much easier by the fact that the Germans only operated by day and made no attempt to exploit their success by night. There was, however, an adverse impact on sleep, which was impossible in daytime due both to infantry attacks and, less damaging by way of casualties but much more so in terms of morale, to dive bombing. Bob himself experienced the latter shortly after returning from his meeting with

Freyberg. Needing a wash, he had just stripped off and filled his helmet with water when the Stukas arrived. 'I have never felt more utterly naked in my life,'[3] he wrote later.

During 27 May A Battalion held its line from the road west of Suda into the hills on the landward side, with D Battalion and 28 Maori Battalion further back near the road junction close to which Graham had set up Bob's HQ. As darkness fell, D Battalion fell back to prepare a line further south between Stylos and Babali Hani, leaving a detachment, composed largely of Spanish Republicans, to hold a position just before the junction. However, believing it to be untenable, many of the Spaniards withdrew without orders and rejoined their battalion, whilst those who remained in position were later cut off.

The last Allied troops passed through A Battalion's line at about 21.00 and, with patrols still in contact with the enemy, the battalion withdrew at 03.00 towards Stylos. Three troops fell into an ambush, which was beaten off with light casualties. Just before midnight, however, Colvin appeared at Bob's Rear HQ to say that his line had been outflanked; but shortly after daylight on 28 May his second-in-command, Major Ken Wylie, led a spirited counter-attack on the advancing Germans with some success. During that day the battalion withdrew further through D Battalion's position five miles south of Stylos. Waugh visited them and asked to see Colvin, finding him under a table from which he only reluctantly emerged after the German dive bombers had left the sky

On the morning of 28 May, on his way to Brigade HQ with Freddy Graham and supposing that they would be well covered by D Battalion's positions, Bob found himself in an ambush. German mountain troops had managed to work their way across to the road and were lying in wait. Layforce had unexpectedly been allocated the last three Matilda infantry tanks on the island, two of which had been given instructions to rendezvous nearby but were initially nowhere to be seen. By what Bob later described as 'an incredibly lucky coincidence',[4] at just that moment the two men saw the tanks under camouflage nets nearby, just off the road.

> Why they and the Germans had not seen each other before I cannot imagine, but be that as it may it did not take Freddie and myself as long as it takes to write this to jump into them and, camouflage nets and all, drive with some satisfaction slap through the German ambush scattering them in all directions. They retreated rapidly towards the west into country over which we could not follow them.[5]

Later that day, Bob managed to contact Brigadier Hargest, who now commanded all the New Zealand troops remaining on the island, and was lucky to find with him his Australian counterpart, Brigadier Vasey. He wrote later:

> Their view was that the three of us should co-ordinate the withdrawal without reference to anyone else as it was useless to expect coherent orders from above. They took a poor view of Weston and his staff and said so without mincing their words. Consequently we discussed plans and agreed what lines we should hold and for how long.[6]

In the words of the subsequent Inter-Services Committee report on Crete:

> Close collaboration between Brigadier Hargest, commanding the 5th New Zealand Brigade, Vasey, commanding the 19th Australian Brigade, and Colonel Laycock, commanding Layforce, alone enabled the initial part of the withdrawal to be conducted in security.[7]

Bob had left A Battalion in what he thought was a very suitable position on some high ground with a fine field of fire, from which he believed the Germans could be held for some time. To his horror, on his way back from inspecting D Battalion's new position he met several detachments of A Battalion retreating towards him. When he asked what they were doing leaving a defensive position without orders, they assured him that they had received a direct order from their commanding officer. Although a counter-attack led by Captain Jocelyn Nicholls partially restored the situation, the position had been abandoned quite unnecessarily. Colvin, who had clearly completely lost his nerve, was relieved of his command and, although Wylie was appointed his successor, the remnants of the two battalions were now effectively merged under Young.

D Battalion, together with 2/8 Australian Battalion, bore the brunt of the action on 28 May, with many casualties, and so Bob, accompanied by Waugh as Graham was worn out, set out to visit Young again that evening. Young was not entirely pleased to see them, because he was in a poor position, albeit the best that could be found; also, Bob had discarded his tin helmet and was 'rather stupidly',[8] as he later admitted, wearing his red banded service dress cap, which Young pointed out was drawing enemy fire. Michael Borwick, Young's adjutant, whilst agreeing that the hat attracted unwelcome attention, later recorded another view of Bob:

> I went down the road with Bob Laycock for him to see for himself – he was a great morale booster by himself, full of fun and made jokes the whole time. One enemy fighter had a go at us, so we landed in an undignified heap. I cannot remember who was on top.[9]

By early afternoon the battalion was engaged in heavy fighting and its HQ was very nearly surrounded before the enemy troops were pushed back with heavy losses. That night, the battalion withdrew a long way further south to Askyphos, where it was joined by A Battalion.

Bob's HQ had been in Babali Hani, but it moved during the night of 28/29 May much further south to Ayios Antonios. The staff had not gone 100 yards when five mortar bombs landed on the house. They boarded one of the very few trucks available, but it had to be abandoned when they reached a point in the road where it had been cratered against orders and was being repaired by a party of engineers. The last of the tanks, which had recently proved their worth on a number of occasions, was also left behind, its engine running but with oil and water drained so it would seize up.

In the plan agreed with the two brigadiers Layforce was due to establish a new line south of Vryses. However, in the light of its casualties and, even more, its exhaustion after two days and nights without sleep, Weston decided that it should be relieved by the New Zealanders and withdraw further south. Brigade HQ was located near Imvros, where Weston's own HQ was also sited at the time. The two battalions both made their way to Askyphos during 29 May, with D Battalion taking up positions flanking the ravine south of the village through which the road led to Sphakia, whilst A Battalion rested in the ravine itself.

For the whole of 30 May Layforce remained in these positions, and that evening Bob and Waugh went to find Freyberg, whose HQ was situated in a cave near Sphakia. He gave each of them half a cupful of sherry and a handful of beans, and Bob asked him about the order of embarkation. The reply was simple: 'You were the last to come so you will be the last to go'.[10] Freyberg, however, made it clear that he was referring to the fighting troops, all of whom would have priority over the very many stragglers who had become separated from their units and were now rapidly becoming a rabble. Shortly afterwards he left the island by flying boat. On their return journey, Bob and Waugh found the going too difficult in the dark and spent the night in a little shrine on a hilltop. They found some recreation in completing *Times* crossword puzzles, a book of which Bob had bought in Egypt.

On 31 May D Battalion moved further back to a new line to the east of Sphakia covering the final evacuation route to the beach. A Battalion was relieved in its old position by the Maoris and also took up a new position covering the beach itself, with the battalion split into left and right flanks. Early that afternoon Bob and Waugh went to see Weston in the cave formerly occupied by Freyberg. This led to the following entry in the Layforce war diary, which was written up by Waugh well after the events it recorded:

> Final orders from CREFORCE for evacuation (a) LAYFORCE positions not to be held to the last man and last round but only as long as was necessary to cover withdrawal of other fighting forces. (b) No withdrawal

> before order from H.Q. (c) LAYFORCE to embark after other fighting forces but before stragglers.[11]

Weston, according to Bob, was thoroughly despondent, warning that there was a shortage of ammunition and food was in very short supply. Bob replied that his men, having picked up large quantities of abandoned ammunition during the retreat, had more than they could possibly shoot off, and had also been trained to forage for themselves. He was amused later in the day when his soldier servant, Corporal Cook, on being asked what was on the menu for dinner, replied, 'Two roast fowls and a sucking pig. This was a slight exaggeration, for the meal consisted of "an old hen which had obviously run several times round the island and some pieces of pork from a pig of doubtful age".'[12]

That evening Bob received a message from Weston to report to him again without delay. This was a key meeting and Bob recorded it later in his memoirs:

> On arrival at his headquarters I found him looking more utterly dejected than I can describe. He looked at me without appearing to see me for a moment or two and then said very slowly and very quietly: 'I am now going to say something which, even in my most ghastly nightmare, I never dreamed that I could say to a British officer on the field of battle. Take down this order.' I turned to Freddy who produced a notebook and pencil. Again in a voice so subdued that we could hardly hear him General Weston started to dictate.
>
> 'From GOC Crete to Remnants Creforce. You will provide yourself with a white flag. Tomorrow morning at first light you will seek out the Commander of the German forces and surrender to him.'
>
> When he had finished, Freddy handed the message to me. I gazed at it for some time before asking Weston whether he would consider it very insubordinate if I flatly refused to obey it. Weston's reply was not, as might so easily have been the case, that it was not for me to reason why. Instead he told me that it was clearly necessary to find a senior officer to explain the situation formally to the enemy … He told me that he himself had been ordered to leave the island in a flying boat that was due to arrive shortly, that Vasey and Hargest were about to embark and that I, as a full Colonel, would be the senior officer left on the island.
>
> I pointed out that the Commandos still had plenty of fight left in them. Either I could stay and organize guerrilla warfare in the hills (which some of the Commandos eventually undertook on their own initiative) or, as there were still ships lying off Sphakia, I could evacuate as many of my own men, including my Brigade Staff, as could get down to the beach in time.
>
> I must admit to being somewhat relieved when Weston, after some thought, gave it as his opinion that the second alternative seemed much

more likely to pay a dividend to our future war effort. In coming to this decision he had taken into account that, as the Germans were making no attempt to give us the coup de gras [*sic*], the responsibility of Layforce to provide a rearguard to a force which was due to surrender in a few hours time had lapsed.

With regard to finding a senior officer to surrender to the Germans, he agreed that as a full Colonel prepared to continue the war was worth more to our side than a Lt. Colonel who gave every appearance of doing no such thing, it was more appropriate for the latter to undertake the role than the former … I now had his permission to delegate my responsibility and that I was at liberty to evacuate my Brigade Headquarters and as many of my men as possible.

I left Weston to go out to his seaplane and went in search of my understudy. When I found him I handed over the surrender orders. Poor man, he was very unhappy.[13]

Graham's account of this key episode is very different, although the conclusion is much the same. He wrote later that he was already at Weston's HQ without Bob, where he identified himself as the Layforce Brigade Major and was ordered directly by Weston to take down the surrender order. He also wrote that Bob had been there earlier and that, when the two met up again shortly afterwards, Bob told him that when Weston had ordered him to make the surrender, a staff officer had 'intervened to say that Layock still had two Battalions of his Brigade in Egypt. On hearing this Weston changed his mind and ordered Layock to take his Brigade HQ and as many of his force (which was now about 400 all ranks) as he could out that night.'[14]

Weston wrote in his own despatches that he sent for Colvin to make the surrender, clear evidence that Bob himself was free to go. Graham confirmed that Colvin was present in Weston's cave and that one of the three copies of the order was given directly to him, with one retained by Weston and one by Graham.

The order subsequently appeared in Weston's despatches and, albeit with one key difference, was later appended by Waugh to the Layforce War Diary. The latter reads as follows:

From: Major-General Weston.
To: Lt. Col. Colvin.

In view of the following facts:

(a) My orders direct me to give preference in evacuation to fighting troops. This has reduced the active garrison below what is required for resistance.

> (b) As no rations are left this Saturday night most of the troops are too weak owing to shortage of food and heavy strain to organise further resistance
> (c) The wireless will give out in a few hours and the risk of waiting for instructions from Mideast cannot be accepted as this will leave the Officer Commanding without guidance as to his course of action.
> (d) There is no possibility of further evacuation.
>
> I hereby order you to collect what senior Officers are available before tomorrow and communicate this order to them.
>
> I further order you to go forward at first light tomorrow and capitulate to the enemy.
>
> Signed. Weston. Major-General.[15]

The last two paragraphs in the version recorded in Weston's despatches are different:

> I therefore direct you to collect such senior officers as are available in the early hours of tomorrow and transmit these orders to the senior of them.
>
> These orders direct this officer to make contact with the enemy and to capitulate.[16]

In the War Diary Waugh recorded that Weston dictated the surrender order to Graham at 21.00 on 31 May. For 22.00 the entry in the war diary is as follows:

> On finding that entire staff of CREFORCE had withdrawn, Col. Laycock, accompanied by B.M. and I.O. proceeded to SPHAKION to obtain authority for withdrawal.
>
> On finding that entire staff of CREFORCE had embarked, in view of the fact that all fighting forces were now in position for embarkation and that there was no enemy contact, Col. Laycock, on own authority, issued orders to Lt. Col. Young to lead troops to SPHAKION by route avoiding the crowded main approach to town and to use his own personality to obtain priority laid down in Div. orders.
>
> LAYFORCE reached SPHAKION in good time for boats but were unable to penetrate rabble; flank dets. were able to reach beach but main body remained ashore.
>
> Col. LAYCOCK accompanied by B.M. and I.O. embarked H.M.S. KIMBERLEY.
>
> Total numbers of LAYFORCE evacuated 23 officers, 186 O.Rs.[17]

Bob sent Waugh's batman, Private Tanner, with the orders. After a difficult climb back up the road, Tanner found Young, who said that he would try to comply. In the event it proved impossible for the bulk of Layforce to break through the rabble of stragglers on the main track to the beach. Only A, B, one section of E and G Troops of A Battalion on the left flank managed to catch the last boats, as they found a minor and unimpeded path. The rest of what remained of A and D Battalions were taken prisoner on the following day. The surrender was not made by Colvin, who handed the order to Young, who was his senior, in accordance with Weston's direction. Young himself was saved from a most distasteful task by the discovery that the CO of 2/7 Australian Battalion, Lieutenant Colonel T. G. Walker, was more senior still. On Bob's recommendation, Young and Wylie were both awarded the DSO, whilst Tanner, who succeeded in catching the very last boat, was mentioned in despatches.

Bob's actions have come in for serious criticism by some historians. He has been both accused of disregarding an order from Weston on the afternoon of 31 May that Layforce should leave after all other fighting forces and censured for leaving himself without the greater part of his command. The first charge is the more difficult to defend, as it relies heavily on Bob's own account of his last meeting with Weston, according to which Weston overrode the earlier order. The Graham version arrives at the same conclusion, but relies on hearsay. The only other man close to the events in question, albeit not present at that meeting, was Waugh, who wrote subsequently:

> Weston said that we were to cover the withdrawal and that a message would be sent to us by the embarkation officer on Sphakia beach when we could retire.
>
> At about 10 o'clock that evening there was no sign of the enemy and the approaches to the beaches were thronged with non-fighting troops. Bob and I and Freddy, with servants, therefore set off to find the beach officer Colonel Healey, and ask authority to withdraw. We pushed our way through the crowds who were too spiritless even to resist what they took to be an unauthorised intrusion and arrived on the beach to find that there was no one in charge, Colonel Healey having left earlier by aeroplane. Bob then took the responsibility of ordering Layforce to fight their way through the rabble and embark.[18]

Bob clearly believed that not only did he already have explicit permission to leave with his staff, but also that, in the absence of any authority allocating priorities on the beach, he could take the rest of Layforce with him. In such circumstances, saving what he could from the wreckage of the campaign was the correct military decision. However, it hangs on his recollection of the Weston meeting, for which there is no third-party corroboration other than Graham's somewhat different hearsay version.

The second criticism, that he should have remained behind with his troops, presents more of a moral issue. This question would probably not have attracted much attention – after all Freyberg, Weston and Vasey had also left behind large numbers of those they had commanded – had it not been for the publication in 1955 of Waugh's novel *Officers and Gentlemen*, the second volume of the *Sword of Honour* trilogy, in which his own wartime experiences were thinly disguised. The dedication of the book to Bob – 'To Major General Sir Robert Laycock KCMG CB DSO. That every man in arms would wish to be' – provoked a telegram from Waugh's friend, Ann Fleming,[19] which the author recorded in his diary:

> Ann Fleming, to my horror, has telegraphed 'Presume Ivor Claire based Laycock dedication ironical'. I replied that if she breathes a suspicion of this cruel fact, it will be the end of our friendship.[20]

In the novel the character most closely based on Bob, Tommy Blackhouse, falls down a ladder on the ship to Crete and breaks his leg, thus avoiding any responsibility for the debacle. Ivor Claire, on the other hand, a debonair member of the Commando raised by Blackhouse, deserts his men on Crete and manages to get back to Egypt. Claire is not based on any single real person, but is a blend of some of the officers of 8 Commando, although none of these, apart from Waugh himself, was on Crete. Bob, who considered that he himself had been let off lightly in the novel, later described Claire as a 'mixture of Eddie Fitzclarence, Bones Sudeley and Peter Beatty and, I expect, Randolph, though part of the character is not unlike his great friends Philip Dunne & Peter Milton'.[21]

Fleming was clearly being mischievous and was taken aback by Waugh's response, which was vitriolic. However, the use of the words 'this cruel fact' have been taken as evidence of Waugh's belief that Bob's and his own evacuation without the majority of Layforce was in some way dishonourable. What needs to be understood is Waugh's own state of mind at the time and his recollections of Crete thereafter. A man whose otherwise unsoldierly qualities belied his considerable personal courage, he was absolutely appalled by the behaviour of many of the soldiers during the retreat, and particularly of Colvin, who was the model for the character, but not the role, of the fictitious Major Hound.

In 1976 Graham was asked if Waugh thought that Bob should have stayed behind. His reply was: 'He never said, or hinted so. Perhaps because he had a personal horror of being captured!'[22] The second sentence was confirmed by Bob's account of their walk back from the first meeting with Weston on 31 May, during which Waugh asked Bob if he could have leave of absence to see the Roman Catholic padre. Bob asked him why:

> 'I am determined not to suffer the ignominy of capture,' replied Evelyn, 'and I wish to ask him whether it would be considered suicide if I drowned in an attempt to swim back to Egypt.'[23]

It proved impossible to locate the padre, and Bob observed:

> Whether or not he would have struck out on his long swim had the necessity arisen I do not know for, as it turned out, we embarked on the last ship to leave the island. By the look on his face at the time I gathered that Evelyn believed this to be a dishonourable thing to do though it made sense to me for, at least, we lived to fight another day.[24]

It does seem likely that Waugh's shame at their flight from the island was, to some extent, shared in his own mind with Bob, in spite of his admiration for a man who had become his mentor and was to remain his supporter.

There was, on the other hand, not a hint of official disapproval of Bob's actions, let alone anything stronger, in Weston's despatches, the Inter-Services Report or any other official or semi-official account of the campaign. On the contrary, notwithstanding the demise of Layforce shortly afterwards, with the inevitable impact on Bob's short-term prospects, his personal standing remained high, and in due course his career resumed its steep trajectory. Moreover, his immediate subordinate, George Young, who was unable to get his men and himself away, believed strongly that Bob's actions were justified and that:

> Whilst battalion commanders are duty bound to go into captivity with their men in such situations, formation commanders, because they have no direct contact with the troops under their command, are under no such onus.[25]

Bob's own reflections on his escape from Crete, whilst expressing justification for his decision to leave, did, nevertheless, introduce more than a suggestion of doubt about doing so:

> Was I right in using arguments which influenced Weston to countermand his original orders, should I, personally, have embarked that night knowing that nearly three-quarters of my command was still ashore? Probably not. There is much to be said in support of the principle that the Captain is the last to leave the sinking ship. At the time, however, my motive seemed reasonable enough and I am confident that my Brigade Staff, with the

possible exception of Evelyn, heartily agreed with my contention that we would be more use to our country by returning with the remnants of Nos. 7, 50 and 52 Commandos to rejoin Nos. 8 and 11 in Egypt than by spending the rest of the war in a prisoner of war camp. Once the order to surrender was given I maintained that every able-bodied man who succeeded in getting back to Egypt had done the right thing. '*Qui s'excuse s'accuse*.' I have never been happy about leaving Young and his gallant men behind.[26]

Chapter 12

Disbandment

Like his companions, Bob had had very little sleep since they first left Alexandria and so, having drunk several mugs of hot, sweet tea, he made up for some of what he had lost. Although a number of German planes were picked up on the radar, none attacked and *Kimberley* made a trouble-free passage. One of the first people Bob met after landing on 1 June was his brother Peter, who had just arrived from Tobruk in 'Pedlar' Palmer's schooner, the *Maria Giovanni*. He sent a telegram to his parents to tell them of the reunion, but nothing to Angie, as he had not told her that he was going to Crete. In fact she had found this out from another source, so was greatly relieved to hear from Bob's sister Rosemary that he was back in Alexandria. It was several days before Bob had time to write to her with a brief description of his adventures.

With his HQ re-established at Sidi Bishr, Bob reported to GHQ in Cairo on the following day. Arthur Smith told him that he would have to give evidence to the Inter-Services Committee which was being put together under the chairmanship of Colonel Guy Salisbury-Jones, the former Chief Staff Officer of the British Military Mission to Greece. Salisbury-Jones, who was well-known to Bob, had accompanied the Greek royal family to Crete, where Bob had met him briefly on the roadside during the retreat.

Smith then dropped a bombshell, telling Bob that there was no possibility of providing reinforcements for Layforce from volunteers within Middle East Command. The Prime Minister was demanding offensive action in the Western Desert, and there were not enough troops as it was. In the meantime, however, C Battalion, which was due to arrive back in Egypt from Cyprus within the next two days, had been selected for a role in the imminent Allied invasion of Vichy French-held Syria, which was all too likely to lead to further casualties.

Bob was too late to have any involvement with C Battalion's actions on the Litani River in the Syria-Lebanon campaign, in their way the most successful of all those carried out by Layforce during its short history. The operation was mounted in support of the left flank of the invasion force, whose immediate path was blocked by the Litani. The intention was for three separate parties to land north of the river and neutralize the Vichy defences, allowing 7 Australian Division to cross and advance up the coast. The battalion embarked in *Glengyle* on 6 June with the objective of landing very early the next morning, but in all too familiar fashion the sea proved to be too rough. On the following night the surf had subsided sufficiently to permit the landings, and all three parties embarked satisfactorily in their landing craft. By this time, however, surprise had been lost and the commandos landed with the moon behind them and the sun in their eyes. In these circumstances they were lucky not to incur heavy losses on the beaches.

Y Party in the centre under Lieutenant Colonel Pedder and Z Party on the left under Captain George More, the Adjutant, both landed on the correct beaches. Initially there was only modest opposition, and More's party was particularly successful, both capturing guns and other equipment and taking prisoners. With no sign of the Australians, however, it was forced to retire across the Litani, which it managed successfully, other than one detachment which was forced back to the beach, where it surrendered, having taken a number of casualties. On the next day the prisoners were released by their Vichy captors.

Pedder's party, in the meantime, attacked a Vichy redoubt covering the key bridge, which they found had already been demolished. The attack continued, however, so that the Australians could construct a pontoon bridge at the site. Resistance was fierce and Pedder was killed, as was the second-in-command of the party. With the other officers and many men dead or wounded, command devolved on the Regimental Sergeant Major, who succeeded in taking the nearby barracks, thus preventing the enemy from reinforcing the redoubt.

X Party on the right under Geoffrey Keyes was landed on the wrong side of the river mouth. However, he established contact with the Australians, from whom he borrowed a boat, which he used to ferry his men across the river under heavy fire, eventually gathering enough to capture the redoubt and enable a pontoon bridge to be constructed. This was effectively the end of the battle, in which C Battalion had distinguished itself, albeit at a considerable cost. Five officers had been killed and total casualties amounted to 123 men, about 25 per cent of the battalion's strength. Keyes, who took over command, in which he was subsequently confirmed, re-concentrated the battalion at Haifa before it returned to Cyprus, where Bob visited it on 23 June.

B Battalion in the meantime had remained at Mersa Matruh, but on 8 June Sudeley, Dunne and Churchill sailed to Tobruk, followed on the next day by nine officers and 109 other ranks. On arrival they were bombed on their way to the transit camp and lost two dead and four injured. The intention was to make a number of raids on German and Italian positions, but Sudeley's nerve failed after some postponements and he insisted on the detachment being withdrawn again, returning himself to Alexandria in advance. This caused considerable embarrassment to Bob, who was in Cairo when Sudeley reappeared. He had to write a very difficult letter to Major General Leslie Morshead, the Australian commanding the Tobruk garrison, offering the rather lame excuse that Sudeley had believed that the members of his battalion should return to take up other appointments due the imminent disbandment of Layforce. In the event, this episode caused considerable distress to Daly and more generally within B Battalion, in which morale plummeted.

Following a meeting in Cairo on 12 June, it had indeed been decided to disband Layforce, and Morshead and other interested parties were sent a letter on the subject on 15 June. A Battalion had been reduced to 150 all ranks under Nicholls. B Battalion was still substantially intact, but very unhappy. C Battalion stood at only 75 per cent of its full strength. D Battalion had effectively ceased to exist, apart from a number of casualties who had been evacuated from Crete before the surrender. The Brigade HQ was already being run down, with both Graham and Franks posted elsewhere during June, followed on 7 July by Waugh, who was returned to the Royal Marines and shipped back to the UK.

The letter of 15 June made it clear that it would be impossible to guarantee that all those whose six months engagement for Special Service had expired would be permitted to return to their own units in the UK, either at the time or in the future, although applications for posting to the Home Establishment on compassionate grounds would be considered. Personnel of A, B and D Battalions would, however, be allowed to return to their own units in the Middle East. Likewise, officers and men in these battalions who elected to remain in a Special Service unit would be able to do so, but the future organization of this would depend on the numbers who applied. In the meantime, volunteers for guerrilla activities in the Far East were specifically called for. C Battalion would remain on its present organization until operations permitted it to be treated in the same way as the others.

Forty-seven officers and 692 other ranks remained in A, B and D battalions, not much more than a single battalion's full establishment of 36 officers and 537 other ranks. Of these, 17 officers and 315 other ranks expressed a wish to remain in a Special Service role; three officers and 121 other ranks, led by Nicholls,[1] volunteered for service in the Far East and departed shortly afterwards; 11 officers and 182 other ranks decided to return to their own units in the Middle East and India; nine officers and 43 other ranks applied to return to the UK on compassionate grounds; seven officers and 26 other ranks made other specific applications for transfer.

Of the officers of 8 Commando who had sailed for the Middle East, Milton, Stavordale, Sudeley, Usher, Campbell and Ian Collins of No. 3 Troop were selected for posting to the Home Establishment. Campbell, however, remained in the Middle East and Sudeley died before he could get back to the UK, of a condition which stopped his sweat glands working, causing fatal heatstroke. It is possible that this condition may have had an effect on his behaviour in Tobruk.

However, 8 Commando did manage one last hurrah when a small party returned to Tobruk in July. Led by Mike Kealy, with Philip Dunne as his second-in-command, three other officers, including Jock Lewes, and 70 other ranks, it found itself attached to an Indian regiment, 18th King Edward

VII's Own Cavalry, with which it co-operated very cheerfully, carrying out a number of successful patrols to reconnoitre the Italian positions. On 18 July the detachment, split into three parties, each accompanied by Australian sappers, mounted a major raid on a feature held by the Italians known as the Twin Pimples. The small force worked its way around to the rear of the enemy position and, as soon as diversionary fire was opened by the Indians, attacked with great success, killing most of the Italians and blowing up their ammunition dumps. As it was withdrawing, the Italians laid down heavy fire from nearby and one man was killed and four wounded, but this was thought to be a small price for an otherwise successful raid. No prisoners were taken, but two days later Lewes brought one back from a patrol.

On 18 June, in the aftermath of the decision to disband Layforce, Bob sent a signal to Roger Keyes, copied to GHQ Middle East:

> Following for D.C.O. repeated Brigadier HAYDON from Colonel LAYCOCK S.S. Bde. Repeated cancellation of Combined Operations caused continued inactivity of S.S. Bde from arrival here until recently (with exception unopposed and not very satisfactory BARDIA raid in April). Past three weeks, however witnessed extensive use S.S. tps resulting in successful actions but such heavy casualties that disbandment now ordered by C-in-C with exception C Bn now defending Cyprus. A Bn (7 Commando) and D Bn (ME Commando) fought fierce rearguard action CRETE but seventy percent failed return Egypt. C Bn (11 Commando) carried out very successful daring raid SYRIA Colonel PEDDER killed and twenty-five percent unit killed wounded or missing. Captain KEYES returned safely having done excellent work. B Bn (8 Commando) now executing raids WESTERN DESERT. As Bde is disbanded do you require my services in UK.[2]

Wavell, who three days later was to hear of his replacement as C-in-C Middle East by General Sir Claude Auchinleck, immediately asked that the CIGS should recall Bob. He also suggested, apparently contrary to what had been agreed, that the Commandos' troops should be returned to the UK, together with *Glengyle* and *Glenroy*, *Glenearn* having been badly damaged off Crete. A signal came back in due course that the Prime Minister had decided that the Glen ships should remain in the Middle East and that the Commandos should in some way be reconstituted; on 28 June another signal arrived from Dill requesting that Bob should return to the UK by the first available aircraft.

The dates of Bob's departure from Cairo or arrival in England are not recorded in any war diary, but it seems likely that the former was during the second week of July. In any event, he relinquished his appointment as Officer Commanding Layforce on 15 July, on which day he gave up his acting rank of colonel and reverted to his war substantive rank of major, which he had held since 11 October 1940.[3] The delay between the signal from the CIGS and the date of departure was caused by his having to wait for the Salisbury-Jones Committee's report on Crete, which he was to deliver in person. This had to be typed out in great haste and was handed to Bob by Arthur Smith before Smith or anyone else at GHQ had had time to read it. The Chief of Staff impressed on Bob that he should go straight to the War Office on arrival in England and hand it over to Dill and to no one else. Smith did agree, however, that Bob could take a second copy for Roger Keyes.

Bob's journey took him by Sunderland flying boat up the Nile to Khartoum and thence by Lockheed Lodestar across Africa to Lagos. On the way he read the report:

> It was a splendid document, but, as I turned the pages I began to wonder what lay in store for its author after Wavell and Arthur Smith had read it too![4] Salisbury-Jones had not minced his words and by the time one had finished reading it one was left in no doubt whatsoever that the battle of Crete had been lost principally because G.H.Q. Middle East had failed to take even the most elementary measure for the defence of the island.[5]

In Lagos Bob boarded a BOAC Boeing Clipper flying boat, now attired in 'a ghastly pair of reach-me-down grey flannel trousers, a pale blue shirt and a dreadful brown homburg hat'[6] and provided with a passport and papers representing him as an official of the Ministry of Agriculture and Fisheries, so that he could avoid internment in any neutral country The Clipper was an exceptionally comfortable aircraft which even boasted beds for the passengers, and Bob found a congenial companion in Harold Caccia, an Old Etonian of his own vintage who had been a member of the British Embassy in Athens at the time of the German invasion and had been evacuated first to Crete and then to Egypt. They landed in the Gambia for the night, where they were able to swim in the Atlantic before the plane took off in the morning. The next stop was Lisbon, where it transpired that Bob's new passport had an unacceptable visa. Asked if he knew anyone who might vouch for him, he suggested the British Ambassador, Sir Ronald Campbell, to whom he wished to pass on news of his son Robin. Campbell immediately sent a car for him and gave him an excellent lunch, which was followed by an even more excellent dinner with Caccia in a fish restaurant.

The Clipper then flew on towards its destination, Poole Harbour, but the weather closed in and it was diverted to Shannon in Ireland, where an uncomfortable interview with a customs officer ended happily when Bob claimed acquaintance with a popular local horse dealer. In due course Bob made his way to London and the War Office, stopping only at Combined Operations HQ to hand a copy of the Inter-Services Committee Report to Keyes, who was delighted when Bob told him that he had recommended Geoffrey for a Military Cross for his actions on the Litani.

On arrival at the War Office, Bob sought an immediate interview with Dill, whom he had not met since he had enlisted the support of the CIGS to join the Commandos. Dill's Military Assistant asked him to leave the document in the office for onward delivery, which Bob, mindful of his instructions, refused to do. Minutes later he was ushered into the CIGS's office:

> When I went in to see Dill he greeted me with 'Come in, come in, we've been waiting for you for several days. Let's have a look at this offensive document you've brought with you. The wires from the Middle East have been red hot to say that it is scurrilous in the extreme and that they disagree with practically every word in it.' I was not surprised.[7]

An officer was sent round immediately to Combined Operations HQ to demand that Keyes should surrender his copy. In due course the criticisms of the Inter-Services Committee were toned down significantly, and only the sanitized version of the report survives on the record.

His official duties out of the way, Bob went straight to the Berkeley Hotel, where Angie was staying. With the children still in Canada, Angie had felt that she should make a contribution to the war effort and had accordingly become involved in the British Restaurants. The first of over 2,000 of these had been set up in 1940 on the initiative of the Prime Minister, specifically to help those who had been bombed out of their homes or who were experiencing difficulties with rationing. They were run by local authorities, notably the London County Council, or by voluntary organizations, and provided a basic but nourishing meal from a canteen-type operation for 9d. Angie became involved in the administration and also acted as a volunteer at one of the restaurants.

After spending the night in London, Bob and Angie went down to their small cottage at Hawthorn Hill, only to receive shortly afterwards a message from the Prime Minister inviting them both to spend the weekend at Chequers. Bob's recollection of the other guests was that they included General Sir Alan Brooke, at that time C-in-C Home Forces, and General Sir Hastings Ismay, Churchill's Chief of Staff in his capacity as Minister of Defence, which would establish the date from Brooke's diary as 19 July. Bob later recalled:

> At luncheon on Sunday the Prime Minister suddenly turned to me and said, 'I thought I had sent you with the Commandos to the Middle East. May I ask what you are doing back here in this country and why the force which you command has not been used in the role for which it was raised and trained?' In answer to the first I explained that the whole future of the Commandos in the Middle East was dependent on the vexed question of how the heavy casualties we had suffered could be replaced. I had reported to Sir Roger Keyes and now awaited his instructions. The Prime Minister,

> looking slightly belligerent, interposed to say that any instructions I received would probably come directly from him.

In answer to the second question, Bob cited the Bardia raid and the Litani river operation as instances of the correct use of Layforce, but said that GHQ Middle East had never appreciated its capabilities and felt that it had been foisted on them.

The Prime Minister then asked Bob for his opinion of COHQ. Bob expressed his strong personal admiration for Keyes, but said that he believed that the admiral was *persona non grata* with the Chiefs of Staff. Perhaps, he continued, someone younger might be appropriate.

> 'Oh, indeed,' replied the Prime Minister, 'and who have you in mind?' … 'Oh, I don't know,' I remarked, 'I should have thought someone like Dickie Mountbatten.'
>
> It may well be that Mr Churchill was never even remotely influenced by my reply; certain it is, however, that Captain the Lord Louis Mountbatten, as he was then, replaced Keyes not long afterwards.

Bob did not dare to repeat this conversation to Mountbatten until many years later, since when he next met him, in early 1942, Mountbatten told him how upset he had been at his removal from the command of his first capital ship, the aircraft carrier HMS *Illustrious*, before it had finished refitting in Norfolk, Virginia!

The Prime Minister sprang into action immediately. On 23 July he sent Ismay a minute:

> I wish the Commandos in the Middle East to be reconstituted as soon as possible. Instead of being governed by a committee of officers without much authority, Brigadier Laycock[8] should be appointed Director of Combined Operations. The three Glen ships and the D.C.O., with his forces, should be placed directly under Admiral Cunningham, who should be charged with all combined operations involving sea transport and not exceeding one brigade. The Middle East Command have indeed mistreated and thrown away this invaluable force.[9]

He followed it up with another on 16 August:

> 1. I settled with General Auchinleck that the three Glen ships were all to remain in the Middle East and be refitted for amphibious operations as soon as possible.
> 2. That the Commandos should be reconstituted, as far as possible, by volunteers, by restoring to them any of their former members who may wish to return from the units in which they have been dispersed,

and that Brigadier Laycock should have the command and should be appointed Director of Combined Operations.

3. The D.C.O. and the Commandos will be under the direct command of General Auchinleck. This cancels the former arrangement which I proposed of their being under the Naval Commander-in-Chief.[10]

It was not to turn out at all as Churchill prescribed.

Bob was able to take some leave, which he spent mostly with Angie, although he also visited Wiseton and had an audience with the King, who seemed very interested in his activities and asked a number of questions about Angie's mother and her sister Pempie. Charles Haydon then organized for him a lecture tour of all the Commando units in the UK to talk about the operations of Layforce and the lessons learnt from them. By the last week in August he was writing to Angie that he had never been so bored, repeating his lecture twice a day for eight consecutive days, which were largely spent in Scotland.

At the end of August he was informed by the War Office that a passage had been arranged for him back to the Middle East and he duly set off for Liverpool to board the ship. He was unpacking his suitcase when a movements officer arrived and bundled him off again in great haste, explaining that the Prime Minister, extremely annoyed that Bob was being sent by the long sea passage, had decreed that he should be given priority by air. This allowed him to spend two more nights with Angie in London before catching a Sunderland flying boat from Plymouth.

This time the journey was the shortest possible at the time, flying the length of the Mediterranean rather than taking the 'reinforcement route' by which he had travelled to England. The first stage was to Gibraltar, where Bob and the only other passengers, Admiral Sir Frederick Dreyer[11] and his Flag Lieutenant, stayed with the Governor, Lord Gort, whom Bob had not seen since he had served at GHQ BEF and who expressed his bitterness about his treatment after Dunkirk. Another guest was Arthur Smith, on his way back to London on behalf of Auchinleck. Smith was far from pleased that Bob was being sent back by the Prime Minister, telling him that he could see no future for the Commandos for as long as it was impossible to replace their losses.

The next stage was to Malta, where the Sunderland arrived after dark but in the middle of an air raid. As it circled the island at low speed, trailing red streaks from its exhaust, Bob was astonished that the aircraft was not attacked, but the bombers eventually withdrew and it touched down in Marsaxlokk Bay. Bob stayed with the GOC and spent the next morning looking round the shelters which had been constructed out of the natural rock. On the evening of 6 September the Sunderland arrived at Aboukir Bay and Bob travelled directly on to Cairo, where he booked into Shepheard's Hotel.

Chapter 13

Flipper

Shortly after Bob returned, he was sent for by Auchinleck. The C-in-C reiterated the difficulties likely to be posed by the lack of casualty replacements, but promised his support and sent him on to see Major General Neil Ritchie, Smith's deputy. Ritchie was far more sympathetic than his superior. He suggested that Bob should start work on the organization of a new Special Services formation, using whatever resources were to hand. He also told Bob that David Stirling had recently put forward a proposal for a parachute commando which had found favour with Auchinleck and that this should be included in his proposals.

Initially encouraged, Bob set to work. There were clearly certain units in the Middle East which he could include in a new formation, but it would, inevitably, be much smaller than Layforce. A, B and D Battalions were now long since disbanded, and the subsequent delay had meant that most of those who had opted to remain in Special Services had lost patience and applied to be posted elsewhere. The obvious starting point was thus C Battalion, which had returned to Amiriya from Cyprus at the end of the first week of August, whereupon its officers and other ranks were offered the same choices as had been placed before the other battalions a month or so earlier. Bob asked Geoffrey Keyes to come and see him in Cairo and learnt that, after those who had opted for the alternatives had been accepted, the Commando had been reduced to nine officers and 250 men, all of whom had chosen to stay in a reconstituted formation. Together with those from the other battalions who remained unposted, this might provide the basis of one complete commando.

The second constituent part of Layforce which still existed was the Folbot Troop, albeit that it was effectively under Royal Navy control and based on HMS *Medway*, the submarine depot ship in Alexandria. Shortly after Bob's return to Egypt he received a letter from Courtney, who wrote that he had heard that Bob would be commanding all Special Service units in the area, in which case he would be delighted to join. Courtney went on to say that it was imperative that all folbotists should be trained in the light of the section's experiences, as some operations were taking place outside his control and mistakes were being made. He suggested that he himself should return to the UK to form a new section on the back of his experience and that, together with those operating in the Mediterranean, this could be developed into a Folbot Corps.

The next step was to find out what David Stirling was up to. Whilst B Battalion had been idle in Mersa Matruh in June, Jock Lewes had obtained permission from Bob to conduct an experiment with parachutes, which until then had not been used by the Army in the Middle East. Approaching an RAF HQ near Fuka, Lewes persuaded the commanding officer to allow him, Stirling and three others to jump out of a Vickers Valentia transport plane. In spite of the fact that they had had no training apart from being shown the basic principles, everyone landed safely except Stirling, whose parachute had been partially ripped on leaving the aircraft, resulting in his hitting the ground far too fast. He damaged his spine quite badly, even losing his sight for a short time, and was admitted to the Scottish Military Hospital in Alexandria. Whilst there he developed a proposal for a new type of force which would hit the enemy behind his own lines, but from the air rather than the sea.

Stirling argued that landings from the sea were wasteful, since they had to use relatively large numbers of troops and valuable naval units which were highly vulnerable. It would be much better to land small parties by parachute behind enemy lines, although there were circumstances in which they could go in by sea or by land. He proposed that the new organization should be independent, under the direct control of the Commander-in-Chief. He added to the paper a specific proposal for multiple attacks behind the lines in support of a new offensive which he understood was being planned for that autumn.

Stirling's problem, once he was discharged from hospital, was how to get his paper into the hands of the C-in-C. He decided on a frontal attack, brazening his way into GHQ where, after a very unsatisfactory encounter with an officer who had taught him at Pirbright and been distinctly unimpressed, he barged without invitation into Ritchie's office and placed the paper on his desk. To his surprise, Ritchie took it seriously, agreeing to show it to Auchinleck. Having found initial favour, Stirling was authorized to recruit six officers and sixty men from the remnants of Layforce, plus some administrative staff, and to establish a base at Kabrit. The name of the unit, conceived by none other than Dudley Clarke, the creator of the commandos and now fast becoming the master of deception at GHQ Middle East, was to be L Detachment, Special Air Service Brigade.

Recruitment for L Detachment was relatively straightforward as far as the other ranks were concerned. Stirling obtained a good number of volunteers from members of his old No. 3 Troop of 8 Commando, which had been largely absorbed into 2nd Battalion Scots Guards, and recruited the balance from the Depot Commando at Geneifa, where they were awaiting posting. The officers proved to be more difficult. Most of those who had been in 8 Commando turned him down. In Mather's words, 'We really could not give it credence and we thought we knew David too well for it to work.'[1] The one man Stirling was determined to have, however, was Lewes, who was still in Tobruk, whither

Stirling went to persuade him. After some initial reluctance, Lewes agreed to join.

Another officer recruit was Blair 'Paddy' Mayne, formerly of 11 Commando. Mayne was a born fighter, who had represented his university as a heavyweight boxer and been capped both for Ireland and the British Lions at rugby. He did not confine his pugnacious disposition to the battlefield – he had done very well on the Litani – or the playing field; once he had drunk too much alcohol, he was all too inclined to violence. When Bob visited C Battalion in Cyprus on 23 June, before leaving for England, he found Mayne under suspicion of having assaulted a fellow officer in the dark after a mess dinner on the previous night. Keyes was keen to have him court-martialled, but Bob persuaded him to drop the charge and had Mayne flown out of the island. Stirling later found him at Geneifa and had little difficulty in persuading him to join L Detachment. When asked if there would be any fighting, Stirling is said to have replied, 'Only against the enemy'!

Bob produced his first paper on the reorganization on 16 September, a week after he arrived back in Egypt. It set out the history of Layforce and the reasons for its disbandment, before referring to the decision to reconstitute a new force, which would be available for reconnaissance, the securing of beachheads, and sea and airborne attacks on the enemy's flank and rear. He saw the limitations as being the availability of suitable ships and the undesirability of forming a greater number of units than could be more or less continuously employed. From units currently available the force would consist of one General Service Commando of 230 all ranks, one SAS Commando of 70 all ranks and the Folbot Troop of 30 all ranks. He proposed that any reinforcements should not come from the Middle East, but from the Special Services Training and Holding Unit at Lochailort.

There was, however, one other unit which GHQ Middle East was prepared to let Bob have. This was 51 Middle East Commando, which had been left in East Africa when the two other Middle East Commandos had joined Layforce as D Battalion. Its origins were unusual. It was originally raised by Lieutenant Colonel H. J. Cator in Palestine as No 1 Palestine Company, Auxiliary Military Pioneer Corps and was composed of both Arabs and Jews, who were unsegregated. It left the Middle East for Europe in early 1940 and was employed on the BEF's lines of communication. After a brief period defending the English coastline, it was shipped back to Egypt, where it was augmented by further recruitment in Palestine and renamed 51 Middle East Commando. Following a typical period of cancelled operations on the coast of Egypt and Libya, it was sent down to Eritrea, where it joined the British offensive against the Italians, playing a significant role at Keren and Amba Alagi. With the campaign in East Africa concluded in the early summer, it was available for new operations.

With 11 and 51 Commandos, L Detachment and the Folbot Troop, Bob was able to prepare a far more comprehensive paper, which he presented to GHQ at the beginning of October. This looked at the history of the commandos and concluded that the Middle East was actually a more suitable theatre than Northern Europe for their deployment: raids by sea from the UK could never make a serious impact against a well-defended coast, but in the Mediterranean they could attack the Axis lines of communication, from land, sea or air. He then looked at the role of the Glen ships, which he concluded were too slow and vulnerable and could only be used with an escort of destroyers and either an anti-aircraft cruiser or fighter cover. He therefore proposed a drastic reorganization, which could only be justified if raiding remained the primary role of the new force; subversive activities would be better handled by SO2, the forerunner of SOE, or G(R), the department at GHQ responsible for covert operations. He later summarized his proposals:

> In the first place I suggested that the Commando Group should be completely self-contained and independent, not only being equipped with its own means of transport but also that it should recruit and command the personnel who operated the ships, aircraft and vehicles required.
>
> The organisation I advocated consisted of a Headquarters and three Wings. The first, airborne (David Stirling's S.A.S with its own aircraft), the second, seaborne with its own landing ships (I suggested converting two destroyers) and the third, landborne, formed by the existing Long Range Desert Group which was already functioning with admirable efficiency in the Western Desert. I further recommended that this force should be kept in a high state of readiness under the control of the Combined Service Commanders, but that any of the three should have a call on its participation in any operation which commended itself as appropriate to them. Thus, for example, the R.A.F might wish raids to be conducted with the object of destroying enemy fighters on the ground; the Army might require diversionary raids in conjunction with their own land offensives; or the Navy might consider that sabotage operations against 'E' boat or submarine bases might pay a dividend.[2]

Whilst Bob waited for GHQ to digest this, he attended what he found to be a most interesting Combined Operations course at the Combined Training Centre at Kabrit, run by Brigadier M. W. M. MacLeod, a founder member of the Inter Services Training and Development Centre in the UK and one of the early apostles of combined operations. Among his fellow students Bob found, to his pleasure, his two friends from Crete, Brigadiers Vasey and Hargest.

He also caught up with those former members of 8 Commando who had remained in the Middle East. Daly, now a major again, was delighted to have been selected to lead the Middle East Squadron of the GHQ Liaison Regiment, usually known as Phantom and responsible for keeping the commanders in the field in touch with developments during a moving battle.[3] He was joined there by Mather. Randolph Churchill and Robin Campbell were running a new propaganda and censorship branch at GHQ.

Bob was summoned to a meeting at GHQ on 11 October, which was attended by staff officers from the various departments concerned. The reaction to his paper was universally hostile:

> My original proposals were completely unprecedented and, *ipso facto*, totally unacceptable to the General Staff, though in all fairness to the officers who turned them down I must admit that I gave them a legitimate excuse for doing so for they argued that, at this stage of the war, they could not provide the equipment for which I asked; though I suspect that, even had they been in a position to do so, they would still have vetoed my ideas on all sorts of other grounds.[4]

Bob was ordered instead to form what would become the new Middle East Commando, a much less ambitious undertaking, which excluded the LRDG and all mention of the exclusive use of ships and planes. This unit would comprise an HQ and a Depot Troop, the latter responsible for reinforcements under training, No. 2 Troop formed from L Detachment SAS, No. 3 Troop from 11 Commando and former Layforce personnel not on any other establishment, Nos. 4 and 5 Troops from 51 Commando and No. 6 Troop from the Folbot Troop, now called the Special Boat Section. The new unit would be placed directly under GHQ. It was agreed that the reorganization could not be fully implemented until the arrival of 51 Commando from East Africa. As the officer commanding designate, Bob was restored on 15 October to the rank of temporary lieutenant colonel.

It was a far cry not only from Bob's proposals, but also from Churchill's. There was no appointment as Director of Combined Operations, let alone promotion to Brigadier. Although Bob almost certainly did not know the contents of the Prime Minister's memos to Ismay, he was distinctly unhappy, writing to Angie on 18 October that he was very disappointed with his new job and had said so in high places, going on to write two days later that he would probably be sacked for it. He continued:

> Incidentally I hear that Dickie MtB is to be made D.C.O in place of Roger Keyes!! If they don't give me what I have asked for here – for God's sake tell Dickie to ask for me to help him. On second thoughts he will probably do his damndest to keep me as far away from you as possible??!!![5]

Mountbatten was renowned as having an eye for the ladies!

The situation was not helped by a subsequent pitch from G(R) to have control of the Special Boat Section, as it had recently been employed under that department's auspices, in conjunction with the Royal Navy. The other GHQ departments were opposed to this, but the matter was not resolved and hung in the balance.

Bob's unhappiness was expressed in a memo to Auchinleck dated 17 October. He reminded the C-in-C of their meeting in September, when Bob had been invited to consult Auchinleck if any difficulties arose. He continued:

> I believe that I should be serving you ill if I did not represent to you before the force comes into being that it will have little value if it is to be organised, manned, and equipped as at present envisaged.
>
> I have already raised this question with G (Training) who, though inclined to agree that my fears might be well founded, suggested that it would be better to give the organisation a trial before condemning it.
>
> I believe, however, that it is simply a waste of time and potential to wait for a scheme which is foredoomed to failure to show itself a failure in practice.[6]

He went on to say that the impression he had received from the Adjutant General's branch in particular was that the proposed new unit was an unmitigated nuisance. He conceded that L Detachment would, when properly equipped, constitute a unit of considerable potential, but reminded the C-in-C that the Folbot Section was essentially a reconnaissance unit rather than a striking force. The other troops, however, 'though doubtless containing a number of excellent officers and men, cannot be considered the most effective organisation for carrying out operational tasks which will call for an exceptionally high standard of discipline and training.'[7] Finally, he made the point that 'this heterogeneous collection of soldiers'[8] would be entirely reliant on the other services before it could go into action and reiterated his request that they should have their own transport, at least as to landing craft and aircraft, with officers attached from the other services.

The reply came not from the C-in-C, but from Smith. As well as expressing his concern about the impression given by A branch and confirming that Auchinleck was prepared to meet Bob, he came quickly to the crux of the matter:

> The real difficulty about S.S. troops is that we simply have not got the men and we are now thousands of men short of our requirements in ordinary infantry battalions in the Middle East.
>
> I have told the Commander-in-Chief that I really cannot recommend calling for volunteers for an S.S. unit in view of this shortage. This does

> NOT mean that when we get reinforcements we shall not be able to expand the S.S. organisation.[9]

Whether or not Bob saw Auchinleck is not recorded. In any event, for the time being the Middle East Commando remained a unit only on paper, pending the arrival of 51 Commando. The other constituent parts remained entirely separate, but in the meantime both L Detachment and the remnants of 11 Commando were put at the disposal of Eighth Army, which had been recently formed under Lieutenant General Sir Alan Cunningham, in order to support Operation CRUSADER, a new offensive to relieve Tobruk and retake Cyrenaica.

L Detachment's role, in which Bob had no involvement, was to attack the Axis airfields at Tmimi and Gazala, put them out of commission and destroy as many aircraft as could be found. Those selected for the operation were divided into five parties, each of which was to be dropped from a Bristol Bombay aircraft. In the event, the operation, which took place on the night of 16/17 November, was a debacle. None of the parties achieved their objectives. Of the sixty-two men who set out, only twenty-two returned, the rest being killed or captured. However, the efficient way in which the survivors were picked up by the LRDG persuaded Stirling that it would be much better to make the approach to operations overland than by air. This was to be the hallmark of the SAS in the future and, although Lewes was killed shortly thereafter, it grew steadily in strength and reputation.

Meanwhile, 11 Commando had continued to wither away and was now reduced to five officers and 110 men. This, however, was more than sufficient to carry out a plan which Keyes had conceived and which he now put to Bob, prior to it being approved by Cunningham. The plan was for a number of raids to be carried out far to the rear of the Axis front line, the most important and audacious of which was an attack on Rommel's supposed HQ and living quarters, which intelligence indicated was in the small town of Beda Littoria, situated in the Jebel Akhdar, the hilly and relatively fertile area in the bulge of Cyrenaica. One of the objectives, although it featured nowhere in the subsequent orders, was to kill or capture Rommel himself. The other targets were an Italian HQ and wireless mast at Cyrene, a wireless station and intelligence centre at Apollonia and other communications facilities. The raids were to take place immediately before the launch of CRUSADER. Bob was initially highly sceptical:

> When the plan was submitted to me as Comdr. of the M.E. Commandos, I gave it as my considered opinion that the chances of being evacuated after the operation were very slender and that the attack on Gen. R's house in particular appeared to be desperate in the extreme. This attack, even if initially successful, meant almost certain death for those who took part in

> it. I made these comments in the presence of Col. Keyes who begged me not to repeat them lest the operation be cancelled.[10]

To Cunningham and his staff, however, it represented a very low-cost way of striking a blow which, if successful, would do serious damage to the enemy's command structure, his communications and his morale.

During October, two reconnaissance missions were mounted, the first by Captain Jock Haselden, a G(R) officer working with the LRDG, who landed from HM Submarine *Torbay* with an Arab NCO. He surveyed a possible landing beach at Khashm al-Kalb, 18 miles from Beda Littoria, before heading to the town in Arab disguise. After missing a number of designated rendezvous, he was eventually picked up by an LRDG patrol and reported back his findings, which were that the beach would be suitable and that a local Arab agent had confirmed that the house in question had been used by Rommel.

The second mission consisted of Keyes's adjutant, Captain Tommy Macpherson, a corporal from 11 Commando and two officers from the Special Boat Section, who landed from HM Submarine *Talisman* to check out an alternative beach at Ras Hillal on the night of 24/25 October. Although they landed satisfactorily, they failed to make contact with the submarine on their return, attempted to get back overland and were all captured. Ras Hillal was ruled out as having been compromised, and Khashm al-Kalb was designated as the preferred beach.

The order for Operation FLIPPER was issued on 9 November and, on the afternoon of the following day, six officers and 50 other ranks embarked in *Torbay* and *Talisman* in Alexandria. The party was drawn substantially from 11 Commando, with Robin Campbell, transferred from his propaganda work at GHQ, a late addition due to his fluency in German. Keyes led the detachment on *Torbay* with two other officers, Campbell and Lieutenant Roy Cooke, a relatively new recruit. Bob himself was the senior officer on *Talisman*, with Lieutenant David Sutherland, who had recently joined 11 Commando from the remnants of 8 Commando, and Lieutenant H. G. Chevalier, an Arabic-speaking Frenchman who had been working for G(R) in Cyrenaica.

With two lieutenant colonels the structure of the party was top-heavy, and questions have been asked as to why Bob thought it necessary to go along. Some have suggested that this was because a successful outcome would help to expunge a blot on his copybook from Crete. This seems improbable, for two reasons. Firstly, there is no evidence of any criticism at the time, official or otherwise, of his actions on Crete. Secondly, Bob was only too aware of the low probability of success. More likely, in the knowledge that the full deployment of the new Middle East Commando was to be delayed until the end of the year, he was keen to be personally involved in at least one of its interim operations; indeed, he was later to claim that it was difficult to command without some experience of what was going on in the field. Furthermore, Keyes was only twenty-four, with a mere four and a half years of military service to his name, and was widely thought to have been over-promoted. Bob had recommended his confirmation as CO of 11 Commando and therefore possibly felt accountable: his own presence might help to ensure that all went to plan. In any event, he was effectively in charge of the whole operation, with Keyes specifically responsible for the raid on Rommel's supposed HQ.

The two submarines arrived off Khashm al-Kalb on 14 November and both carried out a daylight periscope reconnaissance, which revealed no movement. That night, a folbot was sent ashore from *Torbay*, making contact with Haselden. On its return, *Torbay* prepared to disembark Keyes and his party. Attempts to launch the rubber boats by trimming down the submarine to float them off went wrong time and again, and the exercise took five hours instead of one, but the party eventually managed to get ashore by about midnight. *Talisman*, which had no idea of the difficulties being experienced, was at last signalled to carry out its own launchings, but the swell had increased materially and, time and again, the boats capsized and were swept away. One man was drowned, and in the end only Bob and seven other ranks were able to paddle to the beach.

Cold and wet, the men who had landed waited until it was clear that no more would be coming that night from *Talisman* and then moved about a mile inland to a pre-selected *wadi*, where they lay up for the whole of the next day. The folbot officer, Lieutenant John Pryor, and his crewman, Bombardier Brittlebank, remained behind on the beach.

The loss of nearly half the full party meant that the objectives had to be reconsidered. The raid on Rommel's house was clearly the most important of these, so Keyes, with a detachment consisting of Campbell and seventeen other ranks, the most senior of whom was Sergeant Jack Terry, was ordered to carry this out. Cooke and six other ranks were to accompany him on the approach march and, if Keyes felt that he could manage without them, would then carry out the demolition work on the communications mast near Cyrene. Haselden, who would be leaving to rejoin the LRDG, undertook to cut other communications. Before going he told Keyes that the house now believed to be occupied by Rommel was a different one to that previously identified, and the plan of attack was modified accordingly. Bob and six men, including the two folbotists, were to stay behind to secure the approaches to the beach and to await the arrival of the remainder of the party from *Talisman*, which in the event never happened.

That night, Keyes and his men left to carry out their tasks, feeling their way across very difficult country in steadily worsening weather, cold and wet. They lay up for all of the next day, helped by local Arabs, one of whom then guided them on the second night to a cave in which to rest for the following day. On the evening of 17 November they approached Beda Littoria, where they were stopped by Italian Arab *carabinieri*, whom Campbell managed to persuade that the party was a German patrol. After a brief reconnaissance of their target, Keyes decided that he had no need of Cooke's party, which was sent off to carry out its demolitions.

The accounts of what happened next, provided initially by Terry and used for Bob's subsequent report, then by Campbell and some of the other survivors, and finally by the Germans, are seriously inconsistent. Their common ground is that one group was sent to hold off any attempts to relieve the Germans, whilst another was placed to the rear of the house, with instructions to shoot anyone who emerged without giving the agreed password. Two men were left on guard by the front entrance, whilst Keyes, Campbell, Terry and one other entered the house. Surprise was achieved and Keyes burst into a room occupied by some Germans, a number of whom were killed or wounded. Keyes, however, was killed himself, whilst Campbell was seriously wounded in the leg. As to detail, the accounts differ in material respects, and the full truth will never be known. However, it can be said with some certainty that Campbell was shot by one of his own men when he left the house in the darkness but forgot to give the password. As the German report, which is likely to be one of the more reliable ones, states that only one shot was fired by them, it is likely that Keyes was also shot by his own side in the confusion, possibly even by Campbell.

In the knowledge that Keyes was dead, and realizing that he himself was unable to move and would be a burden to others, Campbell gave orders to Terry to withdraw the whole party. This Terry did, deciding not to lie up but to march all day, eventually reaching the rendezvous agreed with Bob at 17.00. As darkness fell, *Torbay* was spotted lying off the bay. The rubber boats, which had earlier been removed by some Arabs, were located, but a line was needed to pull them out to the submarine. Bob was the only person present with any knowledge of Morse code and he signalled for a folbot to be sent with one. His signalling skills were not, however, particularly good and he was handicapped by his torch having no Morse button, meaning that he had constantly to turn it on and off. His signals and *Torbay*'s were both misunderstood and the submarine disappeared, with the intention of returning the next night.

In the meantime, Cooke's party, which had achieved only partial success in demolishing the communications mast, had been surrounded as it tried to make its way back to the rendezvous and was forced to surrender.

At about midday on 19 November shots were heard from the outlying sentries and a sizeable force of *carabinieri* could be seen approaching. Bob sent men to outflank it, but it soon became apparent that the enemy was in such strength that they would be overcome. He then gave the order to scatter in groups of not more than three men, with the intention of either reaching another beach, off which *Talisman* would be lying on the nights of 21 and 22 November, trying to make contact with the LRDG or waiting for British forces to arrive, in the event

Joe Laycock, Bob's father.

The *Valhalla*, Joe's private clipper.

(L to R) Major General John French, Colonel Douglas Haig and Joe near Colenso during the Boer War.

Kitty Laycock, Bob's mother.

Wiseton Hall.

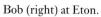

Bob (right) at Eton.

Favourite pastimes:
Hunting …

… and steeplechasing at
Hawthorn Hill (Bob on the left).

The *Herzogin Cecilie*.

Getting in sail.

The main deck,
looking aft.

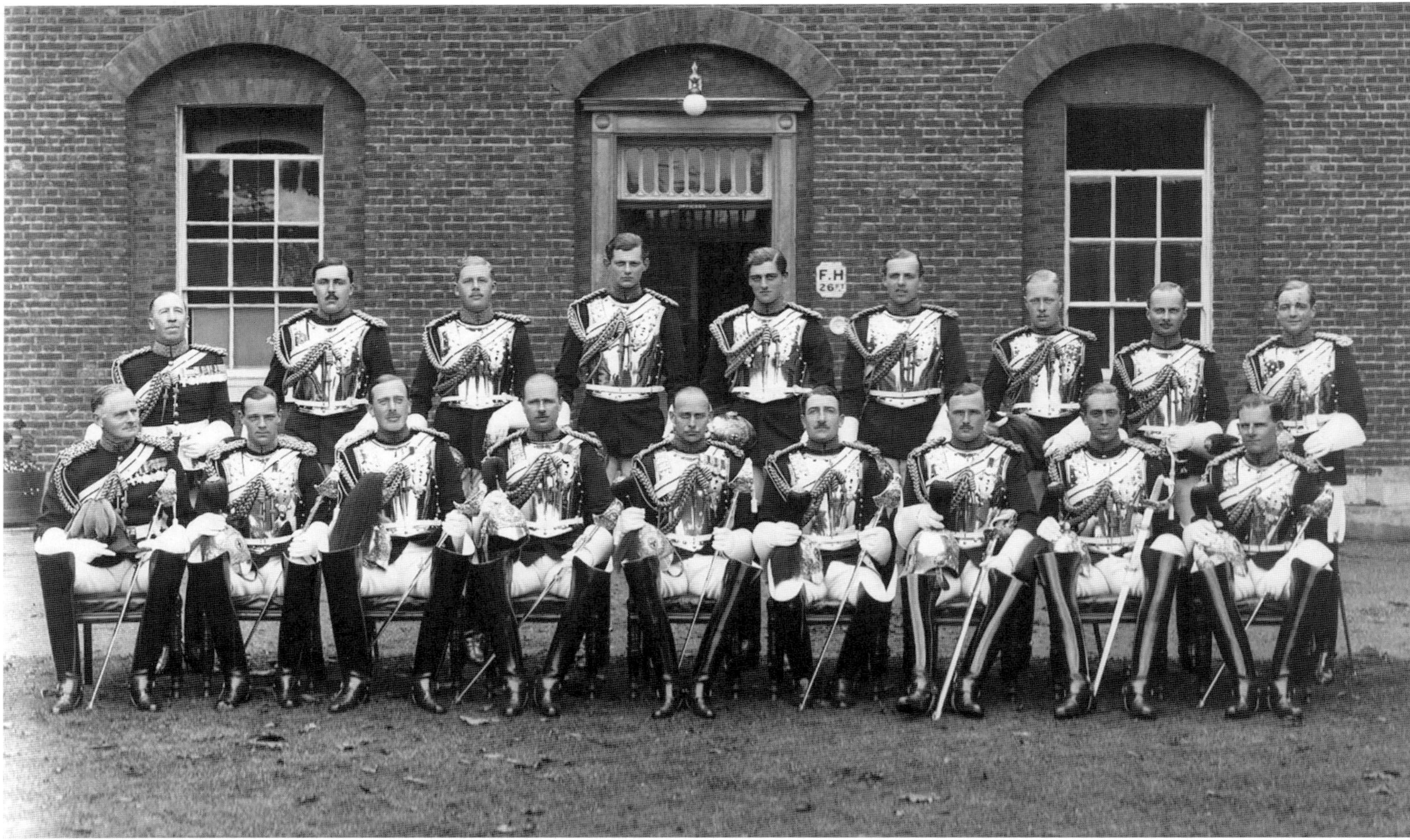

The Officers of the Blues, 1935. Bob, the Adjutant, seated second from left.

Bob and Angie in the late 1930s.

Bob sailing with his great friend, Antony Head.

Joe with Bob's sisters, Joyce and Rosemary.

No. 5 Troop, 8 Commando. Bob seated centre, with Eddie Fitzclarence on his right.

Mechanized Landing Craft off Arran.

Bob after returning from Operation FLIPPER.

Charles Vaughan, the Commandant of the Commando Basic Training Centre. (*Commando Veterans Association*)

Bob, followed by Shimi Lovat, inspecting 4 Commando after the Dieppe Raid. (*Commando Veterans Association*)

(L to R) 'Pops' Manners, Bob and Brian Franks, with the ship's officers, bound for Sicily on HMT *Derbyshire*.

Bob on Sicily with Mountbatten and Head, 13 July 1943.

'Mad Jack' Churchill, CO of 2 Commando.

The senior officers of COHQ in 1942: (L to R) Group Captain A. H. Willetts, Rear Admiral H. E. Horan, Major General J. C. Haydon, Mountbatten, Air Vice Marshal J. M. Robb, Major General G. E. Wildman-Lushington, Commodore R. Ellis.

Photo portrait by Karsh of Ottawa of Bob on his appointment as Chief of Combined Operations.

The officers of 10 (Inter Allied) Commando. Dudley Lister and Peter Laycock are standing third & fourth from left.

Senior officers of the Special Service Group: (L to R) Derek Mills-Roberts, Bob Sturges, John Durnford-Slater and Shimi Lovat. (*Commando Veterans Association*)

Bob inspecting a Royal Marine Commando before D-Day.

Bob accompanies King George VI to Normandy aboard HMS *Arethusa*. On the left is the King's Private Secretary, Sir Alan Lascelles. On the far right is Admiral Sir Bertram Ramsay, the Naval C-in-C for OVERLORD.

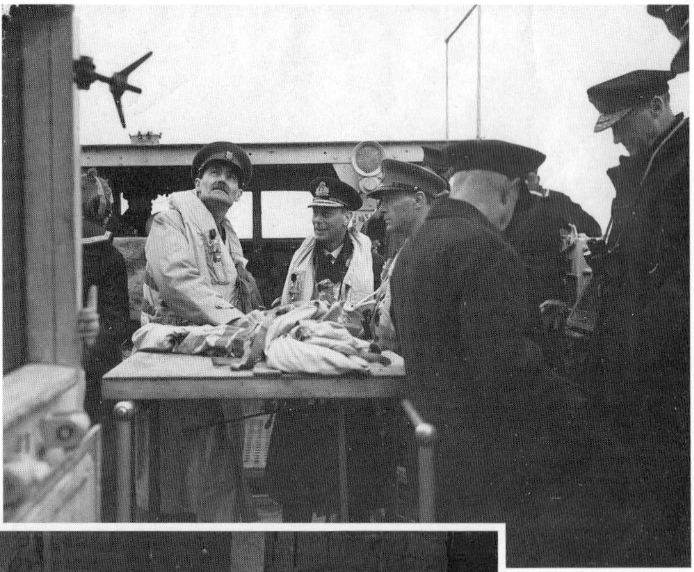

Bob with the other members of the COHQ Mission to South East Asia Command.

Bob visiting the US Army Signals School at Fort Knox, Kentucky.

Bob and Angie, with (L to R) Martha, Ben, Emma and Joe, in the early 1950s.

As a Gold Staff Officer at the Coronation, Bob escorts Sir Winston and Lady Churchill to their carriage after the ceremony.

Bob and Angie on their way to attend the Candlemas Ceremony in Malta with his two ADCs, Mark Agnew (L) and Walter Bonello.

Visitors to Malta: The Emperor Haile Selassie of Ethiopia …

… and Field Marshal Montgomery.

Wiseton Hall after rebuilding in 1960.

Bob at a Commando Association Reunion with (L to R) Charles Vaughan, John Hunt, Charles Haydon and Derek Mills-Roberts.

Bob during his visit to the SAS in Borneo.

Bob in the mid-1960s.

that their offensive had been successful. Pryor had been wounded and was left behind, but the others made off into the scrub.

Bob teamed up with Jack Terry and, having evaded the enemy cordon, the two men headed south into the Jebel Akhdar. The country, whilst difficult to cross in the dark, provided plenty of cover by way of rocks, bushes, *wadis* and caves, so that the fugitives could lie up in the daytime and, with Bob's binoculars, spot any pursuers from some distance away. They adopted a practice of determining which area had been searched during the day and then moving there by night, confident in the knowledge that it would not be revisited. When they found a cave they were able to light a fire for warmth on the cold winter nights.

The only rations which they were able to bring with them, a few tins and a packet of sweets, were exhausted before very long, and for a time they survived on berries. Although the weather had dried up, initially they were able to drink from puddles and, after the first week or so, there was sufficient rain to satisfy their thirst. They sheltered in caves as often as possible, but on one occasion, contrary to their habit, neither man was on guard and they woke to hear a noise at the entrance, where Bob had left his revolver and binoculars. They lay very still, but in due course a man entered the cave. His surprise was as great as theirs, but happily he turned out to be a member of the local Senussi tribe, who were hostile to the Italians and, on the whole, favourably disposed to the British. Bob later said that they would not have survived if it had not been for the Senussi, who brought them unleavened bread and, on one occasion, a whole cooked goat which, by eating everything except the hooves, they managed to make last for days. Terry had been a butcher's boy before joining up, which came in handy.

Apart from constantly living on their nerves, the main problem was boredom. Whilst waiting for the return of the raiding party, Bob had borrowed a copy of *The Wind in the Willows* from Pryor and he carried it away with him, reading extracts to Terry as their sole entertainment.

Far away to the east, Eighth Army had been engaged in Operation CRUSADER since 18 November, and it looked for some time, to Cunningham at least, as if it would fail. Auchinleck, however, encouraged by reports from ULTRA that the Axis forces were very short of supplies, replaced Cunningham with Ritchie but kept control of the battle himself. In due course Rommel was forced to retreat and, on Christmas Day, after 41 days on the run, Bob and Terry spotted what appeared to be their first British troops. The two men were wearing British battledress with Italian overcoats, which they discarded as soon as their hopes were confirmed.

They were immediately taken off to Eighth Army HQ, where their first act was to demolish a jar each of marmalade to satisfy their craving for sugar, which had been almost absent from their diet. A signal was sent to GHQ announcing that Bob had arrived at 21.20 for Christmas dinner. The reply came asking why he was one hour and twenty minutes late. Terry, in the sergeants' mess, was only grateful that he did not have to endure yet another story about Mr Toad!

Bob was flown back to Cairo, where he was invited to stay during his recuperation by Oliver Lyttelton, the Resident Minister of State for the Middle East, to whom his brother Peter was acting as Military Assistant. He had been posted missing on 24 November, which had caused consternation at home. Telegrams and signals were sent immediately announcing his reappearance, but it was 30 December before he was able to write to Angie, apologizing for causing her so much anxiety. The one compensation, he wrote, was that he had slimmed down considerably.[11]

The 'Rommel Raid', as it has become known to history, was in almost every respect a disaster. Apart from killing a small number of Germans and causing some minor damage to their communications, it had achieved nothing. There were only two fatalities, Keyes and Corporal Peter Barrand, the man who had been swept off *Talisman* and drowned during the attempt to launch the boats, but Campbell and Pryor had been wounded, the former suffering the subsequent amputation of his leg. These two and all the others who had landed from the submarine were captured, save only for Bob, Terry and Bombardier Brittlebank, Pryor's partner in the folbot, who made it to safety entirely alone.

Rommel was in fact not only absent from Beda Littoria, he was out of the country in Rome, a fact known to British Intelligence through ULTRA intercepts. This information was possibly withheld in order to protect the integrity of the source, but it is more likely that communication between the intelligence and operations branches on this occasion was poor. There is evidence that he had occupied the house at one time, but he had long before moved his HQ much closer to his front line; indeed, when he heard about the raid he was appalled that anyone should believe that he would command from so far away. The occupants of the house at the time of the raid were members of his administrative staff. Bob certainly knew this by the time that he was visited by Hermione Ranfurly, a family friend[12] who was working in Cairo, on 3 January 1942. He asked Lady Ranfurly to take his account down in shorthand and she recorded it in her diary. He told her that the object of the raid:

> … was to cause maximum damage and interruption to German installations and communications and, incidentally, to raid a house at Sidi Rafa[13] where Rommel was known to stay frequently with the German 'Q' General.[14]

This is at odds with the operational order and Bob's subsequent report, both of which make it clear that this, the first of the four objectives, was far from incidental, having been allocated from the outset to Keyes himself and then prioritized when the number of men available was seriously reduced. Neither source, however, mentions the killing of Rommel himself as an objective, and it was probably regarded as no more than a low-odds bonus, albeit that its achievement would have represented a major coup. The rest of the story recorded by Lady Ranfurly is broadly in line with Bob's report and thus differs from what really happened, at least as far as the attack on the house was concerned.

News of the raid was not hushed up. On the contrary, much was made of it in an effort to boost morale. Keyes was in due course posthumously awarded the Victoria Cross on Bob's recommendation, the usual requirement that there should be three witnesses to the action having been dispensed with. Campbell, who was later repatriated from POW camp due to his injuries, was awarded the DSO and Terry the DCM.

Bob's recuperation was retarded by the development of an abscess in a tooth, which left him 'demented with pain'.[15] However, he had no duty to perform other than to write his report, signed off as 'Lt. Col. R. L. Laycock RHG, O.C. M.E. Commandos'. In fact, by that time he no longer held the appointment, having relinquished it, unbeknown to him, on 25 November, one month after he was posted missing. On Christmas Day he had also lost his temporary rank as a lieutenant colonel. There was no job for him in Middle East Command, but in any event he had been ordered back to the UK.

Mountbatten had come to his rescue!

Chapter 14

Brigade

Bob flew via Khartoum to Lagos, where he boarded a ship back to the UK. He arrived in Liverpool on 28 February 1942, to be met by Angie bearing a letter from Mountbatten. In it Mountbatten wrote that he had sent a telegram on 15 November, just as Bob was landing at Khashm al-Kalb in Operation FLIPPER, to ask for him to be sent home to take over command of the Special Service Brigade from Charles Haydon, whom he had appointed as his Military Adviser at Combined Operations HQ. It is likely that this was the result of representations from Angie, following Bob's letters to her expressing his disappointment at developments in the Middle East. One may well speculate on what would have happened if the signal had arrived a week earlier. It seems entirely possible that Bob would not have become personally involved with a failed operation or endured so many weeks on the run.

Mountbatten and Bob had first met on the polo field in the early 1930s and had come across each other socially on a number of subsequent occasions.[1] It is clear that there was a high degree of mutual admiration and that Mountbatten was, for the time being at least, to become Bob's key supporter, and a powerful one at that. Following his appointment in October 1941 in succession to Keyes as Adviser and then Commodore, Combined Operations, he consolidated his position energetically, expanding the establishment of COHQ from a very modest twenty-three to over four hundred in six months. Churchill was impressed and, a week after Bob's return to the UK, told Mountbatten that he was now to become Chief of Combined Operations and to sit on the Chief of Staffs' Committee, with the acting ranks not only of vice admiral, but also of lieutenant general and air marshal.

On 1 March Bob was appointed Commander of the Special Service Brigade and promoted to acting brigadier. It was only on 12 March, however, after two weeks' leave, that he arrived at his new headquarters at Castle Douglas in south-west Scotland and began to take stock of his new command.

The Special Service Brigade had experienced mixed fortunes since the departure of Layforce in early 1941. It had certainly had its share of disappointments, but these had at least been interspersed with some successes. The first of the latter was Operation CLAYMORE, which was mounted in March 1941 by 3 Commando under John Durnford-Slater and 4 Commando under Dudley Lister, with Haydon in overall command. The target was the Lofoten

Islands off northern Norway. The landings were unopposed and achieved their objective of destroying the local fish factories; moreover, 228 German prisoners were taken, mostly merchant seamen; but the most significant result was the seizure of rotors for an ENIGMA machine, together with its code books.

Over the following months a number of small raids were carried out on the French coast, none of which achieved much, and the same sense of frustration developed as had been experienced by Layforce. It was only in December 1941, following Mountbatten's appointment, that two raids were mounted which would shine a much more favourable light on the Commandos. These were Operations ANKLET and ARCHERY. The first was set up as a diversion for the second, and once again the target was the Lofoten Islands, but this time the operation was mounted by 12 Commando. It landed on 26 December, taking the Germans entirely by surprise. Two radio transmitters were destroyed, some boats were sunk and a number of Germans and Norwegian quislings were taken prisoner, before the force withdrew in good order.

ARCHERY was more ambitious and, for once, it was well planned, with Durnford-Slater, whose 3 Commando was providing most of the troops, working in close conjunction with Haydon, who commanded the military force from his HQ at sea. The target was the island of Vaagso, on the central Norwegian coast. Supported by a strong naval force, the troops went ashore at dawn on 27 December on both the main island at South Vaagso and the neighbouring island of Maaloy. Opposition was much stiffer than anticipated, but the objectives were largely achieved, with the destruction of four fish factories and several military installations, the sinking of a number of ships and the capture of 98 prisoners. Although 17 of Durnford-Slater's men were killed and 53 wounded, the operation was accounted a success overall and, perhaps more importantly in the long term, it played a part in Hitler's decision to reinforce Norway, which he would continue to regard as vulnerable to invasion right up to the end of the War.

The active presence of Haydon in both CLAYMORE and ARCHERY highlighted an anomaly in the Special Service Brigade, which was that its commander was expected to take to the field from time to time, as well as to carry out his primary role, which was to administer all the Commandos in the UK. Haydon, in his new capacity as Military Adviser at COHQ, but temporarily still in charge of the Special Service Brigade, wrote to Mountbatten on 16 February 1942 enumerating the problems this caused. He pointed out that his HQ was in constant contact not only with the eight Commandos (1, 2, 3, 4, 5, 6, 9 and 12), but also with COHQ, the Commando Depot, the War Office and HQ Force 110, which in late 1941 was formed to mount an operation, subsequently aborted, to capture the Canary Islands. When Brigade HQ participated in an operation, the strain on it became excessive. The responsibility for training, in particular, suffered as a result. His proposal was that the Special Service

Brigade should be split in two, with projects allocated fairly to each. If one brigade was planning or carrying out an operation, the more general control of its non-operational units, including training, would be temporarily assumed by the other. The reorganization would inevitably result in a doubling of the staff.

Bob was asked for his own recommendation, which he put forward in a letter to Haydon on 27 March. In contrast to Haydon, he urged that the Special Service Brigade should remain a single formation. He did not cite the advantages, which he claimed were considerable, but he did make the point that the recent creation of Haydon's own department at COHQ would lift much of the administrative burden from the Brigade HQ. Nevertheless, Bob asked that the establishment of officers should be increased, although it would still be less than the number required by splitting the formation in two. He proposed that there should be a Brigade Second-in-Command, with the rank of colonel, who would not only support the Commander but would also be available to lead operations which involved more than one Commando. He requested the retention of Lieutenant Colonel E. G. Atkinson, who had been looking after Staff Duties and Training but was expecting to be posted elsewhere. He asked for an additional Staff Captain, so that the A (personnel) and Q (logistics) functions could be separated, a Brigade Security Officer in addition to the Brigade Intelligence Officer, a Staff Officer RE, a Staff Officer RAOC and a Staff Officer RAMC. The enlarged staff would be larger than that of a normal infantry brigade, but reflected the much greater number of units under command.

Bob's view prevailed and the Brigade remained as it was, with a staff increment as requested, but further rumblings about splitting it would continue and would come to a head in the following year. In the meantime, a number of officers arrived at Brigade HQ to fill both old and new positions. The first was Philip Dunne, who had also arrived back from the Middle East and who replaced Godfrey Nicholson as Liaison Officer. Nicholson, who had led 8 Commando's No. 8 Troop before it was disbanded prior to the departure of Layforce, was a Member of Parliament and now focused his attention on Westminster.

On 18 March Alan Smallman became the Brigade Major, Bob's chief of staff. Smallman had served in 3 Commando, including a spell as Adjutant, but after ARCHERY he was sent off first to talk to factory workers about the Commandos and then to serve as a GSO2 at COHQ, where he found himself involved in planning operations which never came off. One day he was stopped by Bob on the stairs and asked if he would like to join him, having been recommended by Haydon. This he was only too pleased to do.

A number of other old friends arrived. Roger Courtney, as he had hoped, had managed to get himself posted back to the UK to form what became No. 2 Special Boat Section, which was now attached to Brigade HQ. Brian Franks, who had been the Signals Officer in Layforce, in which guise he had accompanied Bob on the Bardia raid, and who was very highly regarded and much liked by him, became the Staff Captain 'A'; towards the end of the year he succeeded Smallman, when the latter went on the Staff College course.

On 11 May Evelyn Waugh reappeared at Bob's side. Waugh had written to Bob shortly after he heard of his arrival back in the UK, expressing his dissatisfaction with his return to the Royal Marines and his wish to rejoin the Commandos. Although the newly forming Royal Marine Commando had applied for him, he much preferred the prospect of a role in the Special Service Brigade. This necessitated his resignation from the Marines, but Bob managed to arrange his transfer to the Blues, albeit only after reassuring the Regimental Colonel that Waugh would never have to serve with them. Whilst waiting for this move to take effect, Waugh was temporarily attached to Brigade HQ, where in due course he was appointed the Intelligence Officer. Smallman, who had not met Waugh before, found that he got on very well with him and enjoyed his 'puckish sense of humour',[2] but speedily established that he had to be talked into doing everything, as ordering him usually failed to work.

Another former member of 8 Commando who for a time seemed likely to be foisted on Bob was Randolph Churchill. Mountbatten was asked in person by the Prime Minister to take him back into the Commandos, and the CCO did not hesitate to agree, apologizing to Bob but arguing that this was a special case. In the event, Randolph decided to join the SAS, but at the end of May he was injured when a truck driven by David Stirling rolled over and Churchill, one of the passengers, damaged his spine so badly that he was hospitalized and later returned to the UK. Bob fully understood Randolph's value as a conduit to the Prime Minister and, once he had recovered sufficiently, asked him to produce a proposal for a Long-Range Sabotage Group. This was duly done, but the activities were thought to be more properly in the remit of SOE.

On 11 April the Brigade HQ relocated to Ardrossan, familiar to the former members of 8 Commando as it was close to Largs and opposite Arran. The offices were in Seafield House, whilst accommodation was in the Glenfoot Hotel and the mess in the Kilmany Hotel. It was as convenient a location as anywhere in the British Isles: although the Commandos were scattered about at seaside locations around the country, much as they had been in 1940, five of them[3] were at that time located in towns on the Firth of Clyde. Bob still had to do a great deal of travelling, meeting his numerous commanding officers, inspecting their units and attending exercises. One of these took place on the Isle of Bute not long after he arrived and involved searching for an enemy who had been unable to embark after a raid. Bob described it to Angie:

> Philip – typical of him – caused alarm & confusion by quietly pointing out to the already nervous and harassed colonel who had set the scheme that the general idea was hardly tactful since I, the inspecting officer, had spent

a good few days running away from the enemy in almost exactly similar circumstances![4]

Bob was also required to pay frequent visits to COHQ, which at least meant that he could see Angie, who had elected to remain in London to continue to run her restaurant. The two of them went down to Broadlands, Mountbatten's house, on occasion for the weekend, but if Bob was in London they would otherwise spend it at Hawthorn Hill.

The rapid enlargement of COHQ meant that Bob at first knew few of the staff, particularly those from the Royal Navy and RAF. One exception was Robert Henriques, who had served in 12 Commando and then been Smallman's predecessor as Brigade Major, before being taken away by Haydon. Henriques, who had also established something of a reputation before the War as a novelist, had been a near contemporary of Bob's at Lockers Park. Another was Wing Commander the Marques de Casa Maury, who was Mountbatten's chief intelligence officer. Bobby Casa Maury, an amateur racing driver who had been part of Mountbatten's social circle, had married Angie's mother, Freda, in 1937. Bob liked him, but was frequently unimpressed by the quality of work of his department, not so much as to its form, which was excellent, but in its content, which was, in his view, all too often deficient.[5]

Bob was particularly pleased to hear that Antony Head had been pulled out of the Guards Armoured Division to head up the COHQ planning team. He was about to see a lot more of him, as the Commandos became involved in a number of operations. The first of these, which took place at the end of March, came too early for Bob or his staff to have anything to do with it. This was Operation CHARIOT, the raid on St Nazaire, in which a party formed substantially from 2 Commando and led by its commanding officer, Lieutenant Colonel Charles Newman, embarked in an old destroyer, HMS *Campbeltown*, which was rammed into the gates of the Normandie dock and subsequently blown up, thereby denying the facility to any large German warship for the remainder of the War. Volunteers from many other Commandos also took part, sailing in a number of motor launches to carry out further demolitions. The operation was judged to be a great success, enhancing the reputation of the Commandos, but came at a considerable cost. Of the 662 Royal Navy, Commando and other Army participants, only 228 returned to England, 169 being killed and the rest captured, other than five men who escaped by way of Spain. Five Victoria Crosses were awarded among the many decorations, including one to Newman, who was taken prisoner, and another to his naval counterpart, Commander Ryder.

Two other operations took place in the spring of 1942, the first being MYRMIDON, an attempt by 1 and 6 Commandos, under Lieutenant Colonel Will Glendinning of the former, to land at the mouth of the River Adour near

Bayonne in south-west France to destroy military installations. It was aborted when a previously unidentified sand bar was seen to block the approach to the landing beach. The second was Operation ABERCROMBY, a landing at Hardelot, in the Pas-de-Calais south of Boulogne, by 100 men from 4 Commando under Shimi Lovat, at that time the second-in-command. The landing was unopposed, although contact was made later with the Germans, but nothing of great moment was achieved.

Lovat, who shortly afterwards succeeded Lister as CO of 4 Commando, was now to participate in one of the War's great disasters, albeit one from which he himself emerged with his reputation enhanced. He first heard of it from Bob, who arrived unannounced during a 4 Commando exercise at Dundonald Castle. Bob found himself initially pinned down by troops firing with live ammunition, but after much waving he was spotted, the firing stopped and he was able to tell Lovat that a major raid had been planned and that two commandos were to be used on the flanks to take out enemy batteries. The choice had fallen on 3 and 4 Commandos, and Lovat and Durnford-Slater were to report to COHQ immediately to be briefed by Haydon.

The target of the raid was Dieppe. With no possibility of an invasion of the Continent in 1942, it had been decided to test the Germans' strength by landing and holding a port for a short period, destroying its defences and any other military installations and sinking ships. The original plan for the operation, which was then to take place in early July, had included landing paratroopers on the flanks to neutralize the threat posed by two batteries. Due to bad weather the operation was postponed and very nearly cancelled, but it was revived in the following month, with the paratroopers replaced by the Commandos, who had been trained to scale cliffs. Moreover, the new Royal Marine Commando was also to be employed for the first time. The bulk of the troops, however, were provided by 2 Canadian Division.

Operation JUBILEE was launched early on the morning of 19 August. The role of 3 Commando was to silence the battery at Berneval, to the east of the town. The men were embarked in small landing craft known as LCP(L)s, but on their way in they encountered a German inshore convoy with its E-boat escort, which attacked and scattered the boats. Only five out of twenty reached the beaches, but the men in four of them were unable to make any progress inland: their boats were then stranded by the tide and most were captured. The men in the fifth craft, led by the second-in-command, Major Peter Young, managed to work their way up to a position from which they could fire at the battery with small arms. They were able to distract the gunners so successfully that the battery thereafter ignored the ships lying offshore, and in due course Young withdrew his men satisfactorily.

To the west of Dieppe, 4 Commando, which like 3 Commando included a small number of officers and men from the newly raised 1st US Ranger

Battalion, landed two parties, one under Lovat, the other under his second-in-command, Derek Mills-Roberts. After fierce fighting by both parties, the battery was taken, the guns demolished and the small force taken off as planned.

The Royal Marine Commando formed part of the reserve. With the main landing force in serious difficulties, Major General Roberts, the Canadian divisional commander, ordered it ashore as reinforcements. However, by that time the Germans had the measure of the battle, most of the landing craft were destroyed or disabled and the commanding officer, Lieutenant Colonel J. P. Phillips, was fatally wounded. The few marines who landed were captured or killed.

Whilst Operation JUBILEE was a complete failure in terms of its objectives, the actions of 4 Commando had been outstandingly successful and Young's party had shown what could be achieved out of very little, given the requisite amount of skill and determination. They were the only bright lights on an otherwise very dark day.

It was by now well understood that the Allies' objectives in both the Mediterranean and north-west Europe could only be fulfilled by mounting a succession of large seaborne landings. One of the lessons of JUBILEE was that the Commandos could fulfil a highly valuable role in such circumstances. Supporting conventional troops in major amphibious operations was now to become their most important function for the remainder of the War.

This had, in fact, already been demonstrated in a faraway operation which predated JUBILEE. Three months earlier, 5 Commando under Lieutenant Colonel W. S. S. Sanguinetti had participated in Operation IRONCLAD, the capture of the port of Diego Suarez at the northernmost point of the island of Madagascar, which it was feared would be made available to Japanese submarines by the Vichy French. The operation, which was otherwise carried out by infantry brigades, was mounted under the command of Major General Robert Sturges, GOC of the Royal Marine Division, and controlled by his staff. As a precursor to the main assault, 5 Commando landed silently and captured two batteries exactly to plan, going on subsequently to participate in other landings, which led in due course to the occupation of the whole island. It arrived back in the UK in November.

With the advent of large scale landings, the old purpose of the Commandos, to carry out 'butcher and bolt' raids on the enemy coast, was largely devolved to special units. The first of these, given the cover name of 62 Commando, but more commonly known as the Small Scale Raiding Force, was set up shortly before Bob took command of the Special Service Brigade; whilst administered by the brigade, it was controlled operationally for the time being by COHQ, in conjunction with SOE. Unlike the other units, it had a dedicated force of motor boats and motor torpedo boats at its disposal and, when its achievements persuaded Mountbatten to increase its establishment, was placed under the command of Bill Stirling.

The successes of 1941 had convinced Mountbatten that Norway should not be ignored, whilst Churchill was always keen to see large numbers of German troops tied up there. However, only one operation of any moment took place there in 1942. In MUSKETOON a small party, formed from 2 Commando and Norwegian members of SOE and led by Captain Graeme Black, landed at Glomfjord to destroy a power station, which supplied an aluminium plant in the area. Their objective was achieved with complete success, but the Germans surrounded and killed or captured all the men other than four who escaped to Sweden. Black, his deputy, Captain Joseph Houghton, and the others were later executed by firing squad in accordance with Hitler's infamous Commando Order.[6] In the light of the changing role of the other Commandos, Mountbatten now ordered the formation of the new 14 Commando to handle any further such raids in Norway and the Arctic. At the end of 1942, in the knowledge that this commando in particular, but possibly others as well, would require more specialist skills, the Commando Snow and Mountain Warfare Training Camp was set up at Braemar under Squadron Leader Frank Smythe, with Major John Hunt as his Chief Instructor; both were already notable mountaineers and the latter was later to achieve fame as leader of the first expedition to conquer Mount Everest.

Even more specialized was 30 Commando, set up in September 1942 on the initiative of Ian Fleming, who was then working for the Director of Naval Intelligence, to operate alongside the forward troops in any landing, with the specific purpose of seizing enemy documents. Manned by technical experts and linguists, all with basic commando skills but trained additionally in others such as safe cracking, it was to feature in all the major Allied landings of the War. Like the SSRF, it was placed under the command of the Special Service Brigade for administrative purposes, but was operationally controlled by COHQ.

The other new creation was 10 (Inter-Allied) Commando. Although 10 Commando had not been raised in 1940 as originally intended, due to the abrupt termination of recruitment late that summer, in mid-1942 it was decided that it should be resuscitated, but this time to consist of troops from the free forces of occupied European countries, specifically France, Belgium, the Netherlands, Norway, Poland and Yugoslavia. There was also a Miscellaneous Troop (No. 3), which consisted of enemy aliens, largely pre-war German and Austrian refugees, who were fluent in German.

Dudley Lister was selected as the commanding officer. Lister had been deeply disappointed when Bob was chosen over him to lead Layforce, and his disappointment was compounded when Bob was selected to command the Special Service Brigade. He began behaving increasingly eccentrically, even to the extent of abandoning his room in a hotel in Troon to live in a tent on the golf course. It was clear to Bob that he was no longer fitted for command in the field. On the other hand, he was admirably suited to raise the new commando, which began forming at Harlech in June.

This also solved another problem for Bob, which was what to do about his brother Peter, who had returned to the UK when Oliver Lyttelton came back to succeed Lord Beaverbrook as Minister of Production. It was clear that he was unlikely to be required by the Sherwood Rangers, which by that time had reformed as an armoured regiment, and in any event he was unenthusiastic about going back to the Middle East. He was an acting major, but initially there was no spare vacancy in the Special Service Brigade for someone of that rank. However, 10 Commando required a second-in-command and Peter got the job. He was to serve in it with distinction for the rest of the War.

During 1942 four other developments took place, all of which were to have a major impact on the Commandos. The first of these, one of Haydon's last decisions before leaving the Special Service Brigade, was the establishment of the Commando Depot, later called the Commando Basic Training Centre, at Achnacarry, the seat of the chiefs of Clan Cameron, not far from Fort William. Until then, each Commando had been responsible for its own basic training, both directly in and around its base and by sending its men for specialist training at Lochailort. Now it was decided that all new recruits should complete the course at Achnacarry, whilst Lochailort was handed over to the Royal Navy for landing craft training. Some of the instructors, including Captains Fairbairn and Sykes, transferred to Achnacarry.

The officer selected to command was a remarkable figure, Lieutenant Colonel Charles Vaughan. He had served in the ranks during the Great War, rising to become a regimental sergeant major before obtaining a commission. He had been the Administration Officer of 3 Special Service Battalion under Lister and then second-in-command of 4 Commando before Lovat. A tremendous disciplinarian, he turned out to be just what was needed to establish and run what turned out to be one of the finest training establishments of the War and the model for commando training ever since. Bob respected him greatly and invariably included him in the conferences which he held from time to time with all his unit commanders.

The second development was the decision of the United States Army to form its own version of the Commandos, the Rangers. Bob was closely involved with getting the new force established, travelling to Northern Ireland on 26 June, a few days after the 1st Battalion began forming with volunteers from 34 US Division, to discuss its training regime and to make arrangements for its members to attend the course at Achnacarry. Unlike many British senior officers, who all too often looked on the Americans as inexperienced newcomers, Bob immediately treated them as equals and was rewarded by their full cooperation. In particular, he established a close personal friendship with the Commanding

Officer, Lieutenant Colonel William Darby and, in order that they should gain experience of operations, arranged for fifty of his men to be attached to 3 and 4 Commandos at Dieppe. Towards the end of the year he was asked to visit 25 US Division to discuss the raising of a second battalion, which duly took place.

The third development was of a different order altogether, but arguably made a greater contribution to defining the Commandos as a discrete part of the British Armed Forces than any other. One of the guiding principles of the Army Commandos was that they should be composed of volunteers, who would be attached from their parent regiments or services, to which, in theory at least, they were likely to return. As a result they continued to wear their own cap badges on the appropriate headgear, which for the majority was the field service or 'forage' cap, although others, notably those from the Household Brigade, wore service dress caps. This resulted in an appearance on parade which was far from homogenous. The exception was 11 Commando, which, to emphasize its Scottish origins, adopted the Balmoral bonnet, with a black hackle instead of cap badges. In due course the Balmoral bonnet was also adopted in the interests of uniformity by 2 and 9 Commandos, although their origins were not at all Scottish.

On investigating the possibilities, 1 Commando, which had considered following the others, expressed a preference for the beret, a black version of which had been worn by the Royal Tank Regiment since 1924 and had now been adopted by the rest of the Royal Armoured Corps, whilst the Airborne Forces were given permission to wear maroon berets in mid-1942. It was argued by 1 Commando that this was a thoroughly sensible type of headgear, easy to maintain and to remove and stow away when necessary. Having decided that the most appropriate colour was green, they had examples made and approached Bob for his approval. He very much liked the idea, believing that it would cement the unity of the Commandos and should become mandatory for them all. He submitted the proposal to Mountbatten, who in turn approached the War Office. Authority for all members of the Special Service Brigade to wear green berets was published on 24 October 1942.

The fourth development would turn out to be the most significant of all. The Royal Marines had already formed one Commando and were actively contemplating raising more.

Chapter 15

Reorganization

If the early years of the War had been frustrating for the Commandos, they were even more so for the Royal Marines. As far back as 1923, the Madden Committee had recommended that they should form an amphibious strike force, but a parsimonious government declined to act on it. In the light of the German invasion of Denmark and Norway in the spring of 1940, a small RM detachment occupied the Faeroe Islands, the recently raised 2nd RM Battalion, still substantially untrained and under the command of Colonel Robert Sturges, took control of Iceland, whilst another force, put together hurriedly from the RM complements of a number of capital ships, held Åndalsnes in Norway to enable British troops to land in support of the Norwegians and later covered their withdrawal. The bulk of the troops for the abortive Dakar expedition came from 101 and 102 Royal Marine Brigades, but other than that part of the MNBDO which saw active service in Crete and suffered the same fate as Layforce, there was nothing more in the way of action. The Royal Marine Division, formed in 1940/41, remained unemployed.

Following his appointment as CCO, Mountbatten, who was finding it difficult to recruit from the Army, approached the Adjutant-General Royal Marines, General Bourne, for help. Bourne agreed that a new commando could be raised from RM volunteers in the UK, and this was duly formed as the Royal Marine Commando in February 1942 and placed under the control of the Special Service Brigade. Bob spent four days with the unit on the Isle of Wight in July 1942, following which it was judged to be ready for inclusion in Operation JUBILEE.

At a meeting attended by Bob at COHQ on 14 September, agreement was reached that a second Royal Marine Commando would be formed. In this case, however, it was decided to convert an existing unit, the 8th RM Battalion, which had originally been formed eighteen months earlier and which was not part of the Royal Marine Division. The original RM Commando was redesignated as 'A' RM Commando and the new one called 'B' RM Commando, but within weeks their titles were changed to 40 and 41 RM Commandos.

This increment to the strength of the Special Service Brigade was made more necessary by the departure overseas of three Commandos in late October, the first deployment in such numbers since Layforce: 9 Commando, under Lieutenant Colonel Ronnie Tod, was sent to augment the garrison of Gibraltar, whilst 1 and 6 Commandos, under Lieutenant Colonels Tom Trevor and Iain McAlpine respectively, joined the force for Operation TORCH, the invasion of French North Africa.

These were precisely the circumstances which Bob had envisaged when he wrote his recommendations on the Special Service Brigade shortly after his return from Egypt. He had asked at that time for a second-in-command, and two months later Will Glendinning moved from 1 Commando to take up the position, with promotion to full colonel. Glendinning was now placed in overall charge of 1 and 6 Commandos and provided with a staff of two officers, one of whom was Randolph Churchill, now recovered from his injuries. As it was thought that the Vichy French would be more likely to surrender to the Americans than to the British, both commandos were augmented by US troops. These did not, however, come from the Rangers, although the 1st Battalion was engaged elsewhere in the invasion, and their training, as it turned out, did not equip them well for what was in store.

For the landings on 8 November, both 1 and 6 Commandos were ordered to seize key French forts and batteries on either side of the Bay of Algiers and further to the west. Half of 1 Commando, led by the CO, took its objective without a shot being fired. The other half, under Tom Trevor's cousin, Ken Trevor, encountered much more determined resistance and incurred casualties; but an attack by Allied aircraft, followed immediately by a charge, caused the French to capitulate. Although 6 Commando experienced difficulties when their boats were ineptly launched and then landed on the wrong beaches by untrained crews, so that the French were fully alerted, once again an air attack persuaded the Vichy defenders to surrender.

The Allies now planned to move as fast as possible into Tunisia, and 6 Commando was sent on ships to take the port of Bône, sailing unimpeded into the harbour. It was joined there by 1 Commando a few days later. Thereafter 6 Commando was attached to 36 Brigade and employed as ordinary infantry, a role to which it was completely unsuited. McAlpine had a nervous breakdown and was evacuated, to be replaced in due course by Lovat's second-in-command, Derek Mill-Roberts, who pulled the commando together and went on to win the DSO. Meanwhile, 1 Commando penetrated further west than any other Allied unit, landing at Bizerta from nine LCMs and four LCAs. It managed very successfully to hold up German reinforcements moving along the coast road, but was eventually attacked in such strength that it had to withdraw with heavy casualties before any Allied troops could come to its relief. Both commandos were now put into the front line as the Allied advance came to a complete halt and, with no replacements for their losses, had to be withdrawn to the UK in the following April.

As the two commandos had been placed under other formations, Glendinning found that he was unable to exercise any control over them. Bob had no news other than a request for more green berets to be flown out and a postcard from Randolph Churchill. As a result, he sent Philip Dunne, who had consistently refused promotion from captain but was proving to be invaluable as a trouble-shooter, out to North Africa in early January 1943 to interview not only Glendinning and his immediate subordinates, but also the relevant Allied commanders.

Glendinning told Dunne that he had suffered from having a very small staff, that he had been unable to persuade his superiors to grasp the proper role of the commandos, which had led to their use as infantry, and that the inclusion of the Americans, whose training and discipline was inferior to that of their British colleagues, had been unhelpful. On the back of his meeting with Glendinning and interviews with Lieutenant General Charles Allfrey, the Commander of V Corps, his BGS and the commanders of 78 Division and 36 Brigade, Dunne concluded that it was actually Glendinning's personality and lack of leadership which had led to his being unable to control the two commandos or protect them from misuse.

There was universal praise for 1 Commando, and it was clear that the overall opinion of the Commandos within the British Army had been greatly enhanced. Although 6 Commando had suffered from poor leadership in the early weeks, Mills-Roberts had impressed everyone and it was felt that he would restore its reputation. For Bob there were some significant lessons to be learnt from the campaign in North Africa, not least that a force of more than one commando sent on overseas operations should be led by a capable and forceful commander, who should be provided with an adequate staff, and used only for what it had been trained to do.

A month before TORCH the Special Service Brigade HQ relocated to Sherborne, with its offices in the Castle. As both RM Commandos were on the Isle of Wight, No. 3 Commando was at Weymouth and No. 4 Commando at Winchester, the geographical emphasis, other than for training, had switched to the south, which was also much more convenient for Bob's frequent visits to COHQ. There were some new arrivals, the most important of whom was Tom Churchill, who had tired of photographic interpretation and, remembering his brief but enjoyable stay with 8 Commando in late 1940, wrote to ask Bob if there was a role for him in the Special Service Brigade. Bob replied that he would be delighted to have him and succeeded in arranging a transfer, although there was no immediate vacancy on his staff. In the meantime, he sent Churchill on temporary attachments to a number of his units, including 2 Commando, which since St Nazaire had been commanded by Churchill's brother Jack. 'Mad Jack' was something of an eccentric, who carried his bagpipes, a Scottish broadsword and a longbow and arrows with him on operations, but he was also a popular and highly effective leader. Tom Churchill also spent some time with Vaughan at the

Commando Depot, before succeeding Atkinson at the Special Service Brigade as GSO1 Staff Duties and Training.

Another welcome addition to the officers' mess was Captain Basil Bennett, the Camp Commandant. In peacetime Bennett had been managing director of the Hyde Park Hotel, in which he had employed Brian Franks. At the age of forty-eight he was considerably older than any of his colleagues and had served in the Rifle Brigade in the Great War, during which he had been wounded three times. Well regarded by Bob and the others, especially Evelyn Waugh, he managed to make significant improvements to the catering in the mess, notably to the wine cellar, and was generally regarded as something of a father figure. Another addition to the HQ was Walter Cowan, who was attached as the Naval Liaison Officer. Captured in North Africa whilst serving with an Indian cavalry regiment, he had been released by the Italians in a prisoner exchange on account of his age.[1]

Bob continued to fulfil a punishing schedule, inspecting units, attending exercises and continuing to apply his own very high standards. Following one of the exercises, Waugh wrote in his diary:

> Bob gave a conference to the troop leaders on the exercise, warning them that their training was elementary and their discipline weak, and threatening to disband them. Where he excels and commands my admiration is that he is able to say this without a sting, so that he rouses no resentment.[2]

One significant advantage of the HQ's new location was that Bob could see more of Angie in London and, on occasion, in Sherborne. She was now running the canteen at COHQ in Richmond Terrace and had also become very closely involved with the Commando Benevolent Fund, which was established on 11 January 1943 on the initiative of Mountbatten to provide financial assistance to the wives, widows and dependent children of those who had served in the Army Commandos. Bob was the first chairman and Angie herself was on the committee; more importantly, as most of the other members were serving officers, she established and ran the Ladies Committee, which carried out most of the fund-raising work during the War. A number of concerts and dances were held, and a major success was arranging for the CBF to be the beneficiary, jointly with the Airborne Forces Benevolent Fund, of the première of Laurence Olivier's film of *Henry V*.

By the beginning of 1943 it was apparent that no further Army commandos were going to be raised and that providing replacements for losses within the existing commandos would continue to present difficulties. One month earlier Bob had met the C-in-C Home Forces, General Sir Bernard Paget, to discuss the problem, only to be told bluntly that Home Forces would be unable to provide any help with recruitment. There were other potential sources, such as Anti-Aircraft Command, which was scaling down from its peak at the height of the Blitz, whilst good junior officers were being recruited directly from their OCTUs, but these were not sufficient to satisfy the demand. It looked as if the only solution would be to cannibalize some existing units, as a result of which 12 and 14 Commandos were first reduced and later disbanded to provide replacements for the others.

Moreover, in the light of the requirement for substantial amphibious operations to establish footholds on the mainland of Europe, it was also becoming very evident that the role of the Commandos had changed. At the Commanding Officers' Conference on 15 January:

> The Brigade Commander stated that owing to the general change in the war situation it was apparent that raiding for the sake of raiding was unlikely to be undertaken. Therefore Commandos must be prepared to carry out a role as specialised and highly trained infantry, possibly for protracted operations. In view of this it was necessary to think ahead of the likely requirements of Units, and consequent changes of establishment.[3]

This involved re-equipping each commando with additional vehicles and heavier weaponry, such as machine-guns and 3″ mortars. Bob, however, was also thinking about a much more fundamental reorganization of the Special Service Brigade itself: on 1 April he sent a paper to Mountbatten and to his own COs entitled 'Role of the Special Service Brigade and the Desirability of Reorganization', identifying three possible futures for the Commandos:

> (a) To be retained in their present form for employment in small scale raids
> (b) To be disbanded
> (c) To be reorganised so that they may participate in large scale operations overseas and in large scale raids mounted from this country, either in a single force or in conjunction with the Field Force[4]

As far as the first was concerned, Bob believed that such a commitment could be met with a force of only three Commandos, raising the question of what would become of the others. Unsurprisingly, he rejected disbandment, arguing that, in their short history, the Commandos had developed a morale, an *esprit de corps* and a fighting efficiency second to none in the British Army and had won admiration and respect from friend and foe alike. He thus settled on the third option but, with no fewer than seventeen units under its direct command – fourteen Commandos, the Brigade Signals Troop, the Commando Depot and the Commando Mountain Warfare Camp – he concluded that the current structure of the Special Service Brigade was too unwieldy.

Having said that, his first recommendation was the formation of yet another unit, to be called the Holding Commando. This was to remedy a major deficiency in the existing organization, which was that, after major raids or lengthy overseas deployments, the Commandos involved were unfit for active service for many months whilst they re-formed and retrained. The solution was for the Holding Commando to take in all those who had undertaken their basic training at Achnacarry and post officers and men to individual Commandos as required.

The second major proposal was a fundamental restructuring, whereby nine of the Commandos would be split into three groups of three, each group commanded by a full colonel with a small staff consisting of a brigade major, a staff captain and an intelligence officer. These groups would be capable of detachment from the Special Service Brigade for operations under other formations as required. The Special Service Brigade would continue to have direct control of 10, 30 and 62 Commandos and of the Commando Depot, the Holding Commando and the Commando Mountain Warfare Camp. Two Commandos, 12 and 14, would cease to exist. Other important proposals included amendments to the war establishments of individual units and the upgrading of weapons and transport in line with Bob's meeting with his unit commanders on 15 January.

Bob did not produce these ideas out of the blue; indeed, he took great care to keep both Mountbatten and Haydon fully informed of what he was going to recommend and reached agreement in principle with the former a month before the paper was submitted. Mountbatten was prepared to put his weight behind the proposals and, in particular, to press at the highest level for the promotion to full colonel of the group commanders.

One of those proposed for this new role was Shimi Lovat, who had, however, recently been approached to move to another job, to which he was giving serious consideration. This may have been in part a consequence of his relationship with Bob, which had not always been an easy one. Bob had received a number of complaints about the behaviour of the CO of 4 Commando and had written to him several months earlier:

> To be absolutely frank with you I think you are inclined to be getting a reputation for arrogance which is a pity. Please rectify this.[5]

Lovat had also been very critical about the formation of the various specialized Commandos, whose role he felt could have been just as well performed by the existing units. Nonetheless, Bob did value him highly as an aggressively minded officer, who had led a first-class unit with great success at Dieppe and was much admired by his own men and by those in other Commandos. He therefore bent over backwards to retain him, asking him to give the newly proposed organization his full consideration before severing his connection with the Special Service

Brigade. He also added his support to a proposal by Lovat to bring the Lovat Scouts into the Commandos: the regiment, which had seen no active service during the War, had been raised by Lovat's father and he had served in it himself. The proposal was turned down, but Lovat was grateful to Bob and this may have influenced his decision, which was to remain in the Commandos.

There was some interesting feedback on Bob's paper from some of the other Commando leaders. Derek Mills-Roberts, for instance, who was still in North Africa, was dubious about the status of the colonels commanding each group, comparing this unfavourably with the parachute brigades he had come across recently, which were all commanded by brigadiers. He suggested that the Commandos would be more influential as a division, with Bob in command and a couple of brigadiers beneath him.

It was 2 May before Haydon returned the paper to Bob with a number of minor amendments, which were all agreed immediately. On 4 May Mountbatten wrote to the CIGS, summarizing the proposals and taking ownership of them himself. He also suggested that in future the Special Service Brigade should be allowed to recruit 40 per cent from the Field Army and 60 per cent from Corps Training Centres.

Unfortunately, the letter was delivered to Brooke on the very day that he, Churchill and the other Chiefs of Staff left for the TRIDENT conference in Washington. The CIGS had many more important issues to address and it was 11 May before he signalled Mountbatten to say that he was unable to accept the proposals without consulting the Adjutant General. He asked Mountbatten to speak to both the Adjutant General and the VCIGS and to have them wire him the results of their discussions. Mountbatten did not write to the VCIGS, Lieutenant General Nye, until 25 May, and it was not Nye but the DCIGS, Lieutenant General Weeks, responsible at the War Office for matters relating to organization, who replied on 3 June, saying that further careful examination was required before he could discuss the proposals with Brooke on the latter's return to the country two days later. On 24 June Weeks wrote again to say that the proposals had been approved in principle and were being submitted to the War Establishments Committee.

Whilst awaiting a decision, Bob had been busy considering the ramifications of the proposed reorganization and particularly the composition and the commanders of the three new groups. On 12 May he wrote to Haydon, proposing that the commanders should be Lovat, with 1, 3 and 6 Commandos, Tom Trevor with 2, 5 and 9 Commandos and Durnford-Slater with 4, 40 RM and 41 RM Commandos. Ken Trevor[6] would step up to command 1 Commando in succession to his cousin, Peter Young would replace Durnford-Slater in 3 Commando and Tom Churchill would, in due course, follow Lovat in 4 Commando, with Lovat's second-in-command, Robert Dawson, acting in the meantime. All the other COs would remain in place.

Before the War Establishments Committee could finally approve it, the reorganization was overtaken by two events. The first of these was the departure overseas of Bob himself, to conduct the operations described in the next two chapters. This did indeed result in a *de facto* reorganization of the Special Service Brigade, although not in the way that he had envisaged. Instead, it was simply the reverse of the earlier arrangement for Operation TORCH, when the Brigade Commander stayed at home whilst his deputy led the expeditionary force. This time it was the deputy who remained behind.

The second event was much more momentous, in terms not only of the immediate organization of the Commandos and their employment for the remainder of the War, but also of their post-war role and composition. This was the wholesale conversion of the Royal Marine Division into Commandos.

The RM Division had existed on paper since August 1940, when Bob Sturges was appointed as its GOC, but the absence of 101 and 102 RM Brigades, which were still in West Africa at that time, meant that the divisional HQ only opened in February 1941. It had been chosen to be part of Force 110 to capture the Canary Islands, only to have that operation cancelled, then selected once again for Operation IRONCLAD in Madagascar and this time be replaced by other formations. It was to suffer yet more disappointment in the autumn of 1943, when General Eisenhower refused Bourne's offer of the division for Operation TORCH, on the grounds that it was composed of only two infantry brigades and lacked most of the supporting arms and services of a standard division. Bourne, however, remained stubbornly insistent on retaining the division as a discrete landing force, and it was only in early 1943, when he was succeeded as Adjutant General by Lieutenant General T. L. Hunton, that a greater degree of flexibility began to emerge within the Corps.

By that time it was already apparent that not only was there an immediate demand for Commandos in the Mediterranean theatre, but that the invasion of north-west Europe would require even more. In addition, it was now being suggested that they would prove valuable in south-east Asia. With little chance of wholesale recruitment from the Army being permitted by the War Office, at least in the UK, Mountbatten turned to the Admiralty to plug the looming gap. Both the First Sea Lord and Hunton turned out to be amenable, but as two RM Commandos were already in existence and an additional six could be formed from the RM Division's battalions, they would only agree to the latter's conversion on the condition that all the Commandos, both RM and Army, came under the overall command of a Royal Marine officer. Sturges was the obvious candidate, not only because of his previous experience in combined operations, but also because he had a sizeable and well trained HQ at his disposal.

Mountbatten capitulated without hesitation. Bob's proposals on structural reorganization were shelved and work began on the creation of a new formation, to be called the Special Service Group.

Chapter 16

Husky

It had been decided in January 1943 at the Casablanca Conference that the next objective for the Western Allies, once they had defeated the Axis forces in North Africa, should be the invasion of Sicily. A planning HQ, Force 141, was set up in Algiers, to which Antony Head was attached as a representative of COHQ, but it was only as the campaign in Tunisia was drawing to an end in May that the senior commanders were able to find time to focus on the operation, codenamed HUSKY. The composition of the ground forces had by then been agreed. They were to consist of Eighth Army under General Sir Bernard Montgomery and Seventh US Army under Lieutenant General George Patton. Once Montgomery was able to find time to study the plans, which proposed dispersed landings, he had them completely recast, so that the two armies would land alongside one another in south-east Sicily, with Seventh US Army on the south coast and Eighth Army on either side of Cape Passero and up the east coast.

Following their creditable performance in North Africa, it was decided at an early stage of planning that both Commandos and US Rangers would be employed in the landings. As far as the British were concerned, the force would consist of 3, 40 RM and 41 RM Commandos. In preparation for this, 3 Commando was sent initially to relieve 9 Commando in Gibraltar, where it stayed for six weeks before being relieved in its turn by 2 Commando and moving on to Algiers and thence to Egypt, in order to rehearse its role in HUSKY with 5 Division, which it would be supporting. Whereas 3 Commando was to sail to Sicily from Port Said and land on the right flank of Eighth Army, the two RM Commandos, whose task was to support 1 Canadian Division on the left flank, were to sail directly from the UK. In addition, one other unit was to land near to but separate from 3 Commando. This was the Special Raiding Squadron, now commanded by Paddy Mayne. It had been created after David Stirling was taken prisoner in Tunisia at the beginning of the year, at which time the SAS had been divided into the SRS and the Special Boat Squadron, the latter commanded by George Jellicoe.

In the knowledge that three Commandos and the SRS would be employed in the Mediterranean and that they were likely to be reinforced by 2 Commando before very long, and in the light of the experience of 1 and 6 Commandos in Operation TORCH, Bob argued forcefully for them to be controlled by

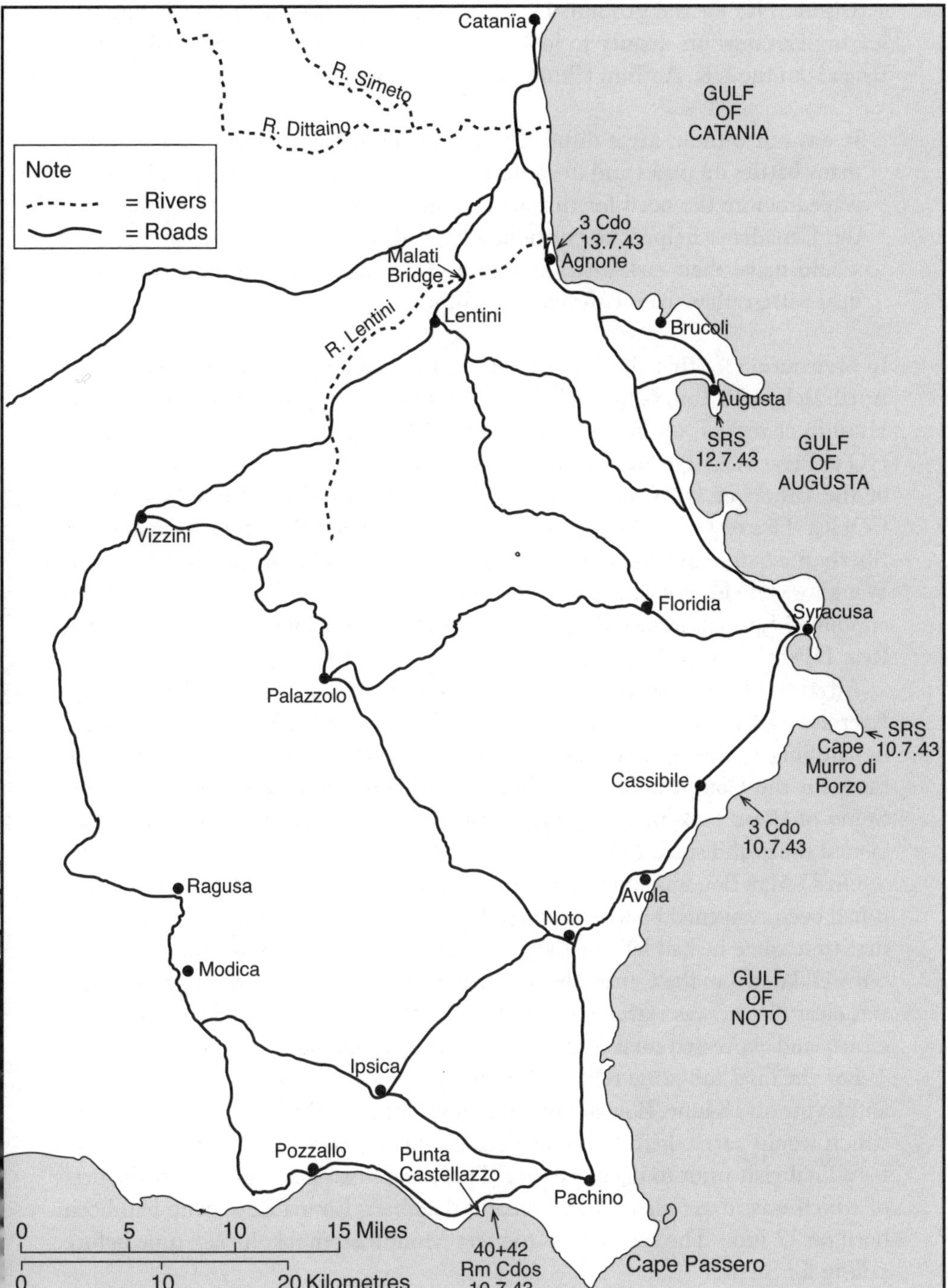

Catanïa
R. Simeto
R. Dittaino
GULF
OF
CATANIA
Note
= Rivers
= Roads
3 Cdo
13.7.43
Malati
Bridge
Agnone
Lentini
R. Lentini
Brucoli
Augusta
SRS
12.7.43
GULF
OF
AUGUSTA
Vizzini
Floridia
Syracusa
Palazzolo
SRS
10.7.43
Cape
Murro di
Porzo
Cassibile
3 Cdo
10.7.43
Ragusa
Avola
Noto
Modica
GULF
OF
NOTO
Ipsica
Pozzallo
Punta
Castellazzo
Pachino
0 5 10 15 Miles
0 10 20 Kilometres
40+42
Rm Cdos
10.7.43
Cape Passero

Eastern Sicily.

a Brigade HQ on the ground. He also sought permission to lead it himself, leaving Lovat as his deputy to look after the remainder of the Special Service Brigade in the UK. As Tom Churchill was to write later:

> It was not without great difficulty that this permission was obtained, and many battles on paper and in conference rooms in the War Office had to be waged before the need for this arrangement was recognised. Our friends the Canadians helped us considerably in this respect, by saying that it would make their task easier if they had a Commando Headquarters to deal with, rather than with separate units.[1]

In preparation for this, the Special Service Brigade HQ was split into two on 12 April. Bob, with Tom Churchill, Franks and Dunne, together with Major Griff Hunt in charge of 'Q' matters and much of the Signals Troop, set up Advance HQ at Prestwick. The officers were comfortably billeted in Troon in the house of the father[2] of Ian Collins, formerly of 8 Commando and now working at COHQ. The rest of the staff, in what was now styled Rear HQ, remained in Sherborne before moving at the beginning of June to Cowdray Park, Midhurst. Waugh was no longer with them. He had never got on well with Lovat and was appointed Special Service Brigade Liaison Officer at COHQ, to be replaced at Rear HQ by Captain Hilary Bray.

Advance HQ was soon joined in Scotland by 40 and 41 RM Commandos. Exercise ALBION was designed by Churchill to give the HQ specific practice in handling a force of Commandos in the field, and further exercises were held, most for the Commandos alone, but two in conjunction with the Canadians. Some of these took place on Arran, the first time that any Commando had visited the island since 1941.

On 27 May Bob was summoned to a conference at the War Office, to find that it had been convened by Montgomery himself, who was visiting the UK for the first time since he had left for Egypt in August 1942. He was a stranger to Bob but well known to the Canadians, who had served under him in England, and it was clear that he was extremely popular with them. He explained his plans very clearly and expressed total confidence that they would be successfully executed.

For the final full-scale rehearsal, carried out on the beaches between Troon and Irvine on 18 June, Bob and his staff embarked in HMT *Derbyshire*, the ship which would carry them to Sicily. Five days later, Bob went down to London for a final visit prior to his departure. There were two main objectives, the first of which was to see his new and second daughter, Emma Rose, who had been born on 12 June. The second was to meet Mountbatten for the last time before sailing for Sicily.

The purpose of the meeting was for Bob to bring the CCO fully up to date with his dispositions for HUSKY, but Mountbatten used the occasion to bring

Bob into the picture about the possible conversion of the Royal Marine Division into Commandos. There is no record of the meeting, but Mountbatten's discussions with the Admiralty and the RM Office were then at an early stage and no decisions had been made as to the composition of the combined organization. Bob did, however, offer a view on this. Some five weeks later, by which time serious differences of opinion had begun to emerge between them, Mountbatten was to write to Bob:

> You will remember that it was you who first suggested that the Army Commandos should come under General Sturges, in order that the Army and the Marine Commandos should be a unified force. I shall always be very grateful to you for that suggestion, because I feel that it was a really important contribution and, incidentally, a very generous one on your part. [3]

Bob was, it seems, responding to this surprising new development off the top of his head, without any chance to pause for reflection. As Haydon was later to tell Mountbatten, 'Brigadier Laycock's mind must, at the time he gave you his opinion, have been filled with the details of Husky',[4] whilst Bob himself wrote, 'I seem to have given the C.C.O a very wrong impression of my recommendation made in great haste before my departure for SICILY.'[5] Bob had actually lunched with Sturges afterwards, during which he repeated what Mountbatten had revealed, but he had no time to consult with his subordinates. He left London the next day to make one final inspection in the south of England before leaving the country.

Advance HQ re-embarked on the *Derbyshire* on 27 June, along with 40 RM Commando, under Lieutenant Colonel J. C. 'Pops' Manners, and the 48th Highlanders of Canada, whilst 41 RM Commando, under Lieutenant Colonel B. J. D. Lumsden, travelled with other Canadian troops in HMT *Durban Castle*. The convoy, which included many more ships carrying 1 Canadian Division, sailed from the Clyde late on 28 June.

The *Derbyshire* had been recently converted into a LSI but was rather more comfortable than the Glen ships. Bob had a bedroom, bathroom and sitting room to himself, which annoyed Philip Dunne, who had to share a cabin. The food was delicious and the drink cheap and plentiful, but there was also serious work to be done. On 1 July the orders for the invasion were distributed to all units, which now had to prepare thoroughly for their specific roles. On 3 July Bob gave a briefing to all the officers, outlining the overall plan so that everyone could understand how they fitted in.

Other than a number of alarms when parts of the escort were detached to deal with possible submarines, only one of which proved to be genuine and was destroyed by depth charges, the voyage was uneventful. The convoy passed

Gibraltar on 5 July and made its way across the Western Mediterranean, which was surprisingly devoid of enemy aircraft. The seas were calm until the convoy arrived off the Maltese island of Gozo on 9 July, when the wind increased substantially and a heavy swell built up, casting doubt on the practicability of landings west of Cape Passero early on the following morning. By late evening, however, the wind had abated and, in spite of a swell remaining, conditions were such that the landing craft could be launched.

At 01.10 on 10 July the LCAs carrying 40 RM Commando and the Brigade HQ were lowered and moved away from the ship, later taking position to the right of a navigational motor launch, with those carrying 41 RM Commando to the left. At 02.30 the ML hove to, uncertain of its position. Nevertheless, 41 RM Commando advanced towards the shore, the craft from the *Derbyshire* following soon afterwards and touching down on the beach near Punta Castellazzo at 03.00, about 400 yards west of the intended position.

Both Commandos and the HQ moved quickly inland, experiencing only modest opposition, although casualties were incurred from machine guns firing on fixed lines, particularly in 41 RM Commando, which lost its second-in-command amongst others. The D-Day objectives, a number of batteries and strongpoints along the coast, were overrun by 06.00. There was some further fighting after daybreak, and 40 RM Commando was ordered to clear the hills immediately in front, which they did quickly, albeit with some casualties. To the east, contact was made with the Canadians.

Brigade HQ established a temporary location soon after landing but moved later to a house further inland, which turned out to have a good supply of wine, notably Marsala. Bob and Dunne insisted on having a photograph taken in front of the hogsheads to send to Waugh, whom they knew was partial to Marsala and would thus be annoyed at not being present. Later that day, Bob attended a conference at 1 Canadian Division's HQ and received orders to move forward again on the next day to conform to the division's advance. After taking up their new position, 41 RM Commando came under mortar fire, but a flanking movement by 40 RM Commando and some heavy mortar support from the Canadians drove off the attackers and, later in the day, the two Commandos were withdrawn into reserve.

On the far right flank of the landings near Cassibile, 3 Commando had had a similar experience, meeting some resistance but capturing the target battery with no casualties. Only Peter Young was unhappy, as his LCA had gone wildly astray and he had missed the action. Durnford-Slater gave him the task of seizing a nearby fort, which restored his good humour.

The SRS had also taken its D-Day objectives at Cape Murro di Porco and, two days later, Mayne and his squadron occupied the port of Augusta by themselves, handing it over to 5 Division on the following day.

On 12 July Bob was ordered to report to Montgomery. He and Churchill took a boat out to HMS *Hilary*, the command ship for the force which had sailed from the UK, flying the flag of Rear Admiral Sir Philip Vian. There they met Montgomery's Chief of Staff, Major General Freddie de Guingand, who told them that the Eighth Army Commander was expected; but although a number of other senior officers came aboard, including Eisenhower, there was no sign of him. Returning to shore, they eventually met him that evening at the HQ of XXX Corps, which was commanded by Lieutenant General Oliver Leese, who was well known to Bob as the former Adjutant of the Eton College OTC. Montgomery was pleased with the performance of the Commandos and talked about other possible operations which were very much in line with what they had been trained to do.

On the next day Bob and Churchill went to Montgomery's Tac HQ and found both Mountbatten and Head there. After further discussions with the Army Commander, Bob escorted the CCO back to his own HQ and then on to 40 and 41 RM Commandos, who were congratulated on their achievements. There was no mention of the conversion of the Royal Marine Division into Commandos, and later that day Mountbatten and Head left for Malta.

On the same day 3 Commando had carried out an operation which was to raise the stock of the Commandos considerably in the eyes of the British commanders, but at a high price. Durnford-Slater was summoned to a conference with Lieutenant General Miles Dempsey, GOC of XIII Corps, at which he was given orders to land behind the enemy lines further up the east coast at Agnone and then to march seven miles inland to seize and hold the Malati Bridge, across which ran the main road to Catania.

Having been told to expect only Italian opposition, which would probably fade away as before, 3 Commando instead encountered German paratroopers, who had recently been dropped into the area. Notwithstanding this, a detachment led by Young reached the bridge and managed to remove demolition charges which had been set there. The Commando then established itself on high ground to dominate the road and succeeded in stopping the traffic, but the Germans threw everything they had at them, including a Tiger tank. Casualties began to rise and, with no relief in sight, Durnford-Slater ordered his men to break up into small parties and make their way back to the British lines.

The operation had failed, but both Montgomery and Dempsey were delighted with 3 Commando's performance and Montgomery later had the bridge formally named after it. Durnford-Slater received a bar to his DSO, Young a bar to his MC and there were numerous other awards. On the other hand 28 men were killed, 66 wounded and 59 missing.

Bob heard about 3 Commando's exploits for the first time on 14 July, when he and Churchill attended a conference in Syracuse to discuss future operations with Dempsey and the Flag Officer Sicily, Rear Admiral Rhoderick McGrigor. Like

Leese, Dempsey was known to Bob, in his case as one of his Company Officers at Sandhurst.[6] The conference continued on the next day, by which time the fate of 3 Commando had become clearer, as a result of which 40 and 41 RM Commandos were moved into XIII Corps to replace it for the next operation.

Strong resistance by the newly arrived Germans meant that XIII Corps was brought to a halt on the Plain of Catania, south of the city itself. Operation CHOPPER was planned to relieve the pressure by landing the two RM Commandos and the SRS north of Catania, into which they would fight their way; they would then form a beachhead in the harbour, from which 17 Brigade of 5 Division would attack the enemy from the rear. All the units involved and Brigade HQ, now augmented by Randolph Churchill, embarked in two LSIs, only to have the operation cancelled due to intelligence on large enemy reinforcements. To compound their disappointment, that night there was a heavy air raid and one of the LSIs was hit, causing numerous fatalities and other casualties.

Over the next few days it became apparent that Eighth Army was held up all along its line and, with no prospect of immediate employment, the Special Service Brigade was temporarily stood down. Tom Churchill managed to find a site for 40 and 41 RM Commandos and the Brigade HQ at Brucoli, which adjoined a good beach where the troops could bathe. On 22 July 2 Commando arrived from Gibraltar to join them, providing a welcome reinforcement after the losses incurred by 3 Commando.

In order to keep the enemy on his toes, a number of feint landings were mounted in Operation LUSTY, carried out on the nights of 25/26, 28/29 and 29/30 July by forces of destroyers accompanied by landing craft. Franks accompanied the ships on the first night, Tom Churchill on the second and Bob on the third, but in spite of shelling the coast road there was no response from the coastal batteries and little evidence that the sorties had made any impact.

With no operations imminent, Bob, Tom Churchill and Dunne flew to Tunis on 1 August and then on to Algiers the next day, to begin planning the Special Service Brigade's role in the next phase of the War, the invasion of mainland Italy. Durnford-Slater was appointed acting Brigade Commander in Bob's absence, with Franks remaining in Sicily as his Brigade Major. The new operations required the Special Service Brigade to be subdivided again, with 2 and 41 RM Commandos employed in Operation BUTTRESS, a landing by X Corps in the Gulf of Gioia on the coast of Calabria, and 3 and 40 RM Commandos and the SRS in Operation BAYTOWN, a landing by XIII Corps on the toe of Italy near Reggio. The Brigade HQ would also be split, with Churchill and Dunne accompanying Bob in BUTTRESS and Franks continuing to act as BM for Durnford-Slater in BAYTOWN. Bob found to his pleasure that the commander of X Corps was Brian Horrocks, whom both he and Churchill had known well as the Chief Instructor at the Staff College in early 1940.

Algiers was the location for both Eisenhower's Allied Forces HQ and General Alexander's Fifteenth Army Group, and there were many old friends in the city. Amongst them was Bill Stirling, who, following the capture of his brother earlier that year, had founded the 2nd SAS Regiment from the remnants of 62 Commando, which had just been disbanded. Bob was interested in exploring future cooperation with the SAS, but Stirling also provided a potential solution to a new problem, which was what to do about Waugh, who had recently been compelled to resign from the Special Service Brigade in the UK.

It had been Bob's intention when he left England to bring Waugh out to join him with the first flight of reinforcements, leaving instructions to that effect at Rear HQ. On 9 July, however, Waugh was surprised to receive a letter from John Sooby, the Acting DAA&QMG at Rear HQ, instructing him to hand over his job to another officer and report to the Commando Depot. He appealed to Lovat, who replied confirming the order and saying that he would not be allowed overseas until passed fit for active service by Achnacarry. Waugh then took his case up to Haydon, who aggressively supported Lovat, and he therefore had no alternative but to tender his resignation, which was immediately accepted. Mountbatten was sympathetic, but refused to overrule his subordinates.

It has been suggested that Bob had never intended Waugh to join him. There is no firm evidence for this, but it is not unlikely. Lovat was later to write that Waugh was 'cordially disliked by every combatant officer in the brigade'[7] and, although this may have been an exaggeration, his continuing pursuit of a varied social and literary life was certainly inconsistent with the commitment required of a Commando officer. It is possible that Bob was finding Waugh something of an embarrassment, but he was nevertheless very angry at his treatment by Lovat and Haydon. It was, however, a *fait accompli*, and all he could do was try to get him accepted elsewhere. He did eventually persuade Stirling to take Waugh, but the latter never served actively with the SAS, although he did go off with Randolph Churchill to Yugoslavia in the late summer of 1944, as part of the British Military Mission to Marshal Tito. Another casualty of the Lovat regime was Basil Bennett, but Bob succeeded in having him transferred to the Special Service Brigade HQ in the Mediterranean.

The Waugh affair was an unwelcome distraction, but no more than that. Of much more concern was what was going on with the reorganization of the Commandos, which had now come to a head. Matters had moved on apace since Bob had left the UK, helped not a little by the CIGS being only too willing to see responsibility for the Commandos devolved onto the Royal Marines. On 18 July, following his return from Sicily, Mountbatten held a meeting with his Chief of Staff, Major General Peter Wildman-Lushington, himself a Royal Marine officer, and Haydon. Haydon was deeply concerned that the wholesale incorporation of the Special Service Brigade into the RM Division 'might prove to be the thin end of the wedge as far as the Army Commandos were concerned'.[8] It would, in particular, sever the link between himself, as the senior Army officer at COHQ, and the brigade. He preferred leaving it as it was. Mountbatten rejected this and, two days later, sent a signal to Bob:

> Am considering proposal to have four Brigades each of four Commandos under Sturges. You would have one Brigade, be deputy Force Commander and Senior Army Brigadier.[9]

Because all non-urgent signals had to pass through AFHQ and Fifteenth Army Group, Bob did not receive it until 25 July, and, when he did, it was corrupted, although the sense was clear. Bob was due to see Montgomery that day and brought the matter up with him. Montgomery was unhappy with the proposal, as a result of which Bob drafted a reply, which read:

> Hope you will postpone decision until after the campaign. I have discussed employment of Special Service troops with General Montgomery who considers reorganisation on a divisional basis most unsatisfactory.[10]

He left the draft with Montgomery, who added the words 'He would like to discuss the matter with you'. Whether or not the signal was sent, Mountbatten had not received it by 28 June, when he sent another signal repeating the contents of his earlier one, but adding:

> Appreciate above suggestion alters proposal now before War Office and that it more than halves the size of your command. Do not propose to proceed unless you agree.[11]

At Haydon's suggestion, Mountbatten then held a meeting with Lovat and the COs of the Commandos in the UK. Haydon himself was not present, as it was felt that they would speak their minds more freely without him. According to a subsequent letter from Mountbatten to Bob, the COs were not keen on rival Army and RM Brigades. Moreover, he continued, they also disliked an alternative suggestion, which appears to have been conceived entirely to placate Bob, that there should be two RM Brigades under their own brigadiers and two Army brigades commanded by full colonels under one brigadier, on the grounds that it would be unnecessarily clumsy and add an extra layer of administration.

In the knowledge that Hilary Bray was leaving for Algiers to join Bob's HQ, in which he was to relieve Griff Hunt temporarily, both Mountbatten and Haydon asked him to carry detailed letters setting out the background. Bob sent a holding signal on 6 August, saying that his considered opinion was that there should be two parallel but separate organizations and that he was sending his full arguments back with Hunt. These were set out in a long handwritten letter to Mountbatten.

In the letter Bob stated that his views were motivated not by his own reduced role but by what he thought was in the best interests of Combined Operations in general and the Special Service Brigade in particular. He went on to say that the opinion he had expressed to Mountbatten before leaving for HUSKY was driven by his understanding at the time that, if the amalgamation did not take place, there would be two separate and rival organizations, one under the CCO and the other under the Adjutant-General RM, which 'would bode nothing but evil for both parties'.[12] Now that he understood that the CCO would control both, he saw no reason why they should not be separate but parallel. When he had met Mountbatten he had harboured concerns that the Army would see no need for the Commandos in future and thought that, in such circumstances, their chances of survival might be improved if they were affiliated to the RM Division. Subsequently, however, Leese, Dempsey and Guy Simmonds, the GOC of 1 Canadian Division, had all expressed great satisfaction with the Commandos, and he now believed that their role in the field was secure.

Bob went on to say that, although the two RM Commandos under his command had performed well overall, they had initially proved to be 'a bit sticky'[13] when sniped and mortared and had needed to be pushed, which would not have been the case with Army Commandos. He attributed this largely to the volunteer background of the latter and felt that their identity, individuality, *esprit de corps* and inspiration would be lost if amalgamated with the RM Division. His preference was thus for his own proposed reorganization of the Special Service Brigade to go ahead, as he believed had been agreed with the War Office, and that both it and the RM Division should report separately to Mountbatten.

Bob was already very much behind events. Notwithstanding Mountbatten's earlier reassurance that the proposals he had set out would not go ahead without his agreement, in fact the wheels had already been set in motion, largely because the Royal Marines were pressing hard to begin converting their battalions. Mountbatten, who was by then at the Quadrant Conference in Quebec, made his decision, sending a signal to Haydon on 16 August:

1. There must be one Special Service Force under General Sturges
2. Army Commandos to continue under Laycock with groups each commanded by a Colonel.
3. This organization to be reviewed one month after Laycock's return.
4. Inform Laycock.[14]

Bob was deeply unhappy with what had happened. On 21 August he wrote to Angie:

> If they are going to mess the Special Service Brigade about they will have to find a new commander and I shall return with ill grace, complaining vitriolically, to be a GII CW or go and learn about armoured cars and command a squadron of the Blues, or, if they will not have me, a Mobile Bath Unit or a Field Bakery – or become a full Sanitary Colonel with a green band around my hat and sit gloomily contemplating the similarity between latrines and Staff Officers who cannot appreciate the value of morale and *esprit de corps*.[15]

Bob's mood was not improved by the receipt of a letter from Haydon, which he described to Angie as 'very rude'.[16] It was certainly extremely blunt, not least because Bob's long letter to Mountbatten had been opened in the CCO's absence by Wildman-Lushington, who had taken the gravest exception to the comparison drawn between the Royal Marine and Army Commandos. Haydon later wrote apologizing for an 'ill-tempered letter',[17] but it was clear that there had been great exasperation at Bob's attitude, which was holding up the reorganization. Mountbatten also wrote on 24 August, telling Bob that he understood his arguments but that the decisions taken must now stand. He also told Bob that he would soon hear 'a very staggering piece of news',[18] which would mean his stepping down as CCO.

It became clear subsequently that the members of the Special Service Brigade in the UK were themselves far from happy with the proposals. Lovat wrote to say that he and the COs had been told by Mountbatten at their meeting with him that Bob was 100 per cent behind the idea of amalgamation, no matter what form it took; they had only later understood that this had been inaccurate, by which time it was too late. In another letter, John Sooby of the Special Service Brigade told Bob that they had been offered just three staff positions, and junior ones at that, out of thirteen at the new Force HQ. He neatly summed up the situation as: 'the Battle has been lost and the Marines have gained possession of the Field.'[19]

It is clear that Mountbatten was determined to drive through the reorganization, which was the only way in which the future demand for Commandos could be satisfied, and that he relied heavily on his selective interpretation of Bob's immediate reaction to the proposals in order to gain acceptance from Lovat and his COs. It is equally clear, in spite of Bob's protestations to Mountbatten, Haydon and even Angie, that he had no ambition for himself. He was in fact deeply disappointed at the turn of events from a personal perspective, so much so that in early September he sent the following signal to Mountbatten:

> Most Secret. Personal for Mountbatten and Haydon from Laycock. Request that I may be relieved of my command on conclusion Avalanche for following reasons. One G.O.C.O.'s letter of 14 Aug shows mistrust

> and disregard of all my recommendations. Two C.C.O.'s letter of 24 Aug repudiates three separate undertakings in his previous signals and letters. I cannot decently interpret this repudiation except as further mark of lack of confidence in me by C.O.H.Q. Three and far more important is my conviction that these proposals which have already been implemented in some respects must eventually prove destructive to tradition morale individuality and technique of Commandos whose interests are paramount with me. I believe that these decisions are ill advised and will cause widespread concern when they are eventually communicated to the officers and men whom I now command.[20]

And there the matter stood, just as Bob was about to participate in one of the most important Allied operations of the War.

Chapter 17

Avalanche

Bob and Tom Churchill had not been in Algiers for much more than a week when Operation BUTTRESS was cancelled in favour of Operation AVALANCHE. The latter would involve landings by Lieutenant General Mark Clark's Fifth US Army in the Bay of Salerno, chosen as the furthest point north over which air cover could be provided from Sicily. X Corps, now commanded by Lieutenant General Sir Richard McCreery, who had had succeeded Horrocks when the latter was seriously wounded by a German fighter in Bizerta, was to land on the left on either side of the town of Salerno, with Lieutenant General Ernest J. Dawley's VI US Corps on the right, close to the ruined ancient Greek city of Paestum.

XIII Corps of Eighth Army would still be carrying out Operation BAYTOWN across the Straits of Messina. Bob confirmed that 3 and 40 RM Commandos and the SRS would be at Dempsey's disposal, and all planning for that part of the Special Service Brigade was now passed to Durnford-Slater and Franks, acting under the orders of the Corps HQ. This allowed Bob and Churchill to focus on 3 and 41 RM Commandos' role in AVALANCHE. Operating under the command of 46 Division, they were to land at the small fishing village of Marina, where the coastline of the Bay of Salerno bends round to become the Amalfi Coast, take the adjacent town of Vietri sul Mare and move inland from there to control the La Molina Pass, through which ran the main road from Naples to Salerno. Meanwhile, 46 Division would be landing on the far side of Salerno and would only be able to relieve the Commandos once it had taken the town. Bob was especially pleased, however, to hear that Bill Darby and his US Rangers would be landing some five miles to his left at Maiore, blocking the coast road from Amalfi and seizing the Chiunzi Pass, through which another road ran from the Plain of Naples.

The change of plan meant that Bob was to stay in Algiers for far longer than he had originally expected. In his absence the last operation carried out by the Commandos in Sicily took place. This was BLACKCOCK, which involved a landing on 16 August by 2 Commando near Scaletta, south of Messina, in conjunction with 4 Armoured Brigade. The intention was to cut off the Axis forces retreating up the coast road from Catania, but the birds had already flown and just one solitary lorry was detained. Another landing then took place even closer to Messina, just north of San Stefano. There was no opposition, and at

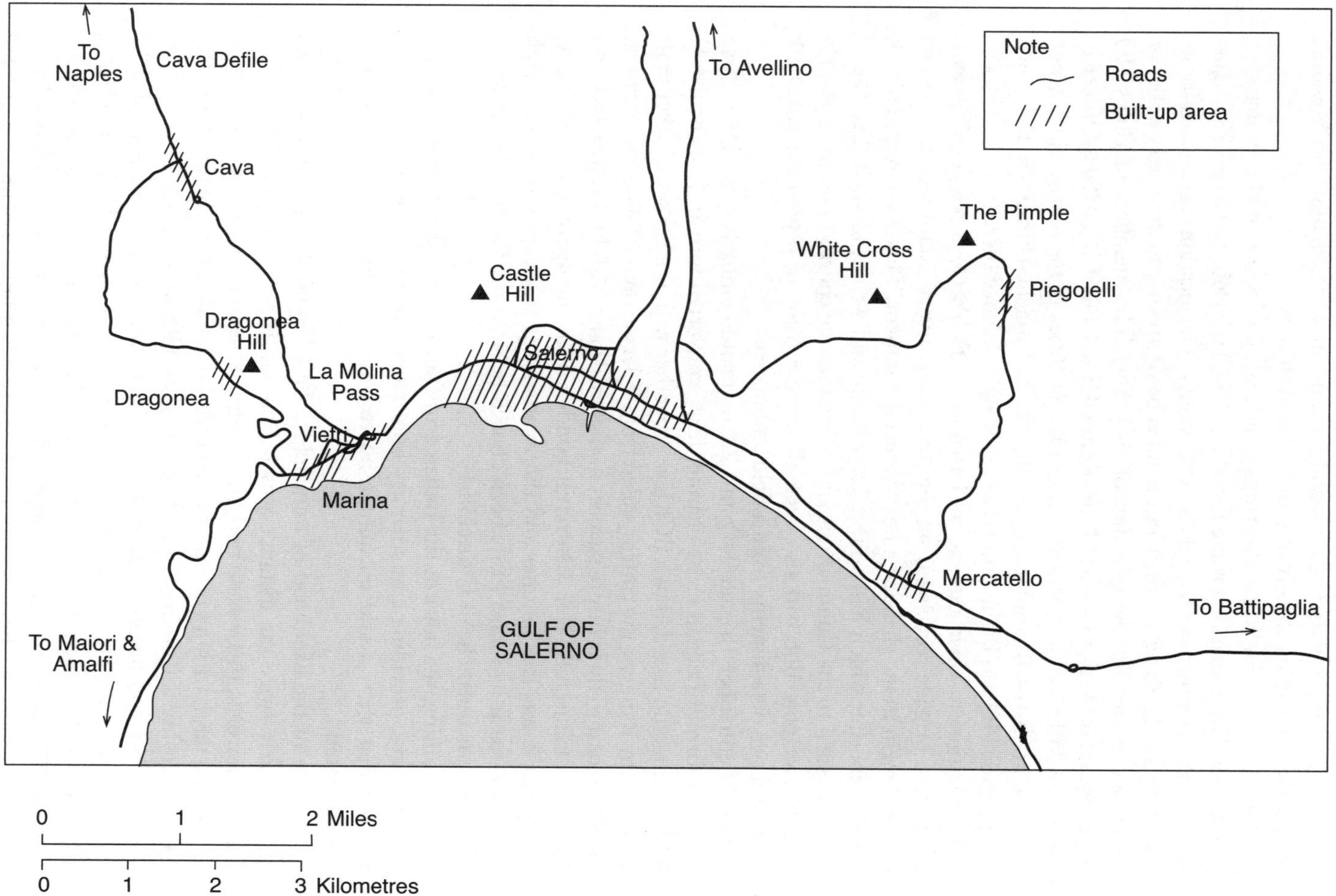
To Naples
Cava Defile
To Avellino
Note
Roads
Built-up area
Cava
The Pimple
White Cross Hill
Castle Hill
Piegolelli
Dragonea Hill
Salerno
La Molina Pass
Dragonea
Vietri
Marina
Mercatello
To Battipaglia
GULF OF SALERNO
To Maiori & Amalfi
0 1 2 Miles
0 1 2 3 Kilometres

Salerno.

09.00 on the following day 2 Commando was the first British unit into Messina, to find the Americans already in possession of the city.

Tom Churchill now flew to Palermo to find a site for 2 and 41 RM Commandos, which would be embarking there for AVALANCHE. Bob arrived on 27 August and the two Commandos over the next few days. The location was chosen for its proximity to the Rangers, the Commandos being treated to their very superior American rations for the duration of their stay. The members of Bob's HQ were invited by Major General Lord Rennell, the Chief Civil Affairs Officer in the Allied Military Government, to use the facilities in his nearby villa, which included hot baths. Randolph Churchill, who had attached himself to Bob when the Brigade HQ was divided into two, took up residence there.

In addition to their rations, and thanks to Bob's close relationship with Darby, the brigade received from the Americans a very useful increment to its establishment in the shape of a heavy mortar company. This was equipped with the 4.2″ mortar, which had a far greater range and weight of shell than the 3″ mortar issued to the Commandos and proved in due course to be an extremely valuable weapon. Bob had also been allocated a troop of 6-pounder anti-tank guns and two detachments from a field ambulance.

On 7 September Brigade HQ and 2 Commando embarked in HMS *Prinz Albert*, a former Belgian cross-channel ferry converted into an LSI, whilst 41 RM Commando boarded two LCI(L)s.[1] Together with the LSIs and other craft carrying the Rangers, the convoy sailed from Palermo on the following morning. Giving a toast to their future success in the wardroom with his brother Jack and Randolph Churchill, Tom Churchill pondered on the operation's codename, given that it was late summer and the weather was still very warm. Randolph observed that it had most likely been chosen because the Germans were about to receive an avalanche of Churchills!

That evening, the news of the Italian armistice was broadcast over the ship's loudspeakers, providing a momentary hope among many of the troops waiting to land that they would encounter no resistance. They were to be gravely disappointed.

Because of the likelihood of minefields, the LSIs hove to seven miles from shore, nearly twice the distance which Bob had thought was too far away at Bardia. However, this was no raid; the Commandos were expecting to be ashore for several days, with no prospect of an early withdrawal back to the ships. The LCAs carrying 2 Commando and the Brigade HQ were lowered at 02.15 on 9 September and began to move towards the shore. They were preceded by two minesweepers clearing a wide channel and the destroyer HMS *Blackmore*, which was to bombard the enemy batteries. There had been some debate during the planning as to whether the approach should be made in complete silence, so as not to alert the defenders, or under cover of a bombardment. Bob decided that the destroyer should open fire on a coastal battery believed to be manned by the Germans shortly before the LCAs hit the beach. This duly happened, and there was no response. Led by Jack Churchill carrying his claymore, 2 Commando landed intact at 03.30 and, having left a troop behind to hold the beachhead, through which Brigade HQ and 41 RM Commando passed twenty minutes later, moved up towards Vietri.

The battery, which was 2 Commando's first objective, turned out to be unmanned, but some prisoners were taken in the vicinity. Two troops were despatched towards Salerno, to be confronted on the way by a Tiger tank. A couple of rounds from a 6-pounder appeared to jam its turret and it withdrew. Meanwhile, 41 RM Commando established itself in the hills on either side of the La Molina Pass, where they also met some resistance, including a Mark IV tank, which was knocked out with a PIAT.

Although there had been no concerted defence, there were still plenty of Germans around. On their separate ways up to Vietri, both Tom Churchill and Bob came face to face with an enemy soldier. Churchill had no time to draw his pistol, whilst Bob fired his and missed. Both were saved by the fast reactions of their batmen, who killed one German and incapacitated the other.

As the day went on, the position became clearer. The Germans still had a firm hold on the La Molina Pass and had brought 41 RM Commando to a halt. They were also resisting strongly in Salerno itself, and although a recce squadron broke through from 138 Brigade, under whose immediate command the Special Service Brigade temporarily came, it was not followed by any infantry battalions. The beach at Marina came under heavy mortar fire, causing casualties, as a result of which the LCAs disappeared without unloading the stores, which included most of the personal kit of the troops. Moreover, the LCA crews spread the news that Vietri had been recaptured by the Germans, prompting a staff officer of 46 Division to come through on the radio with orders for the Special Service Brigade to retake it. Tom Churchill replied that he was speaking from the centre of town, which was fully under British control, and suggested that the staff officer might like to re-check his sources.

The news from the Rangers on the left was good. They had achieved complete surprise and secured the Chiunzi Pass, from the heights of which they could look down on the Bay of Naples. As a result there was no threat, at least, from the direction of Amalfi.

On the following day Brigadier Harding of 138 Brigade arrived at Bob's HQ, now established in a large school in Vietri which had previously served as a German barracks and was full of their clothes and some cases of tinned food. Harding said that he was being threatened from the north and was unable to provide any immediate help other than his Brigade Support Group, which arrived with heavy machine guns and more 4.2″ mortars. He was asked to supply additional 4.2″ mortar and PIAT ammunition, as both were running out, and to arrange naval gunfire support for 41 RM Commando, which was now under heavy pressure. Later in the afternoon, Major General 'Ginger' Hawkesworth, the GOC of 46 Division, also appeared. He was pleased with the Commandos' performance, but unable to promise any relief.

Meanwhile, 2 Commando had been in action for most of the day, wiping out a German machine gun position overlooking Vietri, with some help from Bob doing the spotting for the mortars with his binoculars, and later taking a key hill feature to prevent 41 RM Commando being outflanked on the left. The HQs of both Commandos were hit by mortar fire and at 41 RM Commando the signal section was nearly wiped out, requiring replacements from Brigade HQ. Lumsden was wounded and succeeded by his second-in-command, Major J. R. Edwards. The viaduct carrying the Amalfi road across the valley north of Vietri remained under heavy fire.

On D+2 two battalions from 138 Brigade arrived to relieve the two Commandos, which had suffered serious casualties over the previous forty-eight hours and were withdrawn that evening into a rest area between Vietri and Salerno. The respite was very brief, as at 08.30 the next day they were ordered back into the line, fighting hard and suffering further casualties in the valley and on the hills at either side.

On D+4 2 Commando came under heavy attack again. This time the action took place around the village and nearby hill of Dragonea, where two forward troops of the Commando were overrun and the second-in-command, Major Lawrie, was killed. One troop of 41 RM Commando, led by Teddy Edwards, the acting CO, arrived to assist and, alongside a troop from 2 Commando under Captain the Duke of Wellington and with artillery support from 71 Field Regiment, assaulted the hill and recovered all the positions which had been previously lost. This turned out to be the turning point of the battle, as the Germans withdrew under cover of smoke.

At nightfall the two Commandos were relieved by troops from 138 Brigade and withdrawn into reserve, 2 Commando in Salerno and 41 RM Commando in Vietri. The Special Service Brigade was given responsibility for the defence of the Castle Hill area immediately north of Salerno, with two companies of the 6th Battalion York & Lancaster Regiment, a company of the 138 Brigade Support Group and 272 Field Company RE under command.

D+5, 14 September, turned out to be the quietest day of the battle for the Special Service Brigade, although the two Commandos remained on stand-to throughout, as the position of X Corps was still far from secure. The brigade's positions, especially in Salerno itself, remained under fire from the hills and there was occasional infiltration by German patrols. Although no further casualties were sustained, few of the men got any real rest.

On the following afternoon Bob was summoned to an urgent conference, to hear that the positions of 167 Brigade, part of 56 Division, in the hills to the east of the main road to Avellino, were being seriously threatened. Lorries arrived to take both the Commandos to the village of Mercatello along the coast, where Brigadier Firth of 167 Brigade explained to Bob and his COs that a critical situation had developed around two features known as White Cross Hill and the Pimple; 41 RM Commando was ordered to carry out an attack to clear the hills west of the Pimple, whilst 2 Commando secured the road to the south. The operation began at 17.30, when 41 RM Commando moved forward accompanied by a troop of Sherman tanks. Although these were all halted, the Commando took its objective with only modest casualties. An hour later, 2 Commando moved off, advancing in parallel troop columns, each of which shouted 'Commando' to maintain contact with each other. It returned to its starting position after midnight, bringing with it 136 German prisoners, which was more than the whole of 56 Division had captured to that date. Jack Churchill brought back over forty himself and threatened to kill them all if any attempted to escape.

No sooner had 2 Commando returned than it was ordered back again, this time to take the Pimple itself and the adjacent village of Piegolelli.[2] The latter was captured after close fighting between the houses, and two troops were detached to take the Pimple, which the Germans had occupied in strength. The troops attacked up the hill but incurred serious casualties, including 'Morny'[3] Wellington, who was killed by a grenade.

When dawn broke on 16 September, the two Commandos were holding a line from Piegolelli to the east of White Cross Hill, but the Germans had occupied the Pimple and the ridge to its west in great strength and all attempts that day to dislodge them were fought off. In the hours of darkness on the following morning 41 RM Commando was ordered to assault and capture the Pimple, but the supporting artillery barrage, instead of falling on the Germans, landed squarely in the middle of the Commando, causing many casualties, including Teddy Edwards, the acting CO, who was mortally wounded. By dawn the Commando had been forced to withdraw to its original position. It was no longer fit for combat and was relieved on the following night.

In the meantime, 2 Commando had been keeping up a steady fire with the 4.2″ mortars and heavy machine guns of the Americans and a selection of captured German machine guns, all of which took a significant toll on the enemy. An attack by an infantry brigade was mounted against both the Pimple and White Cross Hill with very limited success, but when another attack was made on 19 September, the Germans were found to have abandoned their positions.

By that time both Commandos had been withdrawn to a rest area near Mercatello. The battle was not yet over, but their part in it was at an end. In ten days of action 12 officers and 59 other ranks had been killed, 15 officers and 207 other ranks wounded, and one officer and 19 other ranks evacuated sick, whilst two officers and 31 other ranks were missing: therefore, they had suffered 346 casualties out of a total establishment of 750, a rate of attrition of 40 per cent.[4] When General McCreery paid the survivors a visit on 22 September he had all ranks assembled so that he could not only explain how they had fitted in to the battle, but also thank them for their hard fighting and sacrifice. He went on to say that they had always looked like soldiers and that the effect of this on the morale of others had been incalculable.

Bob was no longer there, having been ordered by Mountbatten to fly back to England as soon as circumstances permitted. With 2 and 41 RM Commandos now requiring a period of recuperation and reinforcement, there was no prospect of further action for this part of the brigade in the foreseeable future. He was also confident that Durnford-Slater was entirely capable of looking after 3 and 40 RM Commandos and the SRS, which, after being used for some minor landings following BAYTOWN, were shortly to be transferred to the Adriatic coast to support Eighth Army's operations there. He handed over command to Tom Churchill and flew out from an airstrip on the beach on 21 September, accompanied by Philip Dunne.[5]

Bob arrived back in England on 24 September, the day of the announcement of the award to him of the Distinguished Service Order for his leadership in Sicily.[6] There were many letters of congratulation, but probably none was more welcome than that from Haydon, who made the point that Bob had up to then been hard done by in terms of visible recognition. Haydon, who clearly wanted to make peace between them, went on to write:

> The present difficulties through which we are passing we shall laugh at in the future, but at the time they happen they loom large and assume proportions which are not really justified. Five minutes' conversation would, I think, put them right and this I hope we are going to have.[7]

He was, of course, referring to the vexatious issue of the reorganization of the Special Service Brigade and the RM Division, which had yet to be finally resolved. The reason why Mountbatten had wanted Bob back in the UK so urgently was that he himself was leaving COHQ. The 'very staggering piece of news', to which the CCO had referred in his letter to Bob of 24 August, was his appointment as Supreme Allied Commander South-East Asia, and he was in London for briefings and to put together his staff before leaving for India in early October. There was thus just over a week to put matters right, and in the first place Bob's request to be relieved of his command was rejected. Mountbatten was now keen to find a solution which would retain him in the Commando organization.

Matters had moved on, albeit relatively slowly, whilst Bob had been occupied on AVALANCHE. In particular, an important meeting had taken place on 8 September chaired by Wildman-Lushington, the other participants being Sturges, Haydon, Lovat and the senior staff officers from the Special Service Brigade HQ. One of Mountbatten's requirements as SACSEA was a Commando force, and it now appeared that three or four Commandos would be sent out to India by the end of the year. With 9 Commando shortly to leave for the Mediterranean, most of the new RM Commandos yet to complete their training and both 12 and 14 Commando scheduled to be disbanded to provide replacements for losses, it seemed that the requirement would have to be met by Army Commandos, of which 1, 4, 5 and 6 were still in the UK. The requirements for Operation OVERLORD, the invasion of France, would then have to be met entirely by RM Commandos. Lovat, however, pointed out that an additional Army Commando might be required for the Mediterranean, in which case at least one RM Commando would have to be sent to India.

As far as the structure of the new Special Service Group was concerned, Haydon told the meeting that the organization of the Army Commandos into two brigades of four Commandos each, commanded by Colonels, had not been well received by the War Office, but it was agreed that, as this structure met the intentions of the CCO and the Chiefs of Staff, any alternative should be resisted by both COHQ and the AGRM. However, Wildman-Lushington pointed out that a number of anomalies would arise if one Brigadier was to command two separate forces in the Mediterranean and India/Burma. Haydon was asked to go back to Mountbatten to explain the difficulties.

On a more positive note for the Army Commandos, it was agreed that they should now have five of the thirteen staff positions in the Special Service Group, an increase of two over the number reported by Sooby to Bob, and that these would include both the GSO2s on the establishment. Moreover, the positions of AA&QMG, the senior administrative officer, and GSO3 (Air), would be held by Army officers currently on the strength of the RM Division.

Bob's proposal for a Holding Commando had been accepted by all parties and only awaited signing off by the War Establishment Committee. It would, however, for the time being, have both an Army and an RM Wing.

The main problem was the shortage of men in the Army Commandos, put by Lovat at 32 officers and 814 men, without accounting for losses in Sicily and Italy. It was agreed that a letter on recruitment should be drafted for the CCO to send to the Adjutant General at the War Office and that, if an unfavourable reply was received, he should take the matter up with the CIGS.

Following the meeting, Sturges remained unhappy about two issues. The first was the effective command of the Special Service Group, of which he was currently only GOC (Designate), confirmation of which was still awaited from Mountbatten, largely because the CCO was waiting to discuss the situation with Bob. Sturges urged Wildman-Lushington to persuade Mountbatten that this should take effect on 1 October, on which date the new HQ would open at Pinner. Secondly, he felt that the next reinforcement to the Mediterranean after 9 Commando should not be an Army Commando but 43 RM Commando, which had completed its training.

This is how matters stood when Bob reappeared. He was now to embark on a series of meetings with all the parties, but primarily with Mountbatten. There were two major issues with which Bob was concerned: the structure of the Special Service Group and future recruitment into the Army Commandos. On the second of these the Adjutant General in the UK was to prove a difficult nut to crack, but Bob had made considerable progress as regards the Mediterranean theatre whilst still in Algiers, where he had discussed the issue with General Sir Harold Alexander, the C-in-C of the Fifteenth Army Group. Encouraged by the enthusiasm for the Commandos of Montgomery, Dempsey and Leese, he submitted a scheme to Alexander whereby reinforcements could be sought not only in Eighth Army but also in Ninth and Tenth Armies in the Levant and Iraq/Persia. The two latter armies were by this time little more than skeleton formations and Alexander had no responsibility for them. He did, however, permit recruitment anywhere in Fifteenth Army Group, which was a major development, of which 2 Commando was the first unit to take advantage.

It was the reorganization which remained the most important issue. Mountbatten managed to persuade Bob that the full support of the Royal Marines was the only solution to providing enough Commandos to satisfy the demands of three theatres of war. He also explained that the structure of two brigades commanded by colonels under a single brigadier was unpopular not only with the War Office but also with almost everyone else, and was only being entertained to humour Bob himself. Bob, on the other hand, maintained that the Army Commandos, with their very different traditions and conditions of service, should have a senior representative to look after their interests, and that the brigade commanders under the alternative structure would have insufficient time and authority to do this.

The solution, which was to prove acceptable to all parties, was very simple. There would still be four brigades, but instead of comprising either Army or RM Commandos, which would only exaggerate their differences, they would include one or more of each, as this was by now seen to have had worked well in Italy. There would be two Army Brigadiers, Lovat and Durnford-Slater, and two RM Brigadiers, Wilfred Nonweiler and B. W. 'Jumbo' Leicester. Most pertinently, Bob himself would be appointed Deputy Commander of the Special Service Group, with responsibility, among other things, for looking after the particular interests of the Army Commandos.

As far as the allocations of units were concerned, 4 and 6 Commandos were to remain in 1 Special Service Brigade under Lovat in the UK, where they would be joined in due course by 3 Commando from the Mediterranean, with Peter Young succeeding Durnford-Slater as its CO, and by 45 RM Commando once it had finished its training. Durnford-Slater was to take over 2 Special Service Brigade in Italy, retaining 2 and 40 RM Commandos and receiving 9 and 43 RM Commandos, whilst 3 Special Service Brigade was to comprise 1, 5, 42 RM and 44 RM Commandos under Nonweiler and depart for India by the end of the year. Leicester's 4 Special Service Brigade would be the last to become operational, since 41 RM Commando, once it had returned from Italy, would require significant recruitment after its losses at Salerno and 46 and 47 RM Commandos were yet to complete their training. Its sole Army unit would be 10 (IA) Commando.

The Commando Basic Training Centre, the Commando Mountain Warfare Camp, the Operational Holding Commando and 2 Special Boat Section were to come under the direct control of the Special Service Group. Other than the arrival of the newly raised 48 RM Commando in 4 Special Service Brigade in the late spring of 1944 and the placing of 10 (IA) Commando directly under the Special Service Group, this structure turned out to be sufficiently robust to last for the remainder of the War.

Bob had come to the pragmatic conclusion that it was time to accept the inevitable. His role in the new organization satisfied his concerns about the Army Commandos, and he got on well personally with Sturges and felt that he could work with him. Moreover, he had never harboured any antipathy towards the Royal Marines; indeed, it had been his wish to recruit them into 8 Commando in large numbers in 1940, believing that this was their natural role.

It was Bob's intention to return to the Mediterranean at the end of October to settle down the new arrivals there, by which time he hoped to have solved the Army recruiting issues in the UK. By 18 October he was able to claim one success on that front, when the Director of Staff Duties informed him that the Army Commandos were to receive the same priority for recruitment as the Airborne Forces; but he still lacked carte blanche to seek volunteers. Before that happened, however, his career was to be transformed in an entirely unexpected way.

Chapter 18

COHQ

When Mountbatten flew out of Northolt on 2 October 1943 on his way to India, he had sorted out the leadership and composition of the Special Service Group, but had left Combined Operations HQ in a state of flux. Not only had no successor been appointed, but it was also clear that considerable changes would be required in its organization.

It will be recalled that COHQ had originally been set up in 1940 under the then Adjutant-General RM, Lieutenant General Bourne, and that he was replaced shortly afterwards by Sir Roger Keyes. Keyes saw himself very much as holding full responsibility for all combined operations, reporting directly to the Prime Minister. Whereas Bourne had been happy to operate through representatives in the Admiralty, the War Office and the Air Ministry, Keyes insisted on having his immediate subordinates, of whichever service, in his own HQ and accountable personally to him. For these and other reasons he had a less than cordial relationship with the Chiefs of Staff.

Although the numbers at COHQ itself remained small, Keyes did take under his direct control one established facility, the Inter-Service Training and Development Centre at Fort Cumberland, near Portsmouth. At the beginning of the War the ISTDC was the only organization involved in any way in combined operations. It had been set up in the summer of 1938 specifically to study all aspects of assaults from the sea, including methods of landing and the arms and equipment needed to support them. The first Commandant was Captain L. E. H. Maund RN, who was supported by middle-ranking officers from the other two services. Both Maund and the Army representative, Major M. W. M. McLeod, would go on to have long and distinguished careers in Combined Operations, not only in the UK but also in the Middle East and India.

The ISTDC made some highly important recommendations which had a major impact on the development of the techniques for seaborne landings. These included the adoption of the LCA as the principal infantry landing craft, the development of the many other types of more specialized landing ships and craft and the conversion of merchant ships into LSIs. It also looked at the problems associated with landing on defended beaches and developed a number of solutions. It was not, however, in spite of its name, a training establishment, and one of Keyes' first actions on succeeding Bourne was to set up the Combined Training Centre at Inverary, where the theory could be translated into practice, the various types of ships and craft tried out in realistic conditions and the newly established Commandos trained in their use. Its success was such that McLeod, who had succeeded Maund as Commandant of the ISTDC, was sent to set up another CTC at Kabrit on the Bitter Lakes in Egypt, where Bob subsequently attended a course.

By the late summer of 1941 Keyes, as far as the Chiefs of Staff were concerned, was getting above his station. His direct access to the Prime Minister on Combined Operations matters was a major bone of contention, as was his proposal that COHQ should have responsibility for the planning of and training for major operations as well as raids. They decided that his wings should be clipped and formed up jointly to Churchill, who acceded to their request by downgrading his role from Director to Adviser and making it clear that only the Chiefs of Staff could be responsible for advising the Defence Committee and the War Cabinet. Keyes resigned in protest and Mountbatten was appointed.

Astonishingly, within months Mountbatten had obtained all that Keyes had demanded and more. His title was upgraded from Adviser back to Director and then to Chief of Combined Operations, and he was given a seat on the Chief of Staffs' Committee and direct access to Churchill. Moreover, he increased the establishment of COHQ significantly, setting up four main departments: planning, intelligence, training and communications.

Raiding came under Mountbatten's direct control, but it became increasingly clear to him that COHQ should also play a major role in the large Allied landings which, following the entry of the United States into the War, would have to be undertaken in future. Four further CTCs were subsequently established in the UK, at Dorlin House and Castle Toward in Argyll, at Largs and at Dundonald, the last of these also housing the new Combined Signals School. CTCs were also set up at Mahd, Cocanada and Kharakvasla in India.

The need for specialized training became even more evident after the failure of Operation JUBILEE. Operation TORCH came very shortly afterwards, but some lessons had already been learnt, notably the need for much improved beach organization. One major innovation was the use of Headquarters Ships, on which both the naval and army commanders would be located until conditions were such that the latter could transfer their HQs ashore. These majored heavily on communications and more than proved their worth. Happily, the resistance encountered in TORCH was modest, as many other problems were encountered, the resolutions to which were vital to the subsequent success of the landings in HUSKY.

In addition to his tri-service staff Mountbatten recruited a number of civilian experts and especially scientists. These included Professors J. D. Bernal and Solly Zuckerman and the extraordinary Geoffrey Pyke. Many of their ideas were excellent, but some, such as Pyke's proposal for floating airfields of frozen seawater and sawdust, came to nought and established for COHQ something of a reputation for expensive eccentricity. Another recruit, Harold Wernher, an industrialist but also a Territorial Army officer, was brought in to solve the problem of preparing the ports of Southern England for use in the forthcoming Operation OVERLORD and to advise on other supply and transport issues.

There is no doubt that COHQ made a considerable contribution to solving the problems associated with the invasion of north-west Europe, not least because Mountbatten was a vocal supporter of the attractions of Normandy over the Pas-de-Calais. The concept of MULBERRY harbours, for example, had been conceived by Captain John Hughes-Hallett RN, who was at COHQ at the time: he had been involved with the planning of JUBILEE and had served as the Naval Force Commander after the initial postponement, so he knew better than most that taking a defended port from the sea would be out of the question. However, in April 1943, Lieutenant General Frederick Morgan was appointed Chief of Staff to the Supreme Allied Commander (Designate), and his organization, named COSSAC after his own title, was charged with all the planning for Operation OVERLORD. Moreover, although COSSAC continued to work closely with COHQ, it took over responsibility for raiding the Atlantic coast of Europe. At the same time, the control of all landing craft and their crews passed from COHQ to the Admiralty

By the late summer of 1943 it was clear that COHQ needed to be reorganized to meet the changing circumstances, and as one of his many tasks between arriving back from Quebec and leaving for India, Mountbatten was asked to submit proposals on its future, which he sent to the Chiefs of Staff on 20 September. He put forward two proposals. Alternative A was the retention of an independent organization, smaller in size but otherwise similar to the existing one, under the command of one man, who would be responsible to Churchill in his capacity as Minister of Defence but report to him through the Chiefs of Staff Committee. It left open the question as to whether or not that person should belong to the Committee. Alternative B proposed the establishment of a Directorate of Combined Operations in each of the three service ministries, with a Combined Operations Staff formed within the Chiefs of Staff organization and working under the three Directors of Combined Operations in a similar manner to the Joint Planning Staff. Control of the CTCs, the Combined Operations Experimental Establishment (COXE) in Westward Ho!, which in 1942 had replaced the Combined Operations Development Centre, itself the successor to the ISTDC, and the Special Service Group, would have to devolve upon one of the service ministries. This was inherently somewhat unsatisfactory, and Mountbatten also thought that there was still a need for a common approach on planning and training. Therefore he came down in favour of Alternative A.

First to respond was the Admiralty, by way of a memo to the Chiefs of Staff from Vice Admiral Sir Edward Syfret, the Vice Chief of the Naval Staff. The Admiralty had never much liked the whole concept of COHQ and thus, unsurprisingly, opted for Alternative B, which it saw as restoring to it functions which it should never have lost in the first place. Brooke and Air Chief Marshal Sir Charles Portal, the Chief of the Air Staff, disagreed, Brooke insisting that the training, research and development functions of COHQ would be better directed under a single head. The RAF was regarded as the most impartial of the three services, and Brooke proposed that an Air Officer should investigate the issue and report back to the Chiefs of Staff.

The officer appointed to carry out this task was Air Marshal N. H. Bottomley, the Deputy Chief of the Air Staff, who produced his report on 13 October. His overriding recommendation was not dissimilar to Mountbatten's, that COHQ should be maintained as a central organization for the study and development of the techniques of combined operations. He proposed that it should continue to have an Executive consisting of the CCO and four officers – the Chief of Staff and a senior officer from each of the three services. However, rather than just being responsible for their own staffs, whilst the officers heading up the inter-service planning, signals, training and intelligence departments reported directly to the CCO, the members of the Executive should each head up one of four functional groups, which between them would cover all the activities of COHQ and include staff from all three services. The CCO should remain of the rank of or equivalent to Vice Admiral, with the members of his executive one rank lower.

Bottomley did, however, recommend cuts to the current establishment. He proposed that the minor departments of COHQ – Security, Public Relations, Records, Chaplains and Medical Officers – should be either disbanded or significantly reduced, with resulting economies in the Secretariat, that the Planning Staff should become a committee acting in an advisory role to the Chiefs of Staff Committee's own Joint Planners on combined operations matters and that the Intelligence Staff should be reduced to a small section to liaise with each of the services. Only training and communications would be largely untouched. As far as the CCO himself was concerned, Bottomley believed that his reporting line to the Minister of Defence was a matter on which the Chiefs of Staff should advise, but considered that it would be convenient and appropriate for him to do so through the Chiefs of Staff Committee rather than directly.

On 15 October the Chiefs of Staff approved the recommendations of the Bottomley Report, agreeing that the post of CCO should be filled by an officer of Flag, General or Air rank and that, on his appointment, he should be invited to prepare a detailed establishment on the principles set out in the report. This, however, was not to happen for some time, as Churchill was experiencing considerable difficulty in finding Mountbatten's successor.

The Prime Minister's immediate preference was for another senior naval officer, and the First Lord of the Admiralty, A. V. Alexander, was asked for his recommendations. Alexander's first suggestion was Rear Admiral Rhoderick

McGrigor. In many ways McGrigor would have been a good choice. During 1943 he had commanded the amphibious force which captured Pantelleria, and he had subsequently led Force B, which had formed part of the Eastern Naval Task Force for HUSKY. In his capacity as Flag Officer Sicily he had been involved in the planning of all the Commando operations following the initial invasion. Moreover, although he had had a distinguished career at sea, he was also an experienced staff officer, his postings including a spell in the Training and Staff Duties Division at the Admiralty, and he was considered to have done well as Assistant Chief of the Naval Staff (Weapons) in 1941/42.

In the event that Churchill required a Vice Admiral, Alexander's choice was Arthur Power. He, too, had excellent experience both at sea and on the staff and, as Flag Officer Malta, had been closely involved in the planning of both HUSKY and AVALANCHE. Alexander told Churchill that he would prefer Power to go to a senior appointment in the Eastern Fleet, and it does not appear that he was taken into consideration. McGrigor was not rejected, but was put aside for the moment until the Prime Minister had interviewed his preferred candidate.

Throughout his life Churchill had something of a penchant for 'heroes', and both Keyes and Mountbatten fell into this category, the latter for his exploits as a destroyer captain. Rear Admiral Sir Philip Vian was another. He had come to the notice of both the Prime Minister and the public as captain of the destroyer HMS *Cossack*, which entered a fjord in then neutral Norway to liberate British merchant seamen captured by the *Graf Spee* who were being taken back to Germany on the *Altmark*. He had subsequently led a destroyer flotilla in a daring torpedo attack on the *Bismarck* and, in March 1942, whilst escorting a convoy from Alexandria to Malta with a covering force of four light cruisers, had seen off a much more powerful Italian fleet in the Second Battle of Sirte.[1] For the last of these exploits he had been knighted, an exceptional honour for one of his rank. His credentials as potential CCO were less compelling than those of McGrigor, resting on his appointment as commander of Force V for HUSKY and his subsequent role in command of the escort carrier force for AVALANCHE

Vian was a sea officer par excellence; indeed, apart from a short period in the early 1930s, he had never held a shore appointment, and he did not want one now. He was, nevertheless, called back to the UK by Churchill. Briefed by the Admiralty, however, which made it clear that this would not be a career-enhancing move, he had little hesitation in turning down the offer and returned thankfully to sea. McGrigor was then summoned to London, to be given the same briefing and to make the same decision.[2] Mountbatten later claimed that both men had also been warned off by Rear Admiral Charles Daniel, then the Flag Officer Combined Operations at COHQ.

One other possible candidate was put forward by Brigadier Leslie Hollis, the Secretary to the Chiefs of Staff Committee. This was Air Vice Marshal

James Robb, who had actually served in COHQ during 1942 as Deputy Chief of Combined Operations, in which role Mountbatten had thought highly of him. He would have been a good choice, notwithstanding the fact that the involvement of the RAF in combined operations was very much subordinate to that of the two other services. There is no evidence, however, that he was subsequently considered.

It was now mid-October, and Churchill urgently needed to make the appointment. His thoughts turned to Bob, whom he had invited to lunch at Chequers shortly after his return from Salerno. Bob was another hero, in Churchill's mind at least, and he had, moreover, as much practical experience of combined operations as anyone, including over nineteen months leading the Special Service Brigade. He consulted the Chiefs of Staff and, although there is no record of the discussions, there is every likelihood that the price of their agreement was the downgrading of the role of CCO, who would sit no more at the top table, and a significant reduction in the size of the organization. Bob was summoned to see Churchill and offered the job. According to Bernard Fergusson, a friend of Bob's from Staff College and later his subordinate at COHQ, Bob replied that he did not think that he was the right person:

> 'So you shun responsibility, do you?' said the Prime Minister. Laycock replied with some indignation that he had never done so in his life.
>
> 'Well, you're C.C.O.!' said Churchill; and he was.[3]

The appointment was approved by the King, who had recently received Bob in audience, and he was appointed CCO on 22 October 1943, on which day he was promoted to major general. He was thirty-six years, six months and four days old, the youngest age at which anyone in the British or Indian Armies or the Royal Marines was appointed to general officer rank during the War. Not much more than three years earlier he had been a captain.

This was an extraordinary turn of events and an accolade by any standard. Less than two months beforehand, Bob had submitted his resignation to Mountbatten; now he found himself his successor. Even more recently he had accepted a position as Sturges' deputy; now he was being placed in overall control of the Special Service Group. In 1940/41 he had reported to Haydon; now he was his superior.

Bob's position vis-à-vis Haydon was potentially difficult. Haydon was eight years older and had been an acting or temporary major general since joining COHQ in March 1942. He had acted as Bob's mentor for some years and, apart from a temporary chill in their relationship when Haydon lost patience with Bob over his stance on the formation of the Special Service Group, they had always worked well together. He had, perhaps, hoped to be appointed CCO himself and was probably the most qualified person to take the job on, but he had never caught Churchill's eye. Nevertheless, he was typically generous in his letter of congratulations:

> My mind is in a bit of a whirl and I daresay yours is too but I want to say one thing right away and that is that I am ready to do anything I can to help you in any capacity for as long or short a time as you want …
>
> You will, I think, be wise to get your ultimate staff fixed and settled in as soon as you conveniently can but in the meantime there may have to be an interim period and it is that of which I am thinking.
>
> It is a thrill and a tremendous compliment to you and also to the Special Service Brigade. It is an enormous relief to know that they will have you, who knows them so well, as C.C.O. watching over their interests.[4]

It must have been clear to both Bob and the Chiefs of Staff that the apex of COHQ's structure could not stay as it was. It suited the latter well to have a very junior general officer in charge, and it became evident very quickly that his deputies would have to be a rank below him. The three in position, Haydon,[5] Daniel and Air Vice Marshal R. Graham, were all to leave by the end of the year.

The public relations machine at COHQ, which had been honed to perfection under Mountbatten, had a field day with the news, issuing a press release which extolled Bob's youth and his deeds not only in Sicily and Italy, but also at Bardia, on Crete and during the Rommel Raid. This was followed on 23 October by a talk on the BBC by Hilary Saunders, the Recorder at COHQ, which was repeated twice on the following day. A great deal of interest was aroused within the press, both British and foreign, and Henriques was asked to produce a more substantial biography, largely for the benefit of the latter. He, too, gave a talk on the BBC, after David Niven had been approached to do so but was then turned down on account of the size of his proposed fee!

There was a great demand for photographs of both Bob and Angie, with the *New York Times*, *Life* Magazine and the Canadian Press sending photographers along to their flat in Cranmer Court, Sloane Avenue. One of the photographers was the famous Yousuf Karsh of Ottawa, who produced some attractive portraits. These subsequently formed part of an exhibition which toured Canada, and a set was sent to Tilly and Joe, who were still living in that country with Angie's father.

After five days of photos Bob told David Astor, the Public Relations Officer at COHQ, that he wanted no more. He now had to get down to serious work. He had been left a letter from Mountbatten to his 'Successor', whose identity the then CCO did not know at the time of writing; he had had a 'shrewd idea'[6] who it would be, almost certainly Vian, but had been ordered categorically by the Prime Minister not to disclose the name. In the letter Mountbatten urged the recipient to make the best use in the immediate future of Wildman-Lushington, who would be joining him at SEAC as Assistant Chief of Staff as soon as a relief could be found. Mountbatten had agreed with the AGRM that the new CCO could have any Royal Marine officer he wanted. Secondly, he requested that COHQ should act in future as a Rear HQ for SEAC.

An immediate requirement was to make two appointments which were a consequence of Bob's promotion. As Sturges' deputy, Bob proposed Durnford-Slater. Not only was he one of the longest-standing Commando officers, but he was also widely respected throughout the Special Service Brigade and had worked closely with one of the RM Commandos in the Mediterranean. Durnford-Slater returned from Italy immediately, to be told by Sturges not only that would he have responsibility for the welfare of the Army Commandos, but also that he would be in charge of planning the role of the two Commando brigades to be used in Operation OVERLORD. To replace Durnford-Slater at 2 Special Service Brigade in Italy, Bob advised Sturges to appoint Tom Churchill, who travelled immediately from Sicily to Molfetta in Italy to assume control of 3 Commando, 40 RM Commando and the SRS.

Shortly after his appointment Bob received the first draft of the Directive under which he would operate. This was placed on the agenda for the Chiefs of Staff Committee on 10 November, which Bob was asked to attend. He gave notice beforehand of three issues he would like to discuss. The first was whether he would be invited in future to meetings at which his advice was expected to be required, or whether he should study the Agenda and attend as and when he thought fit. The second was clarification of the extent to which he was bound by the Bottomley report on COHQ. The third was a request that he should attend all meetings between the Chiefs of Staff and the Directors of Plans and Intelligence, so that he could be thoroughly conversant with future strategy and the war situation.

The answer to the first was that Bob should attend when required to do so. However, almost certainly on the insistence of Churchill, it was confirmed that Bob would continue to have direct access to the Minister of Defence on matters within his jurisdiction. As far as the Bottomley Report was concerned, the recommendations would have to be implemented significantly as they stood. There was no direction on the request to attend meetings with the Directors of Plans and Intelligence, but the close liaison established between their departments and COHQ may have made this unnecessary.

The revised directive was not issued until 28 November, by which time Bob was thousands of miles away. He had been invited to attend the SEXTANT conference, which was to be held in Cairo from 22 to 26 November. This would bring together Churchill, President Roosevelt and Generalissimo Chiang Kai-shek to agree a common policy on the aims and prosecution of the war against Japan. Stalin did not attend, as the Soviet Union was not at war with Japan, but Churchill and Roosevelt had agreed to meet him in Teheran immediately afterwards.

For Bob this was an immensely valuable opportunity, especially because it would enable him to get to know the British Chiefs of Staff much better. The one with whom he was most familiar was Admiral of the Fleet Sir Andrew Cunningham, who was appointed as First Sea Lord only a few days before Bob became CCO and whom Bob had met on a number of occasions in Egypt whilst at Layforce and afterwards. The first public occasion for both of them in their new roles was the funeral of Cunningham's predecessor, Dudley Pound, at which Cunningham acted as a pall bearer whilst Bob walked in the procession with representatives of the three services. Bob also knew Brooke, but had had little previous connection with Portal. The conference would also enable him to meet for the first time the American Joint Chiefs of Staff, Generals Marshall and Arnold and Admirals Leahy and King. Bob had already been recognized by the Americans as a valued collaborator for his work with the US Rangers, but he would have to foster even closer cooperation in future with Britain's most important ally. Last, and by no means least, he could meet Mountbatten, who was to be at the conference in his capacity as Supreme Allied Commander South East Asia, for a belated briefing.

As cover for his movements Bob pretended to be going up to Scotland, but in fact he flew out from Northolt with Brooke and Portal at 01.00 on 17 November. The Prime Minister was making the journey by sea, so they had the use of his Avro York, *Ascalon*, which was exceptionally comfortable, especially for Brooke, who occupied Churchill's private cabin. They landed at 08.00 in Gibraltar, where they were given breakfast by Lieutenant General Mason-Macfarlane, the Governor, and then flew on to Malta, where they landed uneventfully at 15.00 local time, a welcome contrast to Bob's last arrival there in September 1941, in the middle of an air raid.

Churchill arrived on the same day in HMS *Renown*, accompanied by Cunningham. The next two days were taken up with preparatory meetings for SEXTANT, involving the Chiefs of Staff, the Prime Minister and the three service C-in-Cs in the Mediterranean, Alexander, Admiral Sir John Cunningham and Air Chief Marshal Sir Arthur Tedder. Churchill decided to continue his journey by sea, so Brooke and Bob once again had the use of *Ascalon* to fly to Cairo on 20 November, Portal having decided to visit Tunis on the way.

The conference was held in the Mena House Hotel, near the Pyramids, which housed the conference rooms and all the offices for the various delegations, whilst the participants were housed in villas which had been requisitioned around the hotel and along the road to Cairo. It was in one of these that Bob found himself living, along with Antony Head, who was present with the British Joint Planners.

The SEXTANT Conference was a frustrating one. Brooke lamented in his diary that it should have come after the conference with Stalin, as it was much more important to arrive at firm agreements on the war against Germany, whose defeat had always had priority over the defeat of Japan. The Chinese delegates turned out to be woefully ill-prepared, their most impressive, albeit unofficial, member being Madame Chiang. Their main concern was for the British and Americans to take as much pressure off their own forces as possible by conducting offensive operations in Burma and the Bay of Bengal. Mountbatten, with some trepidation as he was sceptical of Chinese security, presented his plans for the dry weather season of 1943/44, involving an advance along the Arakan coast and a seaborne assault on the Andaman Islands. The Chinese response was confused, and little was achieved by way of their support on the Burma front.

Bob found himself attending conferences nearly every day, of the Chiefs of Staff Committee, which continued as they would have in London, of the Combined Chiefs of Staff, with or without the politicians, and with everyone including the Chinese. He managed to have a good session with Mountbatten and Head, and the three of them had a relaxed dinner together one evening at Shepheard's Hotel away from the conference. He also met many other friends, but was disappointed, yet again, not to see his brother Michael.[7]

SEXTANT ended on 26 November. On the following day the British and Americans flew off to Teheran to meet Stalin, Churchill taking only a small party, which included the Chiefs of Staff but not Bob. He was not to leave Cairo, however, as it had been decided that the Western Allies would continue their discussions there when they returned on 2 December. In the meantime, he took the opportunity to summon Tom Churchill to Cairo from Italy, as it was clear that he was going to find it otherwise difficult to meet him in the near future. He was able to brief him very fully on the changes at the Special Service Group and COHQ, and was also brought up to date on the activities of 2 Special Service Brigade in Italy, where it was being well employed by Montgomery.

It was not until the second week of December that Bob flew back to the UK, by which time he was impatient to implement the reorganization of COHQ and work himself fully into his new role.

Chapter 19

Chief

Bob arrived back from Egypt in time to spend Christmas with the family at Wiseton. Michael was on a month's disembarkation leave, and it seems that this was the first time that Bob had seen his youngest brother, in spite of all his efforts to do so, since Michael had sailed for the Middle East in early 1940. In the intervening period Michael had won an immediate Military Cross as a squadron commander during the Battle of Alam Halfa in September 1942 and been lightly wounded and mentioned in despatches later in the North African campaign. He was now second-in-command of the Sherwood Rangers, which was about to begin training for OVERLORD.

Peter was still second-in-command of 10 (Inter Allied) Commando. This Commando was never to operate as a whole and, during the last few months of 1943, it lost No. 4 Belgian and No. 6 Polish Troops to 2 Special Service Brigade in Italy, and No. 4 Dutch Troop to 3 Special Service Brigade in the Far East. In the summer of 1943 elements of the Commando had joined Forfar Force, which otherwise comprised the remnants of 12 Commando, in a number of very small operations on the Channel coast of France, whose intention was to gather intelligence and bring back prisoners. COSSAC then commissioned a further series of small reconnaissance operations under the codenames of HARDTACK and MANACLE, for which purpose Layforce II was formed by Peter from three troops. These carried out a number of raids in December 1943, with modest success, but the operations were called off early in the New Year, when 21st Army Group became concerned that they might alert the Germans to the location of OVERLORD.

By the end of 1943 the organization of the Commandos into the Special Service Group was complete. In theory its major components were the four Special Service Brigades, but in practice 2 Special Service Brigade in Italy and the Adriatic and 3 Special Service Brigade in the Far East were already on active service under local theatre commanders, whilst both 1 and 4 Special Service Brigades would be transferred to 21st Army Group in February 1944. Although Sturges visited his far-flung formations, it left him on a day-to-day basis with the newly formed Operational Holding Commando, which took in recruits until they were posted elsewhere, the Commando Basic Training Centre, the Commando Mountain Warfare Camp, which had moved to St Ives in Cornwall, the newly formed RM Engineering Commando, which was to second troops on active service as required, and the Special Boat Unit, whose HQ was situated with the Special Service Group at Pinner. The last of these consisted of the Special Boat Section, the RM Boom Patrol Detachment and the Combined Operations Pilotage Parties, all of which provided personnel to force commanders for reconnaissance-related operations.

Under the terms of his Directive* from the Chiefs of Staff, Bob was in control of the Special Service Group, but in practice he was able to leave it entirely to Sturges, whose main focus was on training, the continuing development of commando techniques and the supply of reinforcements to replace battle casualties, although in Italy and the Far East these were now to a significant extent to be found locally. He also had the difficult task in the early days of welding together the Army and RM Commandos, with their very different traditions and conditions of service. This was far from easy, and it was only when they actually fought together that they achieved mutual respect.

Durnford-Slater played an important part in helping Sturges to bind the Special Service Group together, but he also had an active role in planning the participation of 1 and 4 Special Service Brigades in OVERLORD. For this purpose he was invited by Miles Dempsey, who had been selected by Montgomery to command Second Army for the invasion and whom Durnford-Slater had impressed in Sicily and Italy, to form a small HQ within Dempsey's own. This was to work well, as both Montgomery and Dempsey knew exactly what they wanted from the Commandos.

In addition to the Special Service Group, the CTCs, with their associated landing craft, the Signals School, the COXE and the Combined Operations Stores Depot, Bob had two other organizations under his direct command. The first of these was the Combined Operations Bombardment Units, until such time as they were placed under force commanders. These were now integral to all major Allied landings, during which and until the enemy moved out of range, naval gunfire support was essential to the troops engaged in the fighting. Each of the units comprised 146 men, mostly from the Royal Artillery, but with the signals element from the Royal Navy. The core of the unit was the forward observation officers, each of whom, with their own vehicles and a small party, including signallers, would land with the first wave of troops and set up observation posts as far forward as possible. They would then communicate directly with bombardment liaison officers working alongside gunnery officers on board the ships. Bob had been a direct beneficiary of the system at Salerno and it was to prove invaluable during OVERLORD, not only during the landings, when a number of specific strongpoints were targeted, but thereafter to support the advance and to break up enemy counter-attacks. The 15″ guns of battleships

* See Appendix I.

and monitors had a range of 19 miles and the 6″ guns of light cruisers 14 miles, an invaluable increment to the field artillery on land.

The second formation under Bob's command was 105 (Combined Operations) Wing RAF, based at Dundonald, close to the CTC and the Signals School. The main component of the wing was 516 (Combined Operations) Squadron RAF, which deployed a variety of aircraft and whose principal purpose was to provide realistic training conditions at the CTCs by simulating low-level attacks.

There were two other organizations which had been created by COHQ and whose men were entitled to wear the green beret of the Commandos and the Combined Operations shoulder flash, but which no longer came under the CCO's control. The first was the Royal Naval Beach Commandos, who were deployed in every major combined operation from Madagascar onwards, their units landing in the first wave of the assault troops to organize the beachheads and control the landings. By the end of 1943 they were under the command of the Admiralty, although in practice most were allocated to force commanders. The second was the RAF Servicing Commandos, whose units landed in the early stages to make enemy airfields serviceable and to find and commission suitable sites for new airfields. Outside operations they were controlled by the Air Ministry. The men from both the RN Beach Commandos and the RAF Servicing Commandos had to go through the basic Commando course at Achnacarry before moving to specialized training schools.

Bob's main task when he arrived at COHQ was to reorganize its structure in line with Bottomley's proposals. This was easier said than done, as it remained exceptionally busy in the run-up to OVERLORD, during which the CTCs were at full stretch and advice was constantly in demand from formations hitherto unfamiliar with amphibious warfare. The restructuring was nevertheless carried out in January 1944. In Bob's words:

> It has not been easy to carry this recommendation into practice as I had to make radical alterations in a machine which, for all its defects, worked satisfactorily, without stopping the machine whilst the alterations were being made.[1]

Three new Directors of Combined Operations were appointed. The DCO (Naval), Commodore H. W. Faulkner, took responsibility for Experiments, including oversight of COXE, Development and Signals. The DCO (Military), Brigadier C. B. Robertson, looked after Training, Administration and the Special Service Group. The DCO (Air), Air Commodore F. Long, dealt with Policy, Intelligence and Planning. Antony Head, promoted to Brigadier, was in charge of Joint Planning, representing Bob at meetings of the Directors of Plans, advising the Joint Planning Staff on Combined Operations aspects of all future operations and projects, briefing Bob for COS meetings and keeping COHQ advised on future strategy, so that training could be linked to the requirements of operations.

Bob's other key subordinate was the Chief of Staff, his principal adviser and his deputy whenever he was away. This was Brigadier V. D. Thomas RM, who in January 1944 relieved Wildman-Lushington, having previously commanded part of the MNBDO in Ceylon. The other leading member of the staff was the Secretary, Paymaster Commander G. H. Nicholls, who was responsible for the internal administration and organization of COHQ itself. Bob's personal staff consisted of his own secretary, Paymaster Lieutenant Commander I. G. Mason, his personal assistant, Flying Officer E. R. Petrie WAAF and his ADC, Harry Stavordale, still a captain.

Although the structure had been changed in line with the Bottomley recommendations, the numbers at COHQ remained stubbornly high as a result of the continuing demands on its services. Bob inherited a staff of 416. By early May 1944 this had been reduced to 383, and a further 22 were posted out after OVERLORD. However, there was constant pressure on him to make further reductions and, by the end of the War in Europe, the numbers had been further reduced to 278. Among the early departures were a number of civilian advisers, including Pyke, who Bob thought was more trouble than he was worth.

Bob himself, in addition to overseeing the changes, remained exceptionally busy with the substance of his new role, which involved his attending both the Chiefs and the Vice-Chiefs of Staff Committees when so required and visiting his far-flung outposts, from COXE in Devon to the CTCs in Scotland. He was also asked on a number of occasions to give talks on the Commandos and on Combined Operations and, although he was reluctant to spend time in this way, he was unable to avoid some of them. The focus on OVERLORD was all-consuming within COHQ and there was no opportunity for him to go abroad, which was welcome to Angie. She was still working at the COHQ canteen in Richmond Terrace, but devoting a lot of time to the Commando Benevolent Fund, which continued to hold fund raising activities.

OVERLORD was, in many ways, the culmination of COHQ's work, but most of the credit rightly went to Mountbatten. Bob witnessed the landings, but not those on the British and Canadian beaches. Instead, in a tribute to his excellent relationship with the Americans, he was invited by Rear Admiral A. G. Kirk, the Commander of the Western Task Force and 'a most charming and hospitable man as well as being a fine sailor',[2] to accompany him in his flagship, the heavy cruiser USS *Augusta*. Also aboard was General Omar Bradley, Commanding General of First US Army, whose focus that day was not on the successful landings on Utah Beach, but rather the very difficult ones on Omaha Beach. The situation was tense, but by the time Bob returned to Portland on the cruiser

USS *Quincy*, which was in urgent need of replenishing her 8″ ammunition, having fired off 1,200 rounds during the day, the crisis had been averted.

Both 1 and 4 Special Service Brigades were fully committed on D-Day, the former including the two French troops of 10 (IA) Commando and No 3 (Misc.) Troop, with its German speakers, who were to be much in demand. Lovat brought his men ashore near the small port of Ouistreham, on the left flank of the landings, reinforcing 6 Airborne Division, which had made a successful parachute and glider assault on the night before, while 4 Special Service Brigade landed further west. Both brigades were to remain in France, fighting as infantry, for the whole of the Normandy campaign. Lovat was badly wounded on 12 June and succeeded in command of 1 Special Service Brigade by Derek Mills-Roberts.

Durnford-Slater sailed to Normandy in Dempsey's ship and went ashore during D-Day to visit the commando units. He later established his small HQ alongside Dempsey's own, where it was to remain for as long as the Commandos were in France.

The Sherwood Rangers also landed on D-Day as part of 8 Armoured Brigade and successfully accomplished its objectives, but the CO was wounded and Michael took over command. On 11 June, however, tragedy struck. At Point 103, near the village of St Pierre, his tank was hit by a heavy shell and he was killed instantly. Another fatality was his Adjutant, Captain George Jones, the younger son of the head woodsman at Wiseton, who had joined the regiment before the War as a trooper. During the regiment's service in the Middle East he had progressed up the ranks to squadron sergeant major before being selected for a commission.

Michael's death was devastating to his family and particularly to Bob, to whom he had always been close, despite the difference in their ages. However, there was nothing which could be done and Bob's mind was diverted by a hectic schedule. He himself was not to land in Normandy until 16 June, when he was invited to accompany the King on his first visit there. The party, which included Cunningham, Portal, 'Pug' Ismay, Churchill's Chief of Staff in his capacity as Minister of Defence, and the Allied Naval C-in-C, Admiral Sir Bertram Ramsay, embarked in the cruiser HMS *Arethusa*, which sailed from Portsmouth, accompanied by an escort of two destroyers and a constant umbrella of Spitfires. The King, with Bob and the others, spent the whole voyage on the bridge, in spite of very rough seas. On arrival off the invasion beaches, the King and his private secretary, Sir Alan Lascelles, boarded a DUKW to go ashore, where Montgomery was waiting to receive them. They went off to Monty's Tactical HQ at Creully, where the King had lunch and held a brief investiture, but it was not thought safe for him to venture any further. Meanwhile, Cunningham, Portal, Ismay and Bob had transferred to HMS

Scylla, the flagship of the Eastern Task Force Commander and Churchill's first choice as CCO, Rear Admiral Vian, before going ashore at Ouistreham. All then re-embarked in the *Arethusa*, which arrived back at Spithead that evening. Bob returned to Normandy on several occasions over the next two months, not only to visit the Commandos but also to look at the impact of the many innovations of Combined Operations, notably the MULBERRY harbours. One of these, in the American sector, was destroyed in a severe storm at the end of June, but the other, although damaged, continued to make an invaluable contribution to the build-up of material.

Even before the break-out from Normandy cut off the U-boat bases in France, their threat had much diminished, and Bob and Angie considered that it was sufficiently safe to bring Young Joe and Tilly back from Canada, where they had been staying with their maternal grandfather since 1940. They sailed with their nanny from Philadelphia at the end of March in the Portuguese ship, SS *Serpa Pinto*, which was best known for conveying thousands of Jewish refugees to the New World.[3] On arrival in Lisbon, where they were to board a flying boat back to England, the two children managed to escape from their nanny and, having accepted some food from gypsies, contracted food poisoning. As a result they missed the plane, which was just as well, as it was shot down. They arrived back safely, but the ship on which they travelled was torpedoed on its return journey. The nanny, perhaps unsurprisingly, collapsed from anxiety, pernicious anaemia and diabetes on their return, but subsequently recovered.

Later in the year Bob himself went to Canada, as a participant in the OCTAGON Conference in Quebec. He travelled up to Greenock on 5 September to board the RMS *Queen Mary*, which sailed that night, escorted initially by four destroyers and then by a single cruiser, which found it hard to keep up with the liner. Bob was allocated a spacious stateroom, with a sitting room and two bathrooms. Chiefs of Staff meetings were held every day, followed on some days by meetings with the Prime Minister, who was not at all well and frequently in a bad mood. He proved to be extremely difficult on a number of relatively minor diversions from the main thrust of the War, which nearly drove Brooke and the others mad. Bob and the Chiefs of Staff had lunch with him and Mrs Churchill on 7 September, but the Prime Minister was on poor form due to the sulphonamides he was taking. At least the members of his party were able to enjoy films every evening in the ship's cinema.

The *Queen Mary* docked in Halifax on 10 September and the party transferred to a comfortable train, which arrived on the following morning in Quebec, where the British found President Roosevelt and their American counterparts waiting to greet them on the platform. The Churchills, the Roosevelts and their immediate entourages were staying with the Governor General, the Earl of Athlone, at the Citadel, whilst the Combined Chiefs of Staff took over the whole of the Chateau Frontenac Hotel, where the conference itself was held. Bob shared an enormous suite with Antony Head.

In spite of Churchill remaining very difficult to his own side, the conference itself was one of the most productive of the War, so much so that Bob described it to Angie as 'an unqualified success'.[4] The main achievements as far as the British were concerned were an undertaking by the Americans to leave their divisions in Italy for Alexander to conduct his autumn offensive against the Gothic Line and, in the face of strong opposition from Admiral King, who was overruled by Roosevelt and his fellow Chiefs, their acceptance of a British fleet in the Pacific.

Although Bob enjoyed the conference itself, he became tired of the pomp and ceremony, which included a state dinner at the Citadel and numerous other receptions and dinners. The conference ended on 16 September, when Brooke, Portal and Cunningham left for a few days fishing in Northern Quebec. Bob had intended to go with Head to Montreal to meet Angie's father and pick up those of her belongings which she had left behind on her return to England in 1941. Dudley Ward, however, cancelled at the last moment, so Bob and Head went to New York instead. They returned from there with the Prime Minister on the *Queen Mary*, sailing on 19 September and arriving back on the Clyde six days later.

There was never again to be a combined operation on the scale of OVERLORD, but there were many smaller ones. In north-west Europe the next significant landings were on the island of Walcheren. The port of Antwerp had been captured intact on 4 September, but the long approach from the sea up the estuary of the Scheldt continued to be held on both sides. First Canadian Army was unable to clear the southern shore until late October, but Walcheren could only be taken by a joint attack from the South Beveland peninsula and from the sea.

The first wave of landings were carried out on 1 November by 'Jumbo' Leicester's 4 Special Service Brigade, with 41, 47 and 48 RM Commandos landing near Westkapelle on the western tip of the island and 4 Commando near Flushing on the south coast. The former were accompanied by the Belgian and Norwegian Troops of 10 (IA) Commando and the latter by the two French Troops and part of the Dutch Troop,[5] which had returned from the Far East. With so many of his men involved, Peter Laycock, who had recently succeeded Dudley Lister as CO, decided to accompany them. The landings, assisted by the full panoply of combined operations inventions, including an impressive array of specialized landing craft, went substantially to plan and the island was taken.

Combined Operations were by no means confined to north-west Europe, however, and in late November, Bob decided that he should lead a COHQ mission, consisting of himself, Robertson, Long, Commander N. H. G. Austen RN and Stavordale, to the Mediterranean and Far East theatres. His initial

Directive had referred to his responsibility for a common doctrine on combined operations both in the UK and overseas, but a revised Directive, issued in September, was explicit that, although they were under the orders of local commanders, Directors of Combined Operations overseas were to be regarded as his representatives and would apply a doctrine of combined operations approved by him.

The party left on 14 November and flew initially to Naples, then on to Bari. Since Bob had left Italy at the end of September 1943, 2 Special Service Brigade had been continuously employed, initially on the Adriatic coast at Termoli and then on the Garigliano, at Anzio and in the fighting to take Monte Ornito. Most of the brigade's attention had thereafter been diverted to the Dalmatian coast of the Adriatic, where it acted in support of Marshal Tito's partisans amongst the islands, carrying out raids which were far closer to the original activities of the Commandos than to their new role in support of conventional troops. One of these islands, Vis, was held by the Allies and, for a time, the brigade HQ was established there. There had been many successes and one disaster, the latter in June 1944 on the island of Brac, when 'Pops' Manners had been killed and Jack Churchill captured. Subsequently, elements of the brigade had operated in Albania and, more recently, in the liberation of Greece.

Until shortly before Bob's arrival, 2 Special Service Brigade had been vigorously commanded by Tom Churchill, but he had fallen out on a matter of principle with his superior, Brigadier G. M. O. Davy, Commander Land Forces Adriatic, and had been succeeded by Ronnie Tod, the longstanding CO of 9 Commando.[6] The brigade HQ had by then returned from Vis to Molfetta in Italy, and it was there that the COHQ delegation met Tod and visited both 2 Commando under Lieutenant Colonel F. W. Fynn and 40 RM Commando under Lieutenant Colonel R. W. Sankey. They also met Davy and the Commander of the Balkan Air Force, Air Vice Marshal W. Elliott.

The party flew on to Cairo on 16 November, where they stayed overnight at Shepheard's Hotel, before continuing the next day to Baghdad and Shaiba, near Basra, where they were delayed by heavy rain for three days. They arrived in Delhi on 20 November, where Bob stayed with Auchinleck, the C-in-C India, whom he had not seen since leaving Egypt nearly three years earlier. Bob was particularly taken with Lady Auchinleck, whom he described as 'very gay and amusing and most outspoken with a strange vocabulary in which the word "bloody" figures emphatically and frequently!'[7] The party were invited to dinner by Lord Wavell, another old sparring partner of Bob's from Layforce days, before flying off to Bombay in the company of the DCO (India), Major General A. R. Chater, a Royal Marine. Chater's directive followed Bob's very closely, but made him responsible to the three service C-in-C's in India rather than to the COS Committee.

The party visited the CTC at Mahd, thirty miles north of Bombay, the Combined Signals School, two landing craft bases and a bombardment unit, and met a number of senior naval officers. On 28 November they flew to Kandy in Ceylon (Sri Lanka), where they were met in person by Mountbatten, with whom Bob and Stavordale stayed in the Royal Pavilion. Their visit coincided with those of the newly appointed C-in-C Allied Land Forces South-East Asia, Bob's old friend Oliver Leese, and Arthur Power, rejected as a possible CCO by Churchill and now C-in-C East Indies; so a number of birds were killed with one stone. Mountbatten had his own Head of Combined Operations, Brigadier D. W. Price, who had no responsibility for training and was primarily concerned with advising the SEAC planners.

At the beginning of December the COHQ mission returned to India to visit the two other CTCs, at Kharakvasla and Cocanada, before flying on to Burma and visiting Teknaf in the Arakan, where 3 Special Service Brigade was based. The brigade had hitherto seen little in the way of action, other than clearing up after the Japanese HA-GO offensive in early 1944 and holding the Silchar Track from Manipur into Assam against a possible Japanese attack during the siege of Imphal. Brigadier Nonweiler had been invalided back to the UK, and the deputy commander, Peter Young, who had commanded 3 Commando with distinction in Normandy, was acting pending the arrival of Campbell Hardy, fresh from leading 46 RM Commando in the same campaign. In addition to visiting 1 (still under Ken Trevor), 5, 42 RM and 44 RM Commandos, Bob was able to meet Lieutenant General Sir Philip Christison of XV Corps and Major General C. E. N. Lomax of 26 Indian Division, under whose command 3 Special Service Brigade would operate, to hear of their plans for the forthcoming campaign to drive the Japanese out of the Arakan.

The COHQ Mission arrived back to England on 15 December, having stopped once again in Egypt to visit the CTC at Kabrit and in Italy to meet Alexander, recently promoted to Field Marshal and appointed Supreme Allied Commander in the Mediterranean. In one month much had been learnt and a great deal achieved by way of implementing a unified doctrine.

There was one more significant overseas journey for Bob, this time to attend the ARGONAUT conference in Yalta. The British and Americans met initially in Malta, whither Bob flew on 29 January 1945. The key issues for the Chiefs of Staff were Eisenhower's strategy in north-west Europe – the British favoured a concentrated thrust north of the Ruhr, the Americans a broad front approach all along the Rhine – and the question of the withdrawal of further divisions from Italy. On neither did the British receive satisfaction.

The parties flew on to the Crimea on 3 February, Bob travelling in a York which was very comfortably appointed. A four-and-a-half-hour journey by road took the party from the airfield at Saki to Yalta, where the senior members of the British delegation, numbering over thirty, were staying in the Vorontsov

Palace, which Bob described as 'A vast Czarist era house in Scottish Baronial style, but only one bath-room for the whole of the Chiefs of Staff organization'.[8] All the heating was from wood-fired stoves and the grounds were patrolled by security troops, who never stopped saluting. Those at the Vorontsov were at least accommodated in better conditions than the rest of the delegation, who slept six or eight to a room in ramshackle outbuildings. 'Pug' Ismay summed the conference up best:

> From the gastronomical point of view, it was enjoyable; from the social point of view, successful; from the military point of view, unnecessary; and from the political point of view, depressing.[9]

It was the last of these for which the Yalta conference has been remembered, particularly for decisions taken on post-war Europe, notably the frontiers of Poland, the splitting of Germany into four zones and the commitment to democratic elections in liberated countries. The first was to remain highly controversial and the last was reneged on by the Russians.

Little was achieved on the military side, as there was no expectation of direct military cooperation between the widely separated Anglo-American and Soviet fronts. Bob, in particular, found himself with little to do, as Combined Operations were not under specific discussion. There was, however, an enjoyable day off visiting the battlefields of Balaklava and Inkerman and hearing about the capture of Sebastopol by the Germans in 1942 and its recapture in 1944.

Bob had been hoping to return as soon as the conference finished, but, with the crossing of the Rhine now imminent, he and Head were instead ordered to go to Moscow to obtain as much information as possible from the Russian General Staff on river-crossing techniques. The two of them and their batmen travelled by train from Simferopol with Rear Admiral Ernest Archer, the Head of the British Military Mission. The train was excessively crowded except for their carriage, a pre-War model from Belgian Wagons-Lits with eight compartments, one for each member of the party and one for their luggage. The journey took nearly four days and they arrived nineteen hours late.

In spite of Bob's misgivings, the meeting, which took place on 16 February, was a success, with the Russians proving unusually helpful. After another day in Moscow, during which they saw 'Giselle' at the Bolshoi Ballet, Bob and Head travelled to Leningrad by train and then flew to Helsinki and on to Stockholm, where Bob met Mountbatten's sister, the Crown Princess of Sweden, arriving back to England on 19 February.

In December 1944 the much disliked 'Special Service' nomenclature had at last been dropped in favour of 'Commando' for both the Group and the four brigades. There were two major operations in the latter stages of the war in Europe, by 1 Commando Brigade in Montgomery's crossing of the Rhine on 23 March, in which it was instrumental in the capture of Wesel, and by 2 Commando Brigade at Lake Comacchio in support of Eighth Army's last and highly successful offensive in Italy in April. Many smaller operations also took place, and both 1 and 4 Commando Brigades were committed right up until the German surrender. In late 1944 Bob had also been given control of 30 Assault Unit, formerly 30 Commando, but in practice this was invariably employed by force commanders, its teams entering liberated towns in the forefront of the Allied troops to seize all valuable documents and equipment and to take prisoner and interrogate managers and technicians.

The German surrender on 8 May brought increased pressure on Bob to reduce his staff. However, a great deal of experimental work continued to be carried out in respect of new types of landing craft required for the very different conditions of the Far East, for which theatre new training manuals were required, and new CTC staff were being trained to relieve those who were about to be released back into civilian life. He accordingly obtained the agreement of the Chiefs of Staff to a 25 per cent immediate cut, with an additional 25 per cent at the end of the war with Japan.

Chapter 20

Peace

Following the end of the war against Germany, and in spite of continuing hostilities with Japan and major obligations elsewhere, there was immediate pressure, both from politicians on the grounds of cost and from the millions of temporary servicemen, to reduce the size of the armed forces by demobilization.

A number of individuals were demobilized very quickly, among them Lovat, who wrote to Bob to thank him 'for all the loyal support you gave to a very amateur and tactless subordinate'.[1] Lovat was persuaded by Churchill to accept a role in the Government as Parliamentary Under-Secretary of State for Foreign Affairs. He was not to hold that position for long, as Churchill was defeated in the General Election of July 1945, in which Bob himself stood as the Conservative candidate for Bassetlaw, the constituency in which Wiseton Hall stood.

Bob had been approached by the local Conservative Association that April. His initial response was that he thought that the days of Members of Parliament combining their duties with an active military career would soon be at an end, and thus he questioned his suitability. After meetings with the Chief Whip and the local party chairman, the Duke of Portland, he was asked not to reject the offer until he had at least established that he would be able to take two weeks' leave to campaign. He discussed the matter with Brooke, who thought that leave could be arranged, but advised him to consult Churchill. The Prime Minister responded that he should not decline the invitation and that two weeks' leave would be granted to all those not actually engaged in battle. Bob agreed to stand and, from his initial response, it seems that he was prepared to resign his commission if elected.

Bassetlaw had been held by Labour or National Labour since 1929 and the sitting member was Frederick Bellenger, who had served early in the War as a captain in the Royal Artillery in France and Flanders, but had returned to Westminster after Dunkirk. He was personally popular with the electorate, and when the results were declared on 26 July he held Bassetlaw with an enlarged majority of 12,377, in line with the enormous national swing to Labour. Bob was thus unable to emulate the feat of his grandfather Robert, who sixty-five years earlier had been elected one of the two MPs for North Lincolnshire.

Churchill, at least, was grateful, sending a telegram which said simply: 'Thank you so much dear Bob'.[2]

One of the successful candidates was Antony Head, elected as MP for the safe Conservative seat of Carshalton. Due to the delay in declaring the result, Head was able to accompany Bob to the last conference of the War, at Potsdam. They stayed in a pleasant and undamaged villa, whose other occupant was Alexander, but took the opportunity to go into the centre of Berlin. Bob was horrified, writing to Angie: 'There is nothing – literally nothing – left except the shells of some of the buildings.'[3] The weather was hot and sticky and the conference was dull from a military perspective, so he was glad to return to London.

Following the end of the war against Japan in August Bob was to spend much of the next eighteen months looking at the future of Combined Operations, but it was immediately clear that, whatever he recommended, there would be considerable pressure on him to trim the organization yet more, for budgetary reasons if no other. By the summer of 1946 the numbers were down to 126, as a result of which COHQ moved out of Richmond Terrace to a block of flats in Prince's Gate.

On the face of it, Bob's directive changed little between 1943 and 1946, but the underlying situation was very different. The most dramatic development affected the Commandos. In May 1945 Wildman-Lushington returned from the Far East to relieve Sturges at the Commando Group, but in practice he had come to preside over its demise.

Nearly a year earlier, a new committee had been set up under Norman Bottomley, once again seen as a neutral figure, to consider where the future responsibility for amphibious warfare should lie. The Admiralty and the Royal Marines held a strong hand, not least because the opposition of the War Office to their assuming the dominant role had diminished substantially. At an earlier meeting in March 1944, chaired by the Second Sea Lord, Vice Admiral Sir Algernon Willis, and attended by the Commandant General RM, Sir Thomas Hunton, it had been agreed that, as the amphibious functions of combined operations were essentially naval, the Royal Marines should in due course assume the role proposed by the Madden Committee in 1924. The Bottomley Committee, on which Bob himself sat, arrived at the same conclusion, but the demands of the last year of the War meant that no changes could be made at that time. In September 1945, however, its findings were re-submitted to the Chiefs of Staff, who decided that the Commando Group should be wound up, that the Army Commandos should be disbanded and that only one Commando brigade should be retained, composed of three RM Commandos.

In the knowledge that the War Office had only been prevented from doing away with the Army Commandos in 1940 by Churchill himself and had subsequently regarded them with disfavour, Bob had reluctantly accepted that the only way to retain both a Combined Operations organization and a Commando force after the War was to give full responsibility for the latter to the Royal Marines. He had therefore tabled a paper for the COS meeting supporting the recommendations. Brooke was not present at the meeting, but was represented by the VCIGS, Lieutenant General Nye. After Cunningham and Portal had confirmed their agreement to the proposals, the former, who was in the chair, invited Nye to say a few words. Bob later wrote:

> To everybody's amazement but my own General Nye casually remarked that he had nothing to add except that the War Office had never wanted the Commandos and were delighted to see the last of them. Cunningham and Ismay looked pensive and Portal disgusted. The latter asked if I had any further comment to make. I replied that all I could say was that, had the decision been left not to the War Office but to the distinguished Generals who had commanded in the campaigns in France, Germany, Italy and South East Asia, a very different view might have been forthcoming.[4]

This was confirmed at a conference at Camberley in August 1946, over which Montgomery was presiding for the first time as CIGS. In a session on Combined Operations there was a debate on the requirement for Commandos in the future. Monty asked Major General Wimberley, the Director of Infantry, to speak for the War Office, and he produced an indictment of the Commandos on the grounds that they denuded the infantry of their best men. Bob, invited by Monty to make a reply, suggested that one would come better from a former senior field commander with experience of Commandos in battle. Monty picked Dempsey:

> There was dead silence as Sir Miles Dempsey rose to reply but I was not apprehensive as to his verdict. Very quickly he gave it as his opinion that if ever he found himself in command in another war he would never be quite happy unless he knew that there were some green berets in the vicinity.[5]

In late 1945 the changes began to take place. Bob broke the news on 25 October in a talk to 3 and 6 Commandos, which had recently returned from Germany. This was followed immediately by an order of the day and an address which was circulated to every man in the Army Commandos. Two weeks later the process of disbandment began, with the officers and men of Nos. 2, 3, 6 and 9 Commandos being either discharged or returned to their units. No. 4 Commando was subsequently disbanded in Germany and the troops of No. 10 (IA) Commando were returned to their parent countries. Nos. 1 and 5 Commandos escaped the fate of the others for a time, as they formed part of the garrison of Hong Kong. They were in due course merged into 1/5 Commando and then disbanded in February 1947.

The decision to retain a single brigade of only three Commandos meant that the Royal Marines did not escape unscathed. The only formation still operational by early 1946 was 3 Commando Brigade in Hong Kong, which thus became the sole survivor, to this day, of the four brigades in the Commando Group. All the RM Commandos were disbanded except No. 42, which represented those which had served in the Far East in the old 3 Commando Brigade, No. 45, which did the same for 1 and 4 Commando Brigades in north-west Europe and No. 44, which stood for the units of 2 Commando Brigade in Italy and the Adriatic, albeit that it was subsequently renumbered as No. 40.

The other units of the Commando Group were also disbanded,[6] although the Commando Basic Training Centre in due course re-emerged as the Commando Training Centre RM. A new School of Combined Operations, incorporating the Combined Operations Signals School, was opened in early 1946 close to COXE, with Wildman-Lushington as its first Commandant. It was to accept as students officers from all the services. The CTCs, however, were all closed down, and Bob's proposal to open new Combined Training Establishments in Germany, the Middle East and East Africa were rejected on financial grounds.

When Bob announced the disbandment of the Army Commandos, he expected the green beret to disappear with them. However, the propaganda value attached to this symbol was just too great, and a decision was made shortly afterwards to retain it for the RM Commandos.

During 1946 a great deal of Bob's energy was devoted to consideration of the future of Combined Operations. On the positive side Clement Attlee, the new Prime Minister, and the CIGS and CAS had all expressed their support for the continuation of COHQ. Bob, however, was being seriously hampered by a lack of guidance from the Chiefs of Staff on the composition and balance of the three services, the equipment available to them and the nature of the enemy and the ground over which any future war was likely to be fought. He was also dismayed by the scrapping, on the grounds of cost or obsolescence, of a great deal of the specialized equipment used during the War, especially landing craft, as well as the return of all Lend Lease craft and equipment to the Americans and the handing back to their owners of those merchant ships which had been specially fitted out for amphibious operations.

In May 1946 he prepared a draft paper for the Chiefs of Staff requesting more information on the plans and intentions of the service ministries, which would allow him to make a well-considered appreciation. This he submitted for comments to 'Pug' Ismay, who was heading a committee on the reform of the Ministry of Defence. The reply came not from Ismay, but from Major General Sir Leslie Hollis, the Chief Staff Officer to the Minister of Defence, saying that Bob was asking the impossible and that the paper should be recast more precisely to explain his difficulties, ask for guidance on specific issues and include some tentative suggestions as to what policies or actions he might adopt.

The paper was duly redrafted around two broad questions, the first being on what scale and at what stage of a war was a combined operation likely to be required, the second on what enemy was likely to be encountered and in what geographical area. It failed to generate any serious response, which was deeply frustrating; indeed, the attitude of the Chiefs of Staff was encapsulated by Bob in a note which he wrote in preparation for a talk at the Staff College:

> No money, manpower, somehow keep torch CO alight lean years so that rebuild amphibious power times better – meantime do not bother us.[7]

The apparent lack of interest may have been exacerbated by wholesale changes on the COS Committee. Portal had in late 1945 been succeeded by Lord Tedder, Cunningham was off in early June 1946, to be replaced by his namesake, John Cunningham, and Brooke was shortly to hand over to Montgomery. Not only did this create a temporary hiatus, but the new Chiefs were to lack the unity of their predecessors, to the extent that Monty would even refuse to attend meetings at which Tedder was present.[8] In the event, no guidance of real value was received thereafter by Bob.

There was, however, another possible route to enlightenment. Bob had a representative at the British Joint Staff Mission in Washington, through whom he maintained contact with the Americans. He now engineered an invitation to visit the USA during November and December 1946 to find out how they were approaching the issue of combined operations in the post-war environment.

After a briefing at the JSM, Bob met Eisenhower, now the Chief of the Army Staff in Washington DC, who was welcoming and encouraging, and General Alexander Vandegrift, Commandant of the US Marine Corps. They and others made it clear that they thought war with the Soviet Union was inevitable, that they continued to take combined operations very seriously and that therefore, and in sharp contrast to the British attitude, money was no object. Bob then visited a number of training establishments on the eastern side of the country before flying to San Diego, where the Pacific Fleet Amphibious Force was based. The Force Commander was Rear Admiral Arthur Struble, whom Bob had known very well as Admiral Kirk's Chief of Staff for OVERLORD. Since then Struble had gained considerable further experience in command of a Seventh Fleet Amphibious Group during the landings in the Philippines in late 1944 and early 1945.

In addition to visiting a number of other training establishments, including the Air Support School, the Gunnery Support School, the Communications School and the Troop Training Units, the last being the equivalents of the British CTCs, Bob was invited to attend Exercise DUCK as an observer. The exercise was in some respects elementary, as the participants were largely new to amphibious operations, but it demonstrated very clearly that the flame of combined operations was burning much more brightly in the USA than it was in Great Britain. Bob joined Struble aboard USS *Eldorado*, which had been the command ship for the landings at both Iwo Jima and Okinawa, and was impressed by his decision to go ahead with landing a complete division in heavy surf, made possible by new, high-powered landing craft which were able to avoid breaching to.

Although the *Eldorado* was similar to British HQ ships, Bob was further impressed by a recent decision by the US Navy to convert a heavy cruiser into a command ship, stripped of its main guns but faster and more heavily armoured than its predecessors. He was also highly envious of the developments in landing craft design, which went far beyond what had been available during the War.

There was time on the trip for play as well as work. Bob drove down to Tijuana to see a bullfight, but it was cancelled so he went to the races instead, and he stayed for two days with David Niven,[9] who hosted 'a stupendous party for him which went on a very long time and ended in extreme drunkenness'![10] Amongst the guests were Rex Harrison and Douglas Fairbanks Jnr. Bob then travelled to Canada. He had intended to visit Angie's father, but William Dudley Ward died soon after he left the UK. He thus went directly to Kingston, Ontario to deliver a talk at the Canadian Staff College, before travelling on to New York, where he was joined by Angie.

Following his return Bob wrote a memorandum to the Chiefs of Staff, setting out the alternatives as he now saw them, recommending that they should take note of the requirements to lift a single brigade group, the maximum he believed to be possible in the current circumstances, and asking them to decide what course they should adopt if the Admiralty was unable to meet these requirements. The reaction was muted. Bob was, in any event, running out of time to see through any substantive changes, as it had been decided six months earlier that he would hand over to Wildman-Lushington at the end of June 1947, after which the position of CCO or its equivalent was always to be held by a Royal Marine officer.

When the time came, Bob was still only forty and the chances of him obtaining another major general's appointment within the next few years were slim. He had been a substantive colonel since 25 May 1946, with seniority backdated to 22 October 1944, so there was a strong possibility that he would go back no further than brigadier, although it was likely that he would find himself in another office job and almost certainly one less interesting, albeit perhaps less challenging, than CCO. Even a field appointment in 1947 would not have offered the excitement of the Special Service Brigade. He therefore decided to resign his commission and retire into private life.

Bob never disclosed his full reasons for going but, as well as his almost certain demotion, it is quite likely that the exasperation of the last two years had taken its toll and he was simply disinclined to remain in the Army in such circumstances. Moreover, he had a young family, of whom he had seen very little during the War and which had recently grown with the birth of Benjamin Richard Laycock on 4 June.

Bob was, at least, accorded the honorary rank of major general. He had been appointed a Companion of the Order of the Bath in the New Year's Honours of 1945 and had subsequently been made a Commander of the Legion of Merit by the Americans, specifically for his contribution to raising, organizing and training the Rangers, a Commander of the *Légion d'honneur* by the French, a Commander, with Star, of the Order of St Olav by the Norwegians and a Grand Officer of the Order of Orange Nassau, with Swords, by the Dutch.

There was, however, no knighthood, which was perhaps understandable for one so junior, but might nevertheless have been expected for the position Bob had held as CCO. Mountbatten had written a year earlier:

> I want to take this chance of telling you that your C.B. is, in the opinion of everyone with whom I have discussed it, an entirely inadequate reward for your outstanding war service.
>
> I am quite sure that if you had not been a 'youngster', you would have unquestionably have had at least a K.C.B; and if you had been a real Old Blimp I am sure it would have been the G.C.B or a baronetcy.[11]

This reflected the opinion of Sturges, who had written to thank Bob for recommending him for his own KBE in 1945:

> Hells Bells, you got Cdos going, and were my boss so if there was a 'K' about in Combined ops it should have been yours.[12]

For the time being, however, there were no further honours.

After the War ended, Bob and Angie initially kept on their London flat, but also lived in two cottages at Hawthorn Hill, one for them and their cook and the other for the children and their nanny. Young Joe and Tilly went to a small school nearby. In the spring of 1947, however, probably in the knowledge that the family was about to expand, they bought The Old Vicarage at Winkfield, near Windsor, although for some time they retained the farm at Hawthorn Hill. The Old Vicarage was a much larger house with a substantial garden and three fields. It was run by a butler, Simpson, who was eventually fired for drinking too many bottles of Bob's whisky. In addition, there was a gardener, an odd-job man, who lived with his wife in a caravan in one of the fields and played the trombone, and two daily women.

Bob did not take on a full time job. He was asked to stand for Parliament again, both for Bassetlaw in any forthcoming General Election and for North Croydon in a by-election in 1947, but declined. However, he accepted some non-executive appointments, one as a director of Lloyds Bank, another as chairman of the Windsor Hospital Management Committee. His father was now in his eighties and, although still active – he had been County Commandant of the Nottinghamshire Home Guard during the War – was less able to look after the estate than he had been. The Seghill Colliery was nationalized on 1 January 1947, but there were substantial agricultural holdings in the north-east, which Bob inspected from time to time, and at Wiseton, where he and the family were frequent visitors, staying for a longer period each summer.

Bob and Angie had a very large number of friends, some of long standing such as the Heads and the Cotterells, others made during the War, including Evelyn Waugh and Bill Stirling, and there were numerous occasions when they had guests to stay or were entertained themselves. The large house parties which had been regular events in the '20s and '30s were, however, markedly rarer. For a man whose boyhood, adolescence and early career had been devoted to hunting, polo and steeplechasing, it might seem surprising that Bob never again rode for recreation. He had always attributed his success in avoiding capture in the Jebel Akhdar after the Rommel Raid to his knowledge of the habits of foxes and had vowed to give up hunting as a result. However, there was another reason for not riding, which was that he began to experience pain in one of his legs, which was to endure for the rest of his life.

Both Bob and Angie went up to London at least weekly, Bob to attend board and other meetings and to see his friends, sometimes staying overnight at White's. Angie was still very active on behalf of the Commando Benevolent Fund, which continued to hold fund raising events, including a ball at Claridges at which Princess Elizabeth was present, and a concert at the Albert Hall attended by the King and both Princesses. Bob was also on the Committee, which included over the years many of the leading Commando veterans, including Tom Churchill, Charles Newman and Charles Vaughan. He continued to retain close links with his wartime comrades, attending reunion dinners not only of the newly formed Commando Association, but also of the individual Commandos. He was in Westminster Abbey when Winston Churchill unveiled the Commando Memorial there in May 1948[13] and at Spean Bridge, near Achnacarry, when Queen Elizabeth the Queen Mother performed the same function in respect of the spectacular Memorial there just over four years later.

Bob developed a number of interests for which he had had no time hitherto, some of which were unusual for such a masculine person, including needlepoint tapestry. The journalist and author Godfrey Winn, who interviewed Angie and her sister Pempie for a regular feature in *Woman's Illustrated*, commented on a beautiful hand-painted table, on which hundreds of blobs of red, green and blue paint had been interlaced into a complicated pattern, and was astonished to learn that it was Bob's work. Bob also inherited his father's lathe, on which he turned some very attractive artefacts.

Another interest, and a long-held one, was food. Wiseton had at one time boasted a French chef called Monsieur Chateauvert, who had been trained by Escoffier and thus set a very high standard, and Bob had thereafter always asked to meet the chef after a good meal, whether in a private house or in a restaurant. One of the former, at which the quality of the fare was guaranteed, was Fairlawne, the home of his Old Etonian contemporary, Peter Cazalet. The chef there at the end of the 1950s and into the '60s, with whom Bob became friendly, was a young man called Albert Roux, who in 1967 was backed by Cazalet to open Le Gavroche.

On 10 January 1952, Old Joe Laycock died. The implications were considerable and, from a financial perspective, disastrous. Estate duty was levied on an escalating scale, with the top rate on agricultural property in excess of £1 million set at 44 per cent and on all other assets at 80 per cent. Bob was forced to sell all the land in the north-east except that occupied by the Gosforth Golf Cub, half the acreage around Wiseton and a 179-acre farm in Kent. He was to say subsequently that his total wealth was about the same as his father's annual income.

The family did not move permanently to Wiseton, although they stayed frequently and spent much of each summer there. The children adored it, but it was immensely impractical for modern living compared to the Old Vicarage, which, unusually for that time, had central heating. Tilly was by then about to leave school and Joe was at Eton, which was close to Winkfield. Emma and Ben were being educated nearby and the youngest, Katherine Martha, who had been born on 15 May 1949 and was always known by her second name, was still very young. They thus stayed put, whilst Kitty moved down to a house near Reading, where she could easily be visited by Bob and his brother Peter.

Bob's continued residence in Winkfield was convenient for one brief but demanding role which he was invited to undertake, as one of the Gold Staff Officers who acted as ushers at the Coronation of Queen Elizabeth II on 2 June 1953. It is likely that he was chosen personally by the Earl Marshal, the Duke of Norfolk, with whom he had served as a subaltern in the Blues.

Bob's sometime residence at Wiseton Hall did result in one prestigious local appointment, as High Sheriff of Nottinghamshire for 1954. In acting as such he emulated both his grandfather and his father, who had held the office in 1878 and 1906 respectively. Although the High Sheriff was the judicial representative of the sovereign, and thus obliged to attend whenever he or she visited the county, in practice the position was largely ceremonial. As it happened, however, events were to dictate that Bob's year of office would be interrupted by another appointment of far greater significance.

Chapter 21

Malta

One reason for Bob's frequent visits to London was to attend meetings at the Colonial Office, where he became an unofficial adviser. The precise nature of his role is not known, but it may well have been concerned with the military aspects of decolonization, the pressure for which was fast gathering pace. It is likely that Bob's involvement came after Churchill's return to power in October 1951, as he knew many of the members of the new administration, including Ismay, the Secretary of State for Commonwealth Relations, and Alexander, the Minister of Defence, but most notably Antony Head, who had become Secretary of State for War.

The Secretary of State for the Colonies was another old friend, Oliver Lyttelton, in whose house Bob had recuperated following his forty-one days in the desert and to whom his brother Peter had been Military Assistant. Lyttelton was elevated to the peerage as Viscount Chandos at the end of July 1954 and succeeded by Alan Lennox-Boyd. One question which had been vexing the Colonial Office in the months before Lennox-Boyd took office was the choice of Sir Gerald Creasy's successor as Governor of Malta. With one brief exception, between 1813, when Malta ceased to be a protectorate and became a British Crown Colony, and 1946, the governor had always been a military man, usually a very senior general at the end of his career. Following the end of wartime emergency powers and the return to Malta of an elected Legislative Assembly, the Attlee Government decided that the time had come to appoint a civilian and selected one of its own MPs, Sir Francis Douglas. Douglas was himself followed in 1949 by Creasy, a longstanding civil servant in the Colonial Office, who had previously been Governor of the Gold Coast (Ghana).

In the immediate post-war years Malta remained a highly valuably strategic asset of the British Empire, due to its position in the centre of the Mediterranean and its outstanding harbour, used not only by the Royal Navy, but by the navies of NATO. The Colonial Office now concluded that it would be easier for the Governor to deal with the various British and Allied commanders if he had a military background. Moreover, there were some aspects of the political situation on the island which might call for a different approach in future.

Bob was an obvious choice, trusted by Churchill and Lyttelton and strongly supported by Head, who may well have proposed him in the first place. He was duly approached, and agreed to his appointment for a three-year term. By this time he may well have been tiring of his relatively mundane life at home and looking forward to a new challenge. He had visited the island on three occasions, very briefly in 1941 and for longer stays in 1943 and 1945, and had liked it. Mountbatten was Allied Naval Commander-in-Chief in the Mediterranean, albeit nearing the end of his appointment, and was to be succeeded by Admiral Sir Guy Grantham, with whom Bob had become friendly during the War, so his access to the highest naval and military circles was assured. He was also delighted that 3 Commando Brigade was based on the island. Last but not least, Angie was enthusiastic.

On 30 July the Queen approved Bob's appointment, not only as Governor of Malta but as a Knight Commander of the Order of St Michael and St George. The announcement of his appointment was made on 4 August and Bob was hastily knighted by the Queen at Sledmere House in Yorkshire, on her way up to Balmoral. He had to attend a number of briefings before he left London, which delayed his departure until 19 September. In the meantime, he entered into some difficult discussions with the Colonial Office on the matter of finance.

Bob had no problem with his salary, which was £4,000 per annum, with an additional duty allowance of £1,500. The entertainment allowance of £500, however, he regarded as quite unsatisfactory, and he was concerned about reports on the condition of the Governor's main residence, the St Anton Palace, including one from the Queen, who told him that the cold there had been intolerable on her state visit to the island in 1953. His predecessor, a man whose tastes were said to border on the austere, revealed that he had been forced to dip into his own pocket for both entertainment and maintenance, which Bob believed would be beyond his resources. He therefore wrote to Sir Thomas Lloyd, the Permanent Under-Secretary, requesting an increase in the entertainment allowance to £2,000 and permission to submit a report on the St Anton Palace and the Verdala Palace, the Governor's summer residence. Both the increase in entertainment allowance and an increase in the duty allowance were somewhat grudgingly agreed to, but the question of putting the palaces into good order took longer to resolve. Bob in due course submitted a report which recommended strongly that the cost, which he estimated at £10,000, should be defrayed by the British and not the Maltese Government. To illustrate his point he sent a shabby bedside lamp from the main guest room to Lennox-Boyd, who promised his support, as a result of which the work was eventually carried out, although a number of costs associated with running the palaces continued to fall on the Governor.

Whilst Martha and the nanny/governess, Lavinia Jenkinson, flew directly to Malta on 18 September, Bob, Angie, Tilly, Emma and Ben flew to Palermo on the following day. In Palermo they boarded the destroyer HMS *Saintes*[1] for the short voyage, arriving in Grand Harbour on the next morning. Bob was greeted aboard the ship by the Lieutenant Governor, Trafford Smith, who had been Acting Governor since Creasy's departure, the Flag Officer, Malta, and the Prime Minister, Dr George Borg Olivier. Once ashore, he was introduced to the Metropolitan Archbishop, the Chief Justice, Government Ministers and various other dignitaries and was then driven to the seat of administration, the Grand Master's Palace in Valetta, where he took the Oaths of Allegiance and Office and gave a brief address to the assembled audience. Only then, more than two hours after their arrival, were he and Angie able to drive to their residence, the St Anton Palace.

In his address Bob said that his immediate task was the achievement of an even closer bond between Malta and the United Kingdom. This was, indeed, the issue of the moment. Borg Olivier of the Nationalist Party had been Prime Minister since 1951, in a coalition government with Paul Boffa's Malta Workers' Party. Whilst in London for the Coronation in 1953, he had presented a memorandum to the British Government calling for Malta to become an independent dominion in the Commonwealth. This contrasted with the position of the opposition Labour Party, led by Dom Mintoff, which demanded full integration with the United Kingdom, with seats for the island at Westminster and a transfer of responsibilities from the Colonial Office to the Home Office. Neither option was particularly attractive to the British Government and, with no agreement having been reached more than a year later, Lennox-Boyd paid a brief visit to the island shortly after Bob's arrival, during which he offered the possibility of three-party talks in London to discuss the issue. The coalition government, however, held the slimmest of majorities in the Assembly and the defection of one of their members led to its losing an adjournment motion, as a result of which a general election was called for 26–28 February 1955. The Malta Workers' Party did not contest the election, which was won by the Labour Party with 23 out of 40 seats. Mintoff duly became Prime Minister, and the new Assembly was opened by the Duke of Edinburgh on 21 March.

Bob flew back to England for consultations with the Colonial Office shortly after the election, but for the time being there was no progress on the constitutional questions. He was already deeply frustrated with the politicians, although many other prominent figures in the Maltese community had made him and Angie very welcome. He decided to use his higher entertainment allowance to invite as many of them as possible to events at St Anton. Opportunities to do so presented themselves when distinguished visitors came to the island, including the Duke of Edinburgh, the Queen Mother, the Duchess of Kent, Mountbatten and, only weeks after Bob took up his appointment, Haile Selassie, the Emperor of Ethiopia. However, Bob needed no excuse to get to know the key personalities, who included Archbishop Gonzi, a powerful figure who was highly political, and one politician with whom he got on well, Mabel Strickland, owner of the *Times of Malta* and leader of the Progressive Constitutional Party, which had won no seats in the election. He hosted both frequent cocktail parties and, once every three to four weeks during the winter, dinners for thirty-two guests. He was less keen on the latter because of their formality, with guests seated according to the Table of Precedence, whilst his two ADCs were required to ensure that everyone had at least five minutes with him and Angie.

The ADCs were an important part of Bob's retinue. The Colonial ADC was Major Walter Bonello, formerly of the Royal Malta Artillery, who provided continuity and was the primary source of local information. Bob's Personal ADC was chosen by him. When he arrived he inherited as a stopgap a junior Army officer on National Service, who left shortly afterwards. Governors would usually request a young officer from their own regiment, but even before leaving the UK, Bob had told Mountbatten that he thought a Naval ADC would be more suitable. Mountbatten recommended Lieutenant Mark Agnew RN, who had served as a midshipman under him in 1949 and had recently been a watch-keeping lieutenant in HMS *Surprise*, a converted frigate which was employed in the Mediterranean as the C-in-C's yacht. Agnew promptly fell in love with Tilly. They were married on 23 April 1955 at St Paul's Anglican Pro-Cathedral in Valetta and he resigned his commission before the end of the year. His successor was Lieutenant Francis Ponsonby RN, who had been serving locally in HM Submarine *Sanguine*. He was in the post for a year and was prepared to stay for longer, but Bob thought that this might be prejudicial to his career. As a replacement Bob was offered someone he thought was unsuitable and instead took on Lieutenant David Hall RN, who had been working at the Northwood HQ of the C-in-C Eastern Atlantic. Hall fitted in exceptionally well and continued to work for Bob for the rest of his term.

The Personal ADC was considered to be part of the Governor's household and thus lived at the St Anton Palace. The key local member of the household was the butler, and there were other servants, but Bob's individual requirements were initially looked after by his Royal Marine batman, Sergeant McLeod. After a short period McLeod's duties, especially keeping Bob's uniforms in pristine condition, were usurped by Angie's lady's maid, Dorothy, who had been with the family since 1950. Described by David Hall as 'loud and temperamental',[2] she was forceful, but also intensely loyal. The household was completed by Celia Monckton, Angie's secretary, whilst there was a semi-permanent guest in the shape of a young friend, Minty Yarde-Buller, who arrived on a six-week visit in 1956 and stayed on for eighteen months!

In the summer of 1955 the family and household decamped to the Governor's alternative residence, the Verdala Palace. Situated on a ridge, where it was able to enjoy the benefits of a cooling breeze, it was certainly a more pleasant environment in hot weather. However, the shabby state of the palace, the need to take absolutely everything with them, including furniture, and the fact that the children missed the swimming pool at St Anton meant that this practice was not repeated in subsequent years.

Bob's political staff were based in the Governor's Office at the Grand Master's Palace, where he worked every morning and held all his meetings. Other than Trafford Smith, the most senior British member of the Administration was the Legal Secretary, A. M. I. Austin, who was succeeded in 1957 by D. S. Stephens. The Legal Secretary played a key role in advising on constitutional matters, which were to dominate Bob's term. The most senior Maltese member of the staff was Lieutenant Colonel Victor Vella, the Secretary to the Government, who was responsible among other things for the smooth running of the Palace, whilst the Attorney General was Anthony Mamo, who was later to become the second Governor-General and then the first President of an independent Malta.

The Malta Labour Party's victory in the 1955 General Election led to further calls by Mintoff for integration with the United Kingdom on the Northern Ireland model, in which the British Government would be responsible for defence and foreign affairs, whilst the Government of Malta would deal with all other matters. Three MPs would be elected to represent the island at Westminster. Two 'Round Table' Conferences were held that year, in June/July in London and October in Malta. Bob did not attend the first, but was present at the second, at which the large British Government delegation was led by the Lord Chancellor, Lord Kilmuir. The dominant figure was Mintoff, who could be very charming when it suited him, especially when meeting British parliamentarians, but utterly obdurate when it came to negotiation. The talks reached no firm conclusion, but a report was subsequently produced for the British Parliament. In Malta itself, integration was vigorously opposed by the Nationalists and also by Archbisop Gonzi, who believed that the position of the Catholic church would be severely weakened if Malta became part of a country in which the established church was Anglican.

The British Government was persuaded to agree to a referendum on integration, which was held on 11 and 12 February 1956. In spite of the denunciations of Gonzi and a boycott by the Nationalists, the Maltese people voted 77–23 per cent in favour of integration. However, the turnout was less than 60 per cent, enabling Borg Olivier to claim that those voting against and those boycotting the poll constituted between them a majority. Bob went to London shortly afterwards for a series of meetings at the Colonial Office, in which it was decided that no decision could be taken until Parliament had had time to debate the Round Table conference report. He broke his return journey in Rome, where his primary purpose was to hold meetings in the Vatican with the Papal Pro-Secretary of State, Monsignor Tardini, on the guarantees demanded by Gonzi for the Catholic church in Malta. Whilst he was there he had an audience with Pope Pius XII.

With something of a hiatus on the political front, 1956 was otherwise a relatively quiet year for Bob, during which the attention of the world was largely diverted by the Suez Crisis. Numerous visitors arrived in connection with it, including Head and the CIGS, General Sir Gerald Templer, whilst Grand Harbour was exceptionally busy with naval movements. Mintoff, however, did not endear himself to the British Government by describing the Egyptian leader as 'my good friend, Colonel Nasser'.[3]

The political heat began to rise in the winter of 1956/57, with both Mintoff and Bob visiting London for talks. The Nationalist Opposition withdrew from the Assembly at the end of January 1957 in protest against their exclusion from these talks, only to realize that this had been a tactical error, as they risked being further sidelined. The sticking point in the talks was not the constitutional aspects, on which progress was satisfactory, but the economic arrangements, with Mintoff demanding 'equivalence', in other words that Malta's economy would be brought into line with the United Kingdom over a number of years. This would require an extended period of financial subsidies for social services, new industries and the dockyard, and Mintoff demanded that this should be for twelve years, which was unacceptable to the British Government. The question of the dockyard was to become a particular problem, not least because a White Paper issued shortly beforehand by the Ministry of Defence predicted significant cuts to its work for the Royal Navy.

Bob had by that time agreed to an extension of his term as Governor by one year to September 1958. Discussions on the subject had begun in the autumn of 1956, as Bob wanted the decision on his successor to be settled early in order to avoid the hiatus of the previous handover, which had not gone down well in Malta. Lennox-Boyd responded with the suggestion that Bob should stay on so that he could introduce the new Constitution, still thought then to be possible within that time frame. Bob agreed, on the condition that Trafford Smith should stay on as well.

In his letter to the Permanent Secretary at the Colonial Office agreeing to the extension of his term, Bob had written, 'I do not think that it will be a very happy one!'[4] So, indeed, it turned out. He was in London for talks at the Colonial Office early in the New Year, when he also met the new Prime Minister, Harold Macmillan. After a summer of little progress but increasingly rude letters from Mintoff, who went down with a bad case of jaundice, which did nothing to improve his mood, Bob was back in London again in October. Mintoff proved to be as difficult as ever and the talks dragged on for four weeks without any definite conclusion, Bob writing at one stage to Angie:

> God knows how long this farce will continue & yet I don't see how Mintoff can go back to Malta with nothing. He MUST go back soon as the Legislative Assemble opens on 4 Nov. All we have done is get various things accepted in principle but Mintoff has kicked violently at any suggestions for putting them into practice!

The discussions were led on the British side by the Earl of Perth, the Minister of State for the Colonies and became particularly acrimonious when Mintoff flatly refused to consider raising loans or putting up taxes, let alone reducing subsidies.

It was the dockyard which had emerged as the major problem between the two sides. It was becoming apparent that the British Government was unable to guarantee work from the Royal Navy for more than a very limited period, and efforts to replace this with commercial contracts were not likely to cover the shortfall. Mintoff's own power base derived in large measure from the dockyard unions, although he fell out with them in the autumn of 1957, as a result of which he resigned temporarily as Prime Minister in favour of his deputy, Ellul Mercer, only to make up with them shortly afterwards.

The atmosphere deteriorated further as it became clear that the British Government was not prepared to accede to Mintoff's proposal that any dockyard worker laid off should be guaranteed alternative employment. Threats were made of reprisals, such as cutting off supplies and services to British troops on the island. With the mood becoming progressively uglier, Bob travelled yet again to London to meet Lennox-Boyd and Macmillan. He returned to a difficult situation, exemplified by the decision of the Maltese Government to boycott the traditional Candlemas Ceremony on 2 February 1958, on the grounds that Bob was no longer impartial. Instead of integration with Great Britain, the talk turned to full independence, with Mintoff threatening that the Russians would pay much more for use of the dockyard than the British were proposing to do.

In March 1958 Bob flew to London yet again. He had delayed his departure in order to receive the Queen Mother, who stopped briefly in Malta on her way back to London after a world tour. She offered Bob a seat in her plane, and his presence came as a great surprise to the Queen, who met her mother at Heathrow. In addition to his usual meetings at the Colonial Office, Bob had one other reason for going to London: to see a specialist about his leg, which was causing him considerable pain. The specialist diagnosed a slipped disc close to the sacro-iliac joint and recommended that he go into a nursing home for more detailed examination, but Bob was unable to spare the time.

In between the punishing schedule of visits to London and meetings with Mintoff and the other party leaders in Malta, Bob and Angie were at least managing to lead a satisfactory family and social life. By 1957 Joe had left Eton and was at Sandhurst hoping for a commission in the Blues. Tilly and Mark Agnew were in London, where their daughter, Leonie, had been born in March 1956. In that year Ben went to prep school in England, whilst Emma, after two terms in a local convent school, after which she was taught alongside two army children by a governess, also went to boarding school in England in 1958 for the final years of her education. Only Martha remained in Malta for the whole period, initially taught by a governess and then at a succession of schools.

If Bob and Angie were not entertaining in the evening, their favourite recreation was bridge, with a number of like-minded friends. Freda Dudley Ward came to stay for a month every year, during which the game changed to canasta. She was sometimes accompanied by Bobby Casa Maury, although they had divorced in 1954. In the summer of 1957, the Duke and Duchess of Windsor arrived in Malta aboard Loel Guinness's yacht, *Calisto*, and came to dinner at St Anton, whilst Bob and Hall went to lunch on the yacht. In the light of her family history, Angie thought it politic to be away. Many other friends also turned up and most stayed, including David Stirling, although Bob baulked at having Randolph Churchill in the house other than for a meal!

The Laycocks had the use of the Governor's barge, which was a former picket boat with a cabin, coxed by a genial Maltese called Joe Vassallo. When not on official business, this was used extensively for picnics, and Bob became very keen on snorkelling off the beaches around Malta and Gozo. Angie also kept a small sailing boat at St Paul's Bay.

Due to the political situation, Bob took less than half his full leave entitlement, but when he did it tended to be locally in the Mediterranean. The two or three occasions on which he and Angie were invited on a cruise aboard HMS *Surprise* as the guest of the Royal Navy were not treated as leave by virtue of the formal occasions with which they were punctuated. On one of their few proper holidays the family came very close to disaster. They had chartered a motor yacht, the *St Francis*, and were cruising near Corfu, when the weather deteriorated sharply, with heavy rain and a short, steep sea. Ben, on holiday from his prep school, came on deck to be seasick, but as he reached the rail, the yacht gave a violent lurch and he was flung overboard. Luckily he was seen by a deck hand, who sounded the alarm and the ship came round on to the opposite course. A searchlight found Ben, but an attempt to launch the dinghy failed when it filled with water, stove in its side and sank. David Hall then dived in fully clothed and, although not a particularly strong swimmer, succeeded in reaching Ben, who was exhausted. He swam back to the yacht with him, but neither had the strength to use the ladder and they had to be hauled in by hand. Hall was nominated for and subsequently awarded the Royal Humane Society's Stanhope Gold Medal for the most gallant rescue of the year.

In addition to his family and social life, Bob's other pleasure was his connection to the armed forces, not only of Great Britain, but also of its allies. He was always delighted to be invited to spend time with 3 Commando Brigade and also enjoyed going aboard the ships of the Royal Navy: when Montgomery visited the island, he arranged for him to spend a day on the destroyer HMS *Alamein*. Bob particularly impressed the Italians when their sail-training ship, the *Amerigo Vespucci*, called in and he climbed up the rigging and on to the lower mainmast top via the futtock shrouds rather than through the 'lubber's hole'. His relationship with the Americans was particularly good, to the extent that when Admiral Cato D. Glover, the Acting C-in-C of NATO's naval forces in the Mediterranean, learnt that Bob was to visit the Pope once again in Rome, he insisted that he should travel in USS *Forrestal*, at the time the largest aircraft carrier in the world. On this occasion, Bob and Hall were given a private tour of the Vatican and both had an audience with Pope Pius. Bob went again in 1959 to meet the new Pope, John XXIII, but this time he took Angie with him.

These occasions were, however, only diversions from what had become a highly demanding and frustrating job. Notwithstanding his attempts to remain neutral, Bob was increasingly and publicly accused by Mintoff of bias towards the British Government's position. In April 1958 Mintoff resigned again over a proposal from Lennox-Boyd that there should be a five-year period in which the financial and constitutional provisions of integration were implemented, but that during this time Malta would be neither integrated with the United Kingdom nor represented at Westminster. Borg Olivier was invited to form a government, but declined, and Bob was compelled to suspend the Assembly and take direct control of the Civil Service. Demonstrations were held and the General Workers Union called a one-day strike, during which the police were stoned by strikers whilst trying to remove roadblocks. Immediately afterwards, Bob declared a state of public emergency, giving increased powers to the police and banning all meetings and demonstrations for three months.

Bob travelled to London yet again at the end of May, having canvassed the views of all parties other than Labour, which declined his invitation. He was there for two months in intensive talks at the Colonial Office and other government departments, much of which was focused on the dockyard. The conclusion was reached that it should be commercialized, and discussions were held with a number of possible operators, agreement finally being reached with C. H. Bailey Ltd. Once Bob was back in Malta, this was announced, but the Labour Party immediately instructed the unions not to cooperate with the company.

Bob was now asked to extend his term further to the end of May 1959, so when new talks were convened in London for November, he was present. Mintoff was also there, but this time he demanded not integration, but immediate and full independence. When Bob returned to Malta, he broadcast on the radio, placing the blame for the collapse of negotiations squarely on the shoulders of the Leader of the Labour Party and spelling out what the implications of splitting from the United Kingdom would be for Malta's economy and employment. Direct rule by the Governor's Council was imposed, but trouble continued, especially when the Admiralty announced that it was laying off 6,000 workers in the dockyard but that they would be taken on again by C. H. Bailey. Riots broke out, and Rear Admiral Lee-Barber, the Admiral Superintendent, was stoned and chased by the rioters. C. H. Bailey took over formally at the end of March and only twenty-four of the 6,000 workers rejected the offer of a job.

By that time the name of Bob's successor, his old friend Admiral Sir Guy Grantham, had been announced. Bob himself was greatly relieved to be stepping down, as he had found the last few months exceptionally difficult. He was nevertheless admired in London, and by many in Malta, for his patience and forbearance, whilst Mintoff was far from universally popular on the island. Bob's failure to broker a resolution to the constitutional question was widely recognized as the result of the British Government's unwillingness to write what amounted to a blank cheque for Malta and Mintoff's refusal to consider anything else.

Angie was to be missed by many in Malta, where she had enjoyed herself immensely. In addition to her duties as a hostess in support of Bob, at which she was a natural, she carved out a very distinct role for herself as an influential and enthusiastic supporter and patron of a number of local charities, including orphanages and church organizations.

Bob and Angie's departure on 28 May 1959 was as ceremonial as their arrival. They had been invited by the C-in-C Mediterranean Fleet, Admiral Sir Alexander Bingley, to sail in HMS *Surprise* to Nice, where Bob was to meet and brief Grantham. The voyage took the form of a cruise via Minorca and Corsica, and the ship carried Bob's Rolls Royce on board so that they could drive through France back to England. On their arrival in Nice, Bob's back gave out and he was admitted for a short time to the American Hospital. Angie, Hall and Celia Monckton went to the casino in Monte Carlo, where they pooled their meagre foreign currency allowances for Angie to bet all their money on Ben's birthday. The number duly came up!

Chapter 22

Sunset

Bob's accrued leave at the end of his Governorship amounted to 98 days, most of which he and Angie planned to spend on a cruise in the Caribbean at the beginning of 1960. Bob calculated that, if he was to avoid paying UK income tax and surtax on all his income for the year ending 5 April 1960, which combined to produce a marginal rate of nineteen shillings and sixpence in the pound, he would have to stay out of the country for a further three months. Accordingly, that autumn they rented a large house outside Dublin and moved there until the New Year.

This was not a particularly happy period. The house itself, whilst attractive from the outside, lacked many modern amenities, notably central heating. As the electricity supply was highly erratic and the fuses inadequate for appliances such as irons, the family had to rely on open fires to provide warmth. Bob spent as much time as he could in the garden, but Angie was miserable about leaving Malta.

There were other problems. Tilly's marriage was failing and, having espoused communism, she was having an affair with a left-wing journalist whilst working as a journalist herself on the *Evening Standard* in London. Her daughter Leonie, now two years old, was brought to stay with Bob and Angie, but, possibly because of the ructions between her parents, she cried a lot, driving the household to distraction. Joe had resigned his commission in the Army and was uncertain what he should do next: in the meantime, his growing interest in alternative religions and cults irritated his parents. Emma had just left school and was a typically grumpy teenager. Only Ben, now at Eton but back for the Christmas holidays and always cheerful, and Martha, who went to school locally for a term and was quiet and even-tempered, seemed immune from depression.

As Bob and Angie had relations and many friends in Ireland, at least their social life was good. However, there was some relief at the beginning of 1961 when the tenancy ended. In January Ben returned to school and Martha began boarding at Heathfield, whilst Emma went to Blois to learn French. Soon afterwards, Bob and Angie left on their cruise.

The outbound leg of their journey, on the French ship SS *Colombie*, took them to Barbados, from where they flew on to St Vincent and then travelled by plane or ship to Grenada, St Lucia, Tobago and Trinidad, staying for the most part with the Governors of the territories. From Trinidad they visited Caracas, the only place they heartily disliked. Bob, who wrote very amusing letters to his children in verse, described it to Emma as a:

> Ghastly place that ought,
> Or so we thought,
> To be annihilated – for you might as well
> Live there as rent a boarding house in Hell![1]

In Caracas they boarded the SS *Antilles*, of the same shipping line as the *Colombie*, which took a leisurely route via Curaçao, Jamaica, Haiti, Martinique, Guadeloupe, Puerto Rico and Vigo to Plymouth, where they arrived towards the end of March.

The main issue on Bob and Angie's return was what to do with Wiseton Hall: with over 100 rooms, many of which had never been used, the house was totally impractical for modern living and enormously expensive to maintain. There appears to have been no intention to stay on in Winkfield after Malta, and the Old Vicarage was sold. During a long visit to London for the Malta talks in 1957, Bob had written to Angie:

> And now Wiseton. You know that I have been going through hell trying to convince myself that there really is a good excuse for leaving the soil of my youth and a community to which I feel I owe loyalty. Now I reckon I have got it. I have just heard that they are going to sink a new pit our side of the North Road to mine the coal to the east with another pit village between us and Ramskill. This is the final straw and has broken the camel's back.'[2]

He sought an alternative and, almost certainly at the suggestion of Antony Head, looked at Boyton Manor in Wiltshire, not far from the Heads' home near Bishopstone. The house, whose park Bob found particularly attractive, was to come up for sale in the following autumn. It may have been because of the extension to his term as Governor, but he evidently decided not to put in a bid. Instead, putting aside his concerns about the activities of the National Coal Board, he conceived a radical plan to pull down Wiseton Hall and build a much smaller and more practical house on the site.

Whilst only a fraction of the size of its predecessor, the new neo-Georgian house was still large by modern standards, with four spacious reception rooms, eight bedrooms, including a substantial master suite, and all the usual offices. The old stables were untouched and let to a racehorse trainer, who turned out to be extremely bad at paying his rent. The gardens remained much the same, although they had been allowed to run down somewhat and Bob and Angie had to clear a wilderness of brambles and nettles, he with a pick and an axe, she with a tractor. The cricket pitch was retained for the regular use of the Wiseton

Cricket Club, and Bob offered a reward of £5 to any batsman who could hit one of the windows in the house!

During the building process, which took up much of 1960, the family lived in two cottages on the estate, in one of which they slept and Bob had his study, carrying out chemical experiments in the kitchen, whilst the other was used for eating and guest accommodation. Bob and Angie were able to get away for visits to friends such as the Cazalets, Heads and Cotterrells, and also spent time in London, where they were invited to dine with the Queen.

There had been two significant deaths in the Laycock family whilst they were in Malta, Bob's sister Joyce, Lady Daresbury, in November 1958, and his mother Kitty, three months later at the age of eighty-six. To Bob's great regret, he and Angie were unable to attend either funeral, but he had managed to visit his mother on a number of occasions during his frequent journeys to London and found that she had softened considerably in old age. To compound Bob's loss, his half-sister Kathleen also died, in November 1960, at the early age of sixty-two; she had divorced Bill Rollo in 1946 and had married Lieutenant Colonel Daniel Asquith.

Bob resumed his duties as a director of Lloyds Bank on his return to the UK, but with the move from Winkfield he resigned from the Windsor Hospital Management Board. He now picked up a similar appointment as a member of the Sheffield Regional Hospital Board, and was also appointed a Governor of Welbeck College,[3] which was located nearby at Worksop and provided sixth-form education to candidates for the engineering branches of the three armed services and the Ministry of Defence.

He was almost certainly even more pleased by two military appointments in 1960. On 11 April he was made Colonel Commandant of the Special Air Service Regiment in succession to Miles Dempsey, and on 9 May he followed the Duke of Portland as Honorary Colonel of the Sherwood Rangers Yeomanry. Although Bob had never served with the Sherwood Rangers, that appointment maintained a family tradition begun by his father seventy years earlier and continued by his two brothers. After the War the regiment had continued operating tanks, but it converted to become an armoured reconnaissance unit in 1961. Bob's role was not particularly demanding, but he did play a critical and successful part in negotiations with the War Office in 1967, when the Territorial Army was significantly cut back. Many yeomanry regiments were reduced to the lowest category in the new Territorial Army and Volunteer Reserve, with no equipment and no service requirement other than a week's camp. Bob, however, used his influence to ensure that the Sherwood Rangers Yeomanry retained to its singular identity as one of the squadrons of the new Royal Yeomanry, and also that it was one of only four yeomanry regiments at the time to continue in an armoured role.[4] He duly became the Honorary Colonel of the new squadron.

Bob's relationship with the SAS had been much closer. He had been involved with its conception and might well be numbered among its godfathers. Many of the 'Originals', notably David Stirling and Jock Lewes, had served under him in 8 Commando, and he had later supported Bill Stirling in the formation of 2 SAS. Paddy Mayne's Special Raiding Squadron, comprising the remnants of 1 SAS after David Stirling's capture, had served under him in the Special Service Brigade in Sicily. Bob had retained an interest whilst he was CCO and had supported Brian Franks' appointment to command 2 SAS following Bill Stirling's resignation in 1944.

The SAS was disbanded after the War, but the requirement for a deep penetration unit led to the creation of 21 SAS out of a Territorial regiment, the Artists Rifles, under Franks in 1947. This remained a Territorial unit, but a squadron served in the Korean War and then in the Malayan Emergency. The ongoing need for its particular skills led to the formation of a regular unit, 22 SAS, in 1952, and another reserve unit, 23 SAS, in 1959.

At the time of Bob's appointment 22 SAS was experiencing a relatively quiet spell. The Malayan Emergency, in which it had played a minor but nonetheless important role, had come to an end, and the successful Jebel Akhdar campaign in Oman had been concluded in the previous year. The Commanding Officer was Lieutenant Colonel Tony Deane-Drummond, who had served with distinction in 1 Airborne Division at Arnhem. Not long after Bob's appointment, he was succeeded by Lieutenant Colonel John Woodhouse.

Woodhouse was regarded by David Stirling as one of the co-founders of the SAS, although he did not serve in the Regiment until 1950. In Stirling's opinion, he had restored its original philosophy following a period of misuse in Malaya. During the 1950s he had, in particular, devised the rigorous selection process which was thereafter to be the gold standard for recruitment into special forces worldwide. At the time Woodhouse was appointed, operations were continuing in the Arabian Peninsula, notably in the Aden Protectorate, but attention was subsequently diverted to Borneo. This was due to a policy of 'confrontation' by Indonesia, which occupied the larger part of the island and wished to take over the remainder, consisting of the states of Sabah and Sarawak in the newly created Federation of Malaya, a fully-fledged member of the British Commonwealth, and the independent state of Brunei, which had longstanding ties to Great Britain. Elements of the British armed services were deployed, and the SAS and its Australian and New Zealand equivalents were called in specifically to intercept infiltration into these territories by the Indonesians and subsequently to conduct raids into enemy territory under a policy of 'aggressive defence'.

In 1964 Bob asked to visit the two squadrons of 22 SAS on the ground, and the War Office agreed that he should do so. He set off on 5 October, travelling first-class in a BOAC Comet to Kuala Lumpur, where he stayed with Anthony and Dot Head, the former being at the time the British High Commissioner to Malaya.[5] After a briefing there he moved on to Singapore, where he stayed with and was briefed further by Admiral Sir Varyl Begg, the C-in-C Far East. He arrived in Brunei on 9 October, staying with Major General Walter Walker, the Director of Operations and a strong supporter of the SAS. Two squadrons, A and B, were operating in the area, and since Bob's visit coincided with one relieving the other, he was able see them both on active service. He was deeply impressed by their tactics, jungle craft and efforts to win the hearts and minds of the local population, and was gratified to be told by the local army commander that the seventy men in each squadron were doing a job which would otherwise demand a whole battalion of conventional troops. He was particularly taken by the A Squadron Commander, Major Peter de la Billière, who in 1990/91 was to command British Forces in the First Gulf War.

Bob returned the way he had come, staying for several days with the Heads before returning with them to the UK, where he arrived back on 17 October. His written recommendations to the War Office were to add a third squadron to the existing two, which would provide a more manageable cycle of action, rest and training, and to provide them with more and better helicopters. Neither was acted upon!

His return coincided with the end of Woodhouse's term as CO of 22 SAS. In addition to the COs, the Regiment had a Regimental Colonel,[6] who was in overall command of the three SAS units. The retiring Regimental Colonel, Hugh Gillies, wanted Woodhouse to succeed him, and this was supported strongly by opinion in the Regiment and by Bob. The Military Secretary, however, was only prepared to offer Woodhouse a training appointment as a full colonel or a job in public relations. Unsurprisingly, he decided to retire.

Gillies' successor was Colonel John Waddy, who had served as a company commander in the Parachute Regiment at Arnhem. Many in the SAS feared a Parachute Regiment takeover, but nothing was further from Waddy's mind, and before long he was fully accepted. It might have been thought that the choice of someone new to the Regiment was a matter of War Office policy, but in fact Waddy's own successor, Mike Wingate Gray, was appointed immediately after stepping down as CO of 22 SAS.

Whereas Gillies had had a close relationship with Bob, Waddy saw much less of him; Bob's role was certainly not excessively demanding, although he kept in touch directly with the CO of 22 SAS at its base in Hereford and took the chair at the bi-annual SAS Officers' Dinner, just as he did at the Army Commandos Officers' Dining Club.

The one colonelcy which eluded Bob was that of his own regiment. The Colonel of the Blues since 1951 had been Sir Richard Howard-Vyse, and when he died in 1962, Bob was almost certainly the most distinguished former officer of the regiment. The appointment, however, went to Field Marshal Sir Gerald

Templer, and there is no evidence that anyone else was considered. Templer's close personal friendship with Field Marshal Lord Harding, at the time the Colonel of the Life Guards, may have counted in his favour. When Harding stepped down from his own appointment towards the end of 1964, Bob's name was on the short list to succeed him, together with those of Antony Head and Colonel Sir Robert Gooch. Late in proceedings, another name emerged, that of Mountbatten, and it carried the day, with Head making the approach to his and Bob's former mentor on behalf of the regiment. Mountbatten later wrote to Bob, saying that only Angie would appreciate fully his delight at the appointment, because of his weakness for uniforms.

In April 1962, however, Bob did receive another prestigious appointment, that of Lord Lieutenant of Nottinghamshire, the Queen's representative in the county, once again in succession to the Duke of Portland. Although there was no formal royal visit during his period of office, there were occasional visits by other members of the Royal Family, whom he was obliged to escort if he could, being otherwise represented by one of the many Deputy Lieutenants. He sat on occasion as a magistrate, in preparation for which role he had to attend a course at the University of Birmingham, and was required to be present at a large number of functions, many of which, such as giving the prizes at the county boxing match, he found exceedingly tiresome, as he did the chairing of many committees. On the other hand, he enjoyed the increased contact with the armed services in the county.

One committee to which he was appointed had nothing to do with Nottinghamshire. This was set up to plan Operation HOPE NOT, the state funeral of Sir Winston Churchill. As for the Coronation, the organization was in the hands of the Earl Marshal, the Duke of Norfolk, whose former relationship with Bob was almost certainly the reason for his inclusion; but Churchill himself probably vetted the members, as the former prime minister was closely involved with their decisions. Bob told John Waddy about one occasion on which they were discussing which London terminal would be used to convey the coffin by rail to Bladon for burial. Although Paddington would have been the logical choice, Churchill insisted on Waterloo. On being asked why, he growled, 'Because de Gaulle will be there'!

Bob continued to retain an interest in Malta. He and Grantham were guests of the British Government at the Independence Day celebrations on 21 September 1964. Parliamentary democracy had been restored in 1962 under a Government led by Borg Olivier, who had very quickly demanded independence. A referendum was held in May 1964, resulting in a majority in favour of independence, and Malta became a constitutional monarchy,[7] with the Queen as head of state. Mintoff's supporters predictably held demonstrations to show their discontent.

Three years later, with Malta struggling yet again under the impact of British defence cuts, Bob wrote to *The Times* to argue that some of the aid given to former British territories which had subsequently adopted policies which were essentially hostile to Great Britain should be diverted instead to Malta. Although Bob was strongly supported by Mountbatten, who wrote personally to the then Prime Minister, Harold Wilson, little was done to alleviate the situation.

The family was moving on fast. Tilly divorced Mark Agnew in 1963 and married an American lawyer, Sidney Davis, with whom she lived in New York; she had no more children of her own, but after the death of Sidney's brother the couple adopted his two sons. Tilly used to visit her parents frequently. Joe was finding it difficult to settle on any career, dabbling in art and music and spending a lot of time travelling, driving fast cars and flying aeroplanes; eventually, he opened an antique shop in London. Emma married Richard Temple in 1964 and had two daughters, Lucy in 1965 and Alice in 1967. Ben left Eton in 1964 and went on to Sheffield College of Technology to study Building and Structural Engineering, but left early to work in film production and later in catering. Martha spent six months in Spain in 1965 and six months in France in 1966 to learn the two languages and then went to stay with Tilly in early 1967, before returning to share a flat with Ben in London, where she worked in an antique shop.

The new Wiseton Hall proved far more convenient for family and guests, and visits by both were frequent, although Bob had time to pursue his various hobbies and he and Angie regularly holidayed abroad. There was, however, a significant fly in the ointment, in the shape of his bad leg. This had been causing him pain for years, and he had found no cure for it. The original cause, diagnosed as sciatica, was subsequently exacerbated by an arterial condition. This may have been the result of a long history of smoking and alcohol consumption, although after the War Bob gave up cigarettes in favour of less frequent cigars, whilst his drinking was not excessive.

Bob visited a number of specialists and at one time was provided with a box from which wires were attached to his leg whilst he was lying down, probably giving him some form of mild electric shock. Neither this treatment nor a visit to a clinic in Switzerland made any real difference. Amputation was threatened, but instead of this he underwent a less radical operation at the end of 1967, following which there was a marked improvement. One day, following his regular walk to the bottom of the drive and back, he told Martha, who was staying after contracting glandular fever, that he had felt no pain at all. A few days later, on Sunday 10 March 1968, whilst walking back from church in Wiseton village, he suffered a fatal heart attack.

Chapter 23

Reflections

Bob had been only sixty and still vigorous in mind and body, so his death came as a great shock to his family, his friends and those who had served under him. A family funeral was followed by two memorial services, the first on 1 April 1968 in the Guards Chapel in London, which was attended by a large number of friends and representatives of the organizations with which he had been associated. The second, on 5 April in Southwell Minster, was for not only the great and good of Nottinghamshire but also for many others he had known there, some all his life. The Queen was represented at the latter by Rear Admiral Robert Sherbrooke VC, who was to succeed Bob as Lord Lieutenant.

Three years later, Wiseton Hall was sold and Angie went to live in Spain. She returned regularly on visits and never lost her interest in the Commando Benevolent Fund: although she had to resign from the Committee, she accepted the position of President. There was one further tragedy to come for the family when Joe, who had married Lucy Fleming, the daughter of Bob's longstanding friend Peter Fleming, was drowned in a boating accident in 1980 with their eight-year-old daughter Flora.

Bob used to say that he would have liked to have been a research chemist, but that career option would have been entirely impractical in the late 1920s, not to say unacceptable to his father. Instead he became a soldier, at a time of peace when professionalism was in short supply and advancement slow. A more thoughtful officer than many of his contemporaries, he found his occupation socially congenial but professionally stifling, and he was only too ready first to test himself outside his normal environment on the voyage to East Africa and then to branch out from his regiment when an opportunity presented itself, combining his love of science with his training as a soldier by becoming an expert in chemical warfare. By mid-1940, however, with the Phoney War at an end, the prospect of serving on the staff had lost its appeal.

During the War Bob became known as 'Lucky' Laycock. Whilst he himself was later to concede that luck had played a part in his career, he disliked the name intensely, asserting with some justification that his achievements were largely the result of his own efforts and abilities. He should perhaps have comforted himself by recalling Napoleon's preference for lucky generals over merely good ones. The soubriquet was, in any event, perfectly appropriate. Not only did he manage to escape from perilous predicaments on two occasions but, like many who enjoy successful careers in all walks of life, he had the knack of being in the right place at the right time. This was never more so than in his initial appointment to the Commandos. If the appeal for volunteers had come out three weeks later, he would have been on a ship to Egypt on his way to become a staff officer at GHQ Middle East, and his subsequent career would certainly have looked very different. However, it still required a great deal of determination on Bob's part to achieve the result that he so greatly desired. He liked to quote Admiral of the Fleet Lord Fisher, writing a report on one of his subordinates:

> This officer shares one quality in common with myself. In my case it is tenacity of purpose, in his, sheer bloody obstinacy.[1]

When push came to shove, Bob was to prove extremely obstinate, although he knew when a battle was no longer worth fighting, good examples being his conceding in late 1943 that the combining of the Army and Royal Marine Commandos was inevitable and his reluctant acceptance of the demise of the Army Commandos after the War.

In addition to luck, most successful officers also required patronage, and Bob acquired two powerful patrons in the shape of Mountbatten and Churchill. The former came good in the immediate aftermath of what had looked like a fairly disastrous year for Bob in the Mediterranean and later refused his request to resign over the reorganization of the Commandos. Churchill supported Bob after Layforce was disbanded and subsequently turned to him after more senior candidates had rejected a job in his gift. Both had known Bob for many years, Churchill from his childhood.

Notwithstanding the roles played by luck and patronage, it is clear that Bob was invariably well regarded by his superiors. His career in the OTC and at Sandhurst, his appointment as Adjutant of the Blues and his selection as one of a relatively small number of officers in the BEF to go on the Second War Course at the Staff College were indicative of this, as was his nomination by Sergison-Brooke to form the Commando being raised partly in London District. His leadership qualities were also appreciated at an early stage by both Keyes and Haydon. He was one of the four lieutenant colonels chosen to command the short-lived Special Service battalions, and was then selected to lead what became Layforce over the competing claim of Dudley Lister.

Bob's appointments, however, did not always turn out as he might have hoped. Layforce never operated as a whole, as had been originally intended, and its only success, in which Bob had no direct involvement, was the action of 11 Commando on the Litani River, the first example of a Commando operating on the seaward flank in support of conventional troops. It was recognized, however, in London if not in Cairo and not least by the Prime Minister, that Layforce had been badly misused and that the fault did not lie with Bob.

For someone who had joined the Commandos specifically to see some action, Bob's encounters with the enemy turned out to be very brief. Five days on Crete, another five on Operation FLIPPER, followed by the period of evasion, two in Sicily and twelve at Salerno added up to a very modest total, however intense they might have been. However, he did prove to be a brave and decisive leader when it mattered. The last day on Crete became controversial much later, but was not so at the time. Bob's handling of the rearguard was masterly and, in the circumstances in which he found himself, his decisions to save the remnants of Layforce and to leave the island himself, rather than tamely accept incarceration for all, were the correct ones militarily. On Sicily and particularly at Salerno, the actions of the Special Service Brigade attracted the favourable attention of the senior commanders.

Bob was also looked up to by his subordinates. He was much less class-conscious than many of his background and always got on well with the other ranks. He certainly had his difficulties with some officers, Lovat being the supreme example, but was nevertheless respected by them. It was said of him that he lacked personal ambition, although there seems little doubt, in spite of his denials, that his opposition to the reorganization of the Commandos under what was effectively Royal Marine control in 1943 was motivated in part by its impact on his own career. He certainly did not put himself forward to succeed Mountbatten as CCO; indeed, his appointment came as much of a surprise to him as to everyone else.

As CCO, Bob found himself in a difficult position. He was over twenty years younger than Brooke and Cunningham but, although he did not have the same status on the Chiefs of Staff Committee as Mountbatten, he nevertheless had to ensure that his views were heard and his recommendations acted upon. He earned their and Portal's respect by mastering his brief and by standing up for what he believed was the right course of action.

Bob was not infallible and, in particular, there must be a question mark over his selection of some subordinates. His choice of officers for 8 Commando was based on his assessment of what this totally new type of unit would require, together with his belief that war was, for the most part, a boring affair, so that one might as well wage it amongst friends. Those selected certainly turned out to be amusing, but too many were to prove completely unsuitable for special service, although there were some notable exceptions amongst the junior officers, notably Stirling, Lewes, Courtney and Jellicoe. Bob's tolerance of Randolph Churchill is understandable given his longstanding relationship with Randolph's father and, although there is no specific evidence to support this other than the fact that Randolph was in frequent contact with the Prime Minister, it may well have helped his own career. His patronage of Evelyn Waugh is more puzzling: Bob clearly found him an amusing companion, but Waugh was a fish out of water in all other respects, and his retention for so long in the Special Service

Brigade did not go down well with many of its officers. It may, however, be said that Bob gave loyalty just as much as he received it.

Bob has certainly not been immune from criticism, and not just over Crete. Tommy Macpherson, who served in 11 Commando and was captured whilst carrying out a reconnaissance for Operation FLIPPER, wrote much later that Bob 'developed a reputation for endeavouring to take the credit for anything that was successful and distancing himself for anything that was not.'[2] This is puzzling, as there was little to take credit for at the time. One exception was 11 Commando's action on the Litani, and Bob was subsequently quite explicit that he himself had nothing to do with it, although he did use it as an example of what Commandos could achieve. Bob's report on FLIPPER, whilst certainly inaccurate as to the events in Beda Littoria, made no attempt to exonerate himself; indeed, it makes it clear that he himself was taking the decisions and was thus responsible for the outcome.

With the exception of the five years in Malta, where he did well in very difficult circumstances, Bob's post-war life was somehow wasted. Forty was far too early an age at which to retire, as he had skills, experience and connections which could have been put to full-time use in any number of ways. His choice, however, was not an unusual one at that time in the stratum of society to which he and Angie belonged, and it would have provoked no criticism. It did enable them to spend a lot of time with their friends, and friendship was always highly valued by Bob.

Bob was sustained throughout his life by his family, which was exceptionally close. His father was the dominant influence up to the time of his marriage. From then onwards, however, this role passed to Angie. Their marriage could hardly be described as turbulent, but there were moments of difficulty, as both had strong characters, attractive personalities and an occasionally roving eye. Bob voiced his concerns on several occasions about some of Angie's friendships, but, in spite of the difference in their ages, the marriage proved to be robust, and Angie went on to make a particularly important contribution to Bob's role as Governor of Malta.

Bob took his professions as soldier and colonial administrator very seriously, but not life as a whole; indeed, he was able to find the humorous or the ridiculous in most situations, even if they were very difficult ones. His wit can be clearly seen in his memoirs and even more so in the letters to his children, often written in verse. By way of example, after Angie had nearly caused a domestic disaster, he wrote to Martha:

She failed to see the consequences dire,
Which must result if sofa, stuffed with hair,
Is placed some inches from th'electric fire
And this is then turned on – Oh Woe! The air

Was filled with flames and smoke. We had to shout
For help to put the conflagration out.[3]

Another example was his custom at Christmas of sending anonymously 200 cigarettes and a bottle of whisky to the person who had bored him most that year. One of Bob's favourite authors was P. G. Wodehouse, and he accepted Evelyn Waugh in 8 Commando largely on the strength of his enjoyment of Waugh's early novels. On the other hand, he described *Officers and Gentlemen* as 'screamingly funny in parts, but pretty bloody on the whole',[4] regretting that the author no longer stuck to comic themes but 'always has a mission'.[5]

As Bob never went on to higher command in the field or in grand strategy, it is impossible to include him amongst the truly great soldiers of the Second World War. His position in history instead derives from his contribution to the evolution of the Commandos from their uncertain beginnings into the elite and highly specialized force we know today. From the early 1940s, when the Army Commandos were struggling to identify their proper function, often against vigorous opposition from those in high places who deplored their unorthodoxy, to 1946, when it was decided to retain a force of Royal Marines to continue the role at which all the Commandos had subsequently proved so adept, Bob was intimately involved, as a unit and then a formation commander and later as the man in overall control of the whole force.

The final words belong to one who was undoubtedly a great wartime figure, Admiral of the Fleet the Viscount Cunningham of Hyndhope. As C-in-C Mediterranean and subsequently as a member of the Combined Chiefs of Staff Committee, Cunningham was the most senior officer who had seen Bob in his two main roles, as a Commando leader and as Chief of Combined Operations, and he clearly recognized his quality. On his retirement as First Sea Lord in 1946, Cunningham wrote in reply to Bob's valedictory letter:

> It is pleasant to look back on those stirring times in the Middle East. I well remember my first meeting with you and how highly I regarded your exploits in those days. May I say that I am very proud to have been associated with you then & later in conference, there is no one I know of who deserves better of his fellow countrymen than one I shall always regard as a 'very parfait gentle knight'.[6]

Appendix

Directive to the Chief of Combined Operations 28 November 1943

1. You are appointed Chief of Combined Operations.

<u>General Responsibility</u>

2. Under the general direction of the Chiefs of Staff you will:-
   (a) Study practical and technical problems of combined operations including small scale raids and formulate doctrine and staff requirements.
   (b) Advise on all aspects of planning and training for combined operations.
   (c) Co-ordinate basic training policy for amphibious operations for all three Services, and control Combined Training Centres in the United Kingdom.
   (d) Direct and press forward research and development in all forms of technical equipment including craft peculiar to Combined Operations.
   (e) Co-ordinate the development of communications material and inter-communication technique in amphibious warfare.
   (f) Control the Special Service Group except during such times as the whole or part of it is handed over to a Force Commander for operations.
3. In order to fulfil these responsibilities you will give advice to the Chiefs of Staff on matters set out in paragraph 2 above and will be available to attend the Chiefs of Staff Committee when required. In addition you will have direct access to the Minister of Defence on all matters for which you are responsible.

<u>Planning</u>

4. You will be available to give technical advice upon all planning for Combined Operations at all stages. Commanders and Staffs will be informed of your functions and will be requested to take advantage of the facilities you provide.
5. In the case of operations in North-West Europe which are carried out by the Special Service Group only, you will appoint the Commander of the Special Services Troops, who will prepare detailed plans, with your advice, for submission to S.A.C. or COSSAC.

Training

6. You will:-
   (a) Be responsible for co-ordinating the teaching of such Combined schools of instruction or Combined training establishments as it may be found necessary to set up in the United Kingdom, except those established by Force Commanders when your functions will be advisory.
   (b) Command the Combined Training Centres at which the basic training of formations and units in combined operations will be carried out under their Commanders, and with the technical advice of the staffs of the Centres. This advice will be your responsibility.
   (c) Advise, as required, Force Commanders, subsequent to their appointment for an operation, on the technical training of their forces. It is equally incumbent on them to seek your advice on this matter.

Special Service Group

7. The Special Service Group will be under your control. The appropriate Service Ministries will, however, continue to provide through your Headquarters the necessary administrative facilities. Beyond such tasks as you may allot to them, e.g. at the various centres of instruction, these troops will be available for specific combined operations when you will place them under the Commander appointed for that operation.

Co-ordination and Liaison

8. In addition to your responsibilities in the United Kingdom, you will also be responsible for the co-ordination of development in combined assault training and techniques among British authorities overseas, and for ensuring so far as possible the adoption of a common doctrine by Allied authorities both in the U.K. and overseas.

Abbreviations

AA	Anti-Aircraft
AA&QMG	Assistant Adjutant and Quartermaster-General
ACIGS	Assistant Chief of the General Staff
ADC	Aide-de-Camp
AFHQ	Allied Forces Headquarters
AFV	Armoured Fighting Vehicles
AGRM	Adjutant-General Royal Marines
ALFSEA	Allied Land Forces South-East Asia
BEF	British Expeditionary Force
BGS	Brigadier General Staff
BOAC	British Overseas Airways Corporation
CAS	Chief of the Air Staff
CB	Companion of the Order of the Bath
CBF	Commando Benevolent Fund.
CCO	Chief of Combined Operations
CIGS	Chief of the Imperial General Staff
C-in-C	Commander-in-Chief
CMG	Companion of the Order of St Michael & St George
CO	Commanding Officer
COHQ	Combined Operations Headquarters
COS	Chief of Staff
COSSAC	Chief of Staff to the Supreme Allied Commander (Designate)
COXE	Combined Operations Experimental Establishment
CRA	Commander Royal Artillery
CTC	Combined Training Centre
DAA&QMG	Deputy Assistant Adjutant & Quartermaster General
DCIGS	Deputy Chief of the Imperial General Staff
DCO	Director of Combined Operations
DSO	Distinguished Service Order
DUKW	6-wheeled amphibious vehicle
GCB	Knight Grand Cross of the Order of the Bath
GHQ	General Headquarters
GOC	General Officer Commanding
GOC-in-C	General Officer Commanding-in-Chief

GOCO	General Officer Combined Operations
GSO1	General Staff Officer Grade 1
GSO2	General Staff Officer Grade 2
GSO3	General Staff Officer Grade 3
HCTR	Household Cavalry Training Regiment
HMAS	His Majesty's Australian Ship
HMS	His (or Her) Majesty's Ship
HMT	Hired Maritime Transport
HQ	Headquarters
IA	Inter-Allied
IO	Intelligence Officer
ISTDC	Inter Services Training & Development Centre
JSM	Joint Staff Mission
KCB	Knight Commander of the Order of the Bath
KCMG	Knight Commander of the Order of St Michael & St George
LCA	Landing Craft (Assault)
LCI(L)	Landing Craft Infantry (Large)
LCM	Landing Craft Mechanised
LCP(L)	Landing Craft Personnel (Large)
LHA	Liddell Hart Archives
LRDG	Long Range Desert Group
LSI	Landing Ship Infantry
MC	Military Cross
MNBDO	Mobile Naval Base Defence Organization
MP	Member of Parliament
NATO	North Atlantic Treaty Organization
NCO	Non-commissioned Officer
NLO	Naval Liaison Officer
OCTU	Officer Cadet Training Unit
OTC	Officers Training Corps
PIAT	Projector, Infantry, Anti Tank
psc	Passed Staff College
PT	Physical Training
RA	Royal Artillery
RAMC	Royal Army Medical Corps
RAOC	Royal Army Ordnance Corps
RASC	Royal Army Service Corps
RAF	Royal Air Force
RE	Royal Engineers
RHA	Royal Horse Artillery
RM	Royal Marines
RMC	Royal Military College

RMS	Royal Mail Ship
RN	Royal Navy
RNVR	Royal Naval Volunteer Reserve
RTU	Returned to Unit
SACSEA	Supreme Allied Commander South-East Asia
SAS	Special Air Service
SBS	Special Boat Squadron
SEAC	South-East Asia Command
SO	Staff Officer
SOE	Special Operations Executive
SRS	Special Raiding Squadron
SS	Steam Ship
TEWT	Tactical Exercise Without Troops
VC	Victoria Cross
VCIGS	Vice-Chief of the Imperial General Staff
WAAF	Women's Auxiliary Air Force

Acknowledgements

My thanks must go first and foremost to Bob's children, Emma Temple, Ben Laycock and Martha Mlinaric, who have been consistently supportive whilst at the same time accepting that I would have a free hand in writing a biography of their father. As well as giving me their personal reminiscences of Bob and Angie and some very useful background on the family, they unearthed a treasure trove of diaries, memoirs, letters, privately published books and other papers which have never been in the public domain. They also produced many of the photographs which I have used to illustrate Bob's life. Some of the most valuable material was produced by Michael Davis, Tilly Davis' son, who lives in the United States and arranged for it to be brought over to the UK, for which I am most grateful.

I regard it as a great honour that Major General Julian Thompson has agreed to write the Foreword. Julian is not only an eminent historian in his own right, but probably the most famous living Commando soldier, having led 3 Commando Brigade during the Falklands campaign in 1982 and, indeed, acted as ground force commander for the initial landings and engagements. By that time 3 Commando Brigade was no longer an exclusively Royal Marine formation, but included army units in the shape of 29 Commando Regiment Royal Artillery and 59 Independent Commando Squadron Royal Engineers. However, it was also reinforced for the duration of the campaign by two battalions of the Parachute Regiment and, most pertinently, by two reconnaissance troops of the Blues and royals, the successor to Bob's own regiment.

For information on Bob's early schooldays I must thank Roger Stephens, whose career of over fifty years at Lockers Park has left him with an encyclopedic knowledge of its Old Boys. The Library at Eton College was as efficient as always and I would like to thank the Archivist, Eleanor Cracknell, for making my visit there so successful. Anthony Morton, Curator of the Sandhurst Collection, helped me to find the relevant information on Bob's time at the RMC.

Lieutenant General Sir Barney White-Spunner, who was himself commissioned into the Blues and Royals and is the author of the definitive book on the Household Cavalry, answered a number of queries on the Royal Horse Guards between the two world wars and helped me to correct some misconceptions. Stuart Madden and Ted Land of the Household Cavalry

Museum and Archives at Combermere Barracks directed me towards the few sources of information on Bob's early career in the Army, other than his diary.

I am most grateful to Viscount Head, the son of Antony Head, whose career path kept crossing Bob's and who was probably his closest friend both in and out of the Army, for his help and particularly for allowing me to use a number of photographs.

As far as the Commandos were concerned, the outstanding contributor was Desirée Roderick, to whom I am deeply indebted for allowing me to interview her and following this up with a number of letters. Mrs Roderick's first husband, Captain R. F. Broome, served initially in 2 Commando under Bob at Salerno, where sadly he became one of the many fatalities. Her brother, Captain Joe Houghton, also of 2 Commando, was the second-in-command of Operation MUSKETOON in Norway, but although the operation was successful, he was taken prisoner and later executed under Hitler's Commando Order. Mrs Roderick's second husband, Captain, later Doctor John Roderick, also served in 2 Commando and was taken prisoner at St Nazaire.

Mrs Roderick's mother was one of the founders of the No. 2 Commando Next of Kin Association and subsequently became a Trustee of the Commando Benevolent Fund. Mrs Roderick herself became a Trustee of the CBF in 1973 and its Honorary Secretary in 1986; her daughter Angela, who was Angie's god-daughter, followed her mother and grandmother as a Trustee in 1983. Mrs Roderick was thus able to talk from personal experience about many of the leading figures in the Commandos and was also most helpful in referring me to some useful sources.

I am also grateful to Brigadier Jack Thomas, Chairman of the Commando Benevolent Fund and President of the Commando Veterans Association, and to Joe Murtagh, until recently the National Secretary of the CVA, for their help, and to Pete Rogers, the CVA web site archivist, for allowing me to publish a number of photographs from the site.

I had a number of very useful discussions with Philip Eade, who was in the course of writing his new book, *Evelyn Waugh: A Life Revisited*. Although we also debated the circumstances of Waugh's resignation from the Commandos, our main focus was on the events on Crete and I must thank Philip for helping me to clarify my own views on this critical episode.

For Bob's governorship of Malta, my main source was David Hall, who was Bob's ADC for more than half his term. I had a long interview with him, at which Martha Mlinaric was also present, as a consequence of which I came away much better informed on the events, personalities and general background, as well as on the private life of the Governor and his family. I am most grateful to David for his time then and subsequently.

For information on Bob's Lord Lieutenancy of Nottinghamshire I must thank Sir Andrew Buchanan, himself a former Lord Lieutenant, and Gaynor

Brown of the Lieutenancy Office. As far as Bob's colonelcy of the Sherwood Rangers was concerned, I am grateful to Colonel Jonathan Hunt, the historian of the regiment and one of Bob's successors as its Honorary Colonel. Colonel Hunt also pointed me in the direction of Stanley Christopherson's diaries, which enabled me to track the wartime movements of Bob's brothers, Peter and Michael. On Bob's association with the post-war SAS I was helped by Colonel John Waddy, the Regimental Colonel for much of Bob's term as Colonel Commandant.

Apart from the material produced by the family, the single most important source for the book was the Laycock Papers in the Liddell Hart Archives at King's College, London, and I spent long hours there. I am most grateful to Diana Manipud and her colleagues for the most efficient and friendly way in which they satisfied my requirements, which included copying reams of documents. I would also like to thank the staff of the National Archives and the Imperial War Museum, two organizations I appreciate greatly for their standards of service.

At Pen & Sword Henry Wilson has been unfailingly supportive, whilst Matt Jones has handled all the issues relating to the production of the book with the minimum of fuss. I have also been very lucky to have George Chamier as my editor once again.

I could not write without the encouragement of my wife, Sheelagh, and my sons, Tim and Rupert. As ever, Rupert was the first reader of all my drafts, making time in the midst of his very busy professional and family life, for which I am most grateful.

Sources and Bibliography

Interviews

David Hall
Ben Laycock
Martha Mlinaric
Desirée Roderick
Emma Temple

Primary Sources

The National Archives

ADM 1/18084	Definition of responsibilities of Admiralty & COHQ.
ADM 202/402	Crete: Despatches of Major General Weston.
CAB 80/55/12	Employment of 3 Commando Brigade: Memorandum by CCO.
CAB 80/76/87	Directive to CCO 28.11.43.
CAB 120/414	Combined Operations: General.
CO 967/352	Malta: Extension of term of office for Sir Robert Laycock.
CO 1017/478	Malta: Extension of term of office for Sir Robert Laycock.
DEFE 2/43	Combined Operations War Diaries.
DEFE 2/48	RM Commandos War Diaries.
DEFE 2/54	SS Brigade HQ War Diary October 1940–August 1941.
DEFE 2/55	SS Brigade HQ War Diary September 1941–October 1943.
DEFE 2/205	Supplementary report on Operation Flipper.
DEFE 2/699	Early history of Combined Operations.
DEFE 2/710	Evolution, Development & Organization of COHQ.
DEFE 2/711B	Miscellaneous COHQ papers.
DEFE 2/1051	Role & reorganization of SS Brigade and SS Group.
DEFE 2/1066	Laycock biography and other papers.
WO 193/384	Independent Companies.
WO 201/716	Layforce Adjutant General Questions.
WO 201/717	Layforce Commander Personal Papers.
WO 201/720	Report on Operation Flipper.
WO 201/2652	Inter Services Committee Report on Crete.
WO 205/47	Functions of CCO May1943–June 1944.
WO 218/8	8 Commando War Diary June–November 1940.
WO 218/29	SS Brigade War Diary January–December 1942.

WO 218/44	1 SS Brigade War Diary January–December 1943.
WO 218/50	2 Commando War Diary January–December 1943.
WO 218/166	HQ Z Force/Layforce War Diary January–July 1941.
WO 218/168	A Battalion Layforce War Diary January–May 1941.
WO 218/169	B Battalion Layforce War Diary May–June 1941.
WO 218/170	B Battalion Layforce War Diary January–March 1941.
WO 218/171	C Battalion Layforce War Diary March–October 1941.
WO 218/172	D Battalion Layforce War Diary January–May 1941.

Imperial War Museum

The Papers of Major General T. B. L. Churchill, Major General F. C. C. Graham, Major General J. C. Haydon, Captain F. R. C. Nicholls.

Interviews with Earl Jellicoe, Sir Carol Mather, Lieutenant Colonel J. M. T. F. Churchill, Major W. A. Smallman, Lieutenant J. B. Sherwood.

Liddell-Hart Centre, King's College, London

The Papers of Major General R. E. Laycock.

Eton College Library

Term calendars, school lists and *Eton College Chronicle.*

Hartley Library, University of Southampton

Mountbatten Papers.

Private Laycock Papers

Draft memoirs.

Diaries 1927–1932.

Letters from Bob to Angie, Emma Laycock (later Temple) and Martha Laycock (later Mlinaric).

Letters from Brigadier General Joseph Laycock to his mother and sister 1899–1900.

Diary of the voyage of *Herzogin Cecilie* August–November 1931.

List of books read 1928–1968.

Army Service Record.

Other Sources

Army List

Dictionary of National Biography

London Gazette

The Times Digital Archive

Who's Who

Wikipedia and other web sites

Books

Anon, *Log of the Valhalla*, privately published 1894.
Anon, *The Story of 46 Division 1939–1945*, Graz 1946.
Asher, Michael, *Get Rommel*, London 2004.
Asher, Michael, *The Regiment – The Real Story of the SAS*, London 2007.
Beevor, Antony, *Crete – The Battle and the Resistance*, London 1991.
Bryant, Arthur, *The Turn of the Tide – 1939–1943*, London 1957.
Bryant, Arthur, *Triumph in the West – 1943–1946*, London 1959.
Churchill, Tom, *Commando Crusade*, London 1987.
Churchill, Winston S., *The Second World War*, Volumes II to VI, London, 1949–1954.
Connell, John, *Auchinleck*, London 1959.
Cowles, Virginia, *The Phantom Major*, London 1958.
Cunningham, Andrew, *A Sailor's Odyssey*, London 1951.
Danchev, Alex & Todman, Daniel (Eds.), *War Diaries 1939–1945 – Field Marshal Lord Alanbrooke*, London 2001 & 2003 (paperback).
Davie, Michael (Ed.), *The Diaries of Evelyn Waugh*, London 1976.
D'Este, Carlo, *Bitter Victory – The Battle for Sicily 1943*, London 1988.
Dunning, James, *It Had To Be Tough – The Origins and Training of the Commandos in World War II*, Barnsley, 2012.
Durnford-Slater, John, *Commando – Memoirs of a Fighting Commando in World War Two*, London 1953.
Eade, Philip, *Evelyn Waugh – A Life Revisited*, London 2016.
Fergusson, Bernard, *The Watery Maze – The Story of Combined Operations*, London 1961.
Fraser, David, *And We Shall Shock Them – The British Army in the Second World War*, London 1983.
Hall Spencer, John, *Battle for Crete*, Barnsley 2008.
Hastings, Selina, *Evelyn Waugh – A Biography*, London 1994.
Hickey, Des and Smith, Gus, *Operation Avalanche – The Salerno Landings 1943*, London 1983.
Hoe, Alan, *David Stirling*, London 1992.
Holland, James (Ed.), *An Englishman at War – The Wartime Diaries of Stanley Christopherson*, London 2014.
Ismay, Hastings, *Memoirs*, London 1960.
Joslin, H. F., *Orders of Battle – Second World War 1939–1945*, London 1960.
Kemp, Anthony, *The SAS at War 1941–1945*, London 1991.
Keyes, Elizabeth, *Geoffrey Keyes*, London 1956.
Keyes, Roger, *Amphibious Warfare and Combined Operations*, Cambridge 1943.
Konstam, Angus, *Salerno 1943*, Barnsley 2007.
Ladd, James, *The Royal Marines 1919–1980*, London 1980.
Lavery, Brian, *Churchill Goes to War*, London 2007.
Lovat, Simon, *March Past – A Memoir*, London 1978.
Macpherson, Tommy (with Richard Bath), *Behind Enemy Lines*, Edinburgh 2010.

Mather, Carol, *When the Grass Stops Growing*, Barnsley 1997.
Maund, Loben, *Assault from the Sea*, London 1949.
Messenger, Charles, *The Commandos 1940–1946*, London 1985.
Messenger, Charles (with George Young and Stephen Rose), *The Middle East Commandos*, London 1988.
Mitchell-Innes, Barbara, *Joseph Frederick Laycock*, privately published 1936.
Morgan, Frederick, *Overture to Overlord*, London 1950.
Owen, James, *Commando*, London 2012.
Ranfurly, Hermione, *To War with Whittaker*, London 1995.
Rostron, Peter, *The Military Life & Times of General Sir Miles Dempsey*, London 2010.
Saunders, Hilary St George, *The Green Beret*, London 1949.
Stannard, Martin, *Evelyn Waugh – No Abiding City 1939–1966*, London 1992.
Vian, Philip, *Action This Day*, London 1960.
Waugh, Evelyn, *Men at Arms*, London 1952.
Waugh, Evelyn, *Officers and Gentlemen*, London 1955.
Waugh, Evelyn, *Unconditional Surrender*, London 1961.
White-Spunner, Barney, *Horse Guards*, London 2006.
Young, Peter, *Storm from the Sea*, London 1958.
Ziegler, Philip, *Mountbatten – The Official Biography*, London 1985.
Ziegler, Philip (Ed.), *Personal Diary of Admiral The Lord Louis Mountbatten – Supreme Allied Commander South-East Asia 1943–1946*, London 1988.

Notes

Chapter 1

1. Mitchell-Innes, *Joseph Frederick Laycock* p.11.
2. A younger son of the 8th Duke of Leeds. He died in 1895, but Annie lived for another forty years.
3. Letter from Joe to his mother 15.12.1899.
4. 'Bendor' was a reference to the ancient arms of the Grosvenors – 'Azure, a bend d'or' – before they lost a famous case in the Court of Chivalry in 1389, in which the Scrope family, rival claimants to identical arms, was victorious.

Chapter 2

1. Mitchell-Innes, *Joseph Frederick Laycock* p.55.
2. Ibid. p.56.
3. Joe had been appointed CMG in 1917. The Order of St Michael & St George is now awarded for specifically non-military services on foreign and Commonwealth affairs, but in the Great War it was used as a general award for military services.
4. Letter from A. E. Foot to Bob 5.8.25, Family Papers.
5. DEFE 2/1066.
6. Laycock Papers LHA 9/1/1.

Chapter 3

1. The creation of the title was as 'Earl Erne', but 'Earl of Erne' is in common use, not only in the press, but in most works of reference.
2. Cornet was the lowest commissioned rank in some cavalry regiments and was equivalent to second lieutenant. It is now only used in the Blues and Royals and the Queen's Royal Hussars.
3. The First and Second Life Guards had been amalgamated into a single regiment in 1922.
4. The Household Cavalry Mounted Regiment continues to provide Short and Long Guards to this day.
5. *Memoirs* pp.1–2.
6. By coincidence, Turnor and Smith-Dorrien died within six weeks of each other in the summer of 1930, both as the result of accidents. Turnor had only recently succeeded Innes-Ker as Commanding Officer of the Blues.

7. This was by no means universal. Each of the four officers immediately senior to Bob – Henry Abel Smith, Walter Sale, Eion Merry and Peter Grant Lawson – remained in the service, did well in the War and subsequently became the regiment's Commanding Officer.

Chapter 4

1. The film was based on the theatrical version of Hornung's books, which had first been staged in 1903, with Sir Gerald du Maurier in the title role.
2. The donkey man was the crewman responsible for the machinery aboard ship, notably the motors to raise the anchor and pump out water. On the *Herzogin Cecilie* he was a jack of all trades.

Chapter 5

1. Laycock Papers LHA 2/1.
2. Laycock Papers LHA 9/1/1.
3. Now renamed Hyde Park Crescent.
4. Diary 6.12.28.
5. Letter from Bob to Angie 20.9.34.
6. Letter from Bob to Angie 6.10.34.
7. *Memoirs* p.8.

Chapter 6

1. Three years is Bob's recollection in his *Memoirs*. However, the Military Secretary's Department's communication to London District of his selection referred to his tenure lasting until 31 March 1939, just over fifteen months.
2. *Memoirs* p.18.
3. Ibid. pp.49–50.
4. Ibid. p.60.
5. Ibid.
6. Letter from Bob to Angie 20.10.39.
7. Letter from Bob to Angie 8.10.39.
8. *Memoirs* p.90.
9. Ibid p.108.
10. The course was subsequently changed to three periods of six weeks each, with short breaks between them.
11. He took part in the defence of Boulogne in May 1940, in which he earned a Military Cross, and was then appointed GSO2 at the newly formed Guards Armoured Division.

Chapter 7

1. CAB 120/414.
2. Ibid.
3. Clarke, *Seven Assignments* p.207.
4. WO 193/384.

5. Niven, *The Moon's a Balloon* p.225.
6. Sergison-Brooke was the cousin and a very close confidant of Alan Brooke, later CIGS. It is quite possible, albeit documented nowhere, that he was helpful to Bob's later career.
7. This is not strictly true. Bob was only in Beira for a week and, although he did work in the hold of the *Herzogin Cecilie* on unloading from time to time, it was by no means the full-time job which was the impression conveyed.
8. *Memoirs* pp.152–3.
9. The first mention of White's appears to have come on p.17 of Virginia Cowles' biography of David Stirling, *The Phantom Major*, published in 1958. Cowles, an American journalist, biographer and travel writer, was a friend of Bob's even before the War. She would have relished the unorthodox myth over the more prosaic reality.
10. Letter from Bob to Angie 15.10.40.
11. Their fathers were Lord Astor of Hever, who owned *The Times*, and Viscount Camrose, who owned the *Daily Telegraph*.
12. He had an illustrious career in the law after the War which included leading the prosecution in the Lady Chatterley trial.
13. *Memoirs* pp.170-1.

Chapter 8

1. Mather, *When the Grass Stops Growing* p.29.
2. WO 218/8.
3. Ibid.
4. Simon Fraser, Lord Lovat and Chief of Clan Fraser of Lovat, was always known as 'Shimi', a corruption of the Gaelic MacShimidh (son of Simon).
5. WO 218/8.
6. Nos. 1–9 & 11. No 12 Commando was also raised specifically to help counter a German invasion of Northern Ireland, but did not come under Combined Operations until later.
7. Letter from Bob to Angie 26.8.40.
8. Churchill, *The Second World War*, Volume II p.413.
9. HMS *Glengyle* was one of three 'Glen' ships, 10,000-ton, 14-knot cargo vessels converted to LSIs, which could carry twelve LCAs, one LCM (later two) for vehicles and stores and 700+ men in addition to her crew. The others were *Glenearn* and *Glenroy*.
10. *Memoirs* p.232.
11. Ibid. p.234.
12. Young, *Storm from the Sea* p.24.
13. *Memoirs* p.241.
14. Davie (Ed.), *The Diaries of Evelyn Waugh* p.491.
15. Jellicoe IWM interview.
16. There is no hotel of that name now on Arran: it is possible that it was actually the Douglas Hotel.

17. Churchill, *Commando Crusade* p.60.
18. Davie (Ed.), *The Diaries of Evelyn Waugh* p.492.
19. Ibid.
20. *Memoirs* p.263.
21. DEFE 2/43.

Chapter 9

1. Sherwood IWM interview.
2. Laycock Papers LHA 3/4.
3. WO 218/166.
4. *Memoirs* p.266.
5. Ibid.
6. *Memoirs* p.271.
7. Ibid. p.273.
8. Ibid. pp.292–3.
9. It appears to have originally been called Operation MANDIBLES, which is how Bob refers to it in his memoirs, but the Layforce war diary refers only to CORDITE.
10. Courtney was awarded the Military Cross for this.

Chapter 10

1. Cunningham had served as Cowan's Flag Captain from 1926 to 1928 when the latter was C-in-C West Indies. He was later to say that he had spent no happier years at sea.
2. *Memoirs* p.320.
3. Ibid. p.332.
4. Laycock Papers LHA 6/3.
5. Davie (Ed.), *The Diaries of Evelyn Waugh* p.494.
6. *Memoirs* p.354.
7. Mather, *When the Grass Stops Growing* pp. 41–2.
8. *Memoirs* p.356.

Chapter 11

1. Ibid. p.357.
2. Ibid. p.366.
3. Ibid. p.369.
4. Ibid. p.370.
5. Ibid. pp.370–1.
6. Ibid. pp.372–3.
7. WO 201/2652.
8. Memoirs p.374.
9. Messenger, Young and Rose, *The Middle East Commandos* p.87.
10. Davie (Ed.), *The Diaries of Evelyn Waugh* p.507.
11. WO 218/166.

12. *Memoirs* p.379.
13. Ibid. pp.382–4.
14. Papers of Major General F. C. C. Graham IWM.
15. WO 218/166.
16. ADM 202/402.
17. Ibid.
18. Davie (Ed.), *The Diaries of Evelyn Waugh* p.509.
19. The wife of the author Ian Fleming, and sister-in-law to Peter Fleming.
20. Davie (Ed.), *The Diaries of Evelyn Waugh* p.728.
21. Letter to Angie 2.7.55.
22. Papers of Major General F. C. C. Graham IWM.
23. *Memoirs* p.380.
24. Ibid. pp.380–1.
25. Messenger, Young and Rose, *The Middle East Commandos* p.93.
26. *Memoirs* p.388.

Chapter 12

1. Nicholls was killed in May 1942 whilst leading Chinese guerrillas behind Japanese lines.
2. DEFE 2/711B.
3. Unlike acting or temporary rank, which could and usually would be terminated on the expiry of a particular appointment, war substantive rank was to be held for as long as hostilities continued.
4. Not long after Bob's return to the Middle East, Salisbury-Jones was appointed Head of the British Military Mission in South Africa, a wartime backwater. Repeated requests to be given a more active role eventually resulted in his appointment to Eisenhower's staff at SHAEF in 1944.
5. *Memoirs* p.353.
6. Ibid. p.355.
7. Ibid. p.399.
8. Churchill was well ahead of events. It was not until 1 March 1942 that Bob was to attain the rank of acting Brigadier.
9. Churchill, *The Grand Alliance* p.721.
10. Ibid. pp.725–6.
11. Dreyer had retired from the Royal Navy and rejoined when war was declared. At the time he was Inspector of Merchant Navy Gunnery.

Chapter 13

1. Mather, *When the Grass Stops Growing* p.53.
2. *Memoirs* p.411.
3. Daly was taken prisoner during Operation CRUSADER.
4. *Memoirs* pp.410–1.
5. Letter from Bob to Angie 20.10.41.
6. Laycock Papers LHA 6/4.

7. Ibid.
8. Ibid.
9. Ibid.
10. Citation for the award of the Victoria Cross to Lieutenant Colonel Geoffrey Keyes WO 373/19/153.
11. He was later to say that he had lost a pound in weight for every day on the run.
12. She and her husband Dan, a fellow officer of Peter and Michael Laycock in the Sherwood Rangers Yeomanry, had been staying with the Laycocks in Torridon when war was declared.
13. The Arab name for Beda Littoria.
14. Ranfurly, *To War with Whittaker* p.118.
15. Letter from Bob to Angie 30.12.41.

Chapter 14

1. Mountbatten was also an Old Boy of Lockers Park but left well before Bob arrived.
2. Smallman Interview IWM.
3. 1 (Irvine), 3 (Largs), 4 (Troon), 6 (Saltcoats) and 12 (Ayr).
4. Letter from Bob to Angie 10.4.42.
5. Casa Maury was subsequently blamed for the poor intelligence on the German defences of Dieppe.
6. This was issued on 18 October 1942 and required all captured commandos to be executed. Some German generals, including Rommel, refused to obey it. Others were later charged with war crimes for having done so.

Chapter 15

1. He was to go on to serve in 2 Special Service Brigade in Italy and Yugoslavia, for which he was awarded a bar to the DSO which he had won in the Sudan in 1898!
2. Davie (Ed.), *The Diaries of Evelyn Waugh* p.529.
3. Laycock Papers LHA 4/20.
4. DEFE 2/1051.
5. Laycock Papers LHA 6/15.
6. In a letter dated 26 December 1942, Bob told Glendinning that he did not believe that Ken Trevor had the personality or drive to be a CO. He had clearly changed his mind, probably as a result of Trevor's performance in North Africa. Later in the War Trevor was to win a DSO leading 1 Commando in Burma.

Chapter 16

1. Churchill, *Commando Crusader* p.74.
2. William Collins, chairman of the eponymous publishing house.
3. Laycock Papers LHA 6/20.
4. DEFE 2/1051.
5. Ibid.

6. He was known for the same reason to Churchill, who had been a cadet in No. 1 Company in the term behind Bob.
7. Lovat, *March Past* p.233.
8. DEFE 2/1051.
9. Ibid.
10. Ibid.
11. Ibid.
12. Laycock Papers LHA 6/21.
13. Ibid.
14. DEFE 2/1051.
15. Letter from Bob to Angie 21.8.43.
16. Letter from Bob to Angie 3.9.43.
17. Laycock Papers LHA 6/21.
18. Ibid.
19. Ibid.
20. Laycock Papers LHA 6/19.

Chapter 17

1. Landing Craft Infantry (Large), capable of carrying about 200 troops on to the beaches.
2. It is called Piegoletti in the war diaries. This is because there was a contour line running through the map across the double ls.
3. His nickname derived from the courtesy title of Earl of Mornington, which he used from his birth in 1912 until 1931, when his grandfather died and his father succeeded to the Dukedom, at which point he adopted the more senior courtesy title of Marquess of Douro. He himself had become Duke on the death of his father in 1941. He had no children and was succeeded himself by an uncle. Bob wrote a personal condolence letter to the Dowager Duchess, whom he knew socially.
4. These were the 'final' numbers provided in a letter of 30.9.43 to Haydon from Griff Hunt, who had recently returned to the brigade as Staff Captain. They differ from the brigade's operations report and the 2 Commando war diary, in which the casualties total 367.
5. Dunne won a MC at Salerno.
6. Jack Churchill also received a DSO, in his case for his actions at Salerno, which was downgraded from the Victoria Cross for which Bob had recommended him.
7. Laycock Papers LHA 6/22.

Chapter 18

1. The battle was fictionalized in C. S. Forester's *The Ship*.
2. Rejecting Churchill's offer did no harm to the career of either man. Both became Admirals of the Fleet, McGrigor after serving as First Sea Lord.
3. Fergusson, *The Watery Maze* p.294.

4. Laycock Papers LHA 6/23.
5. Haydon went out to Italy to command an infantry brigade, but was promoted back to major general in 1944 as a member of the British Joint Services Mission in Washington.
6. Laycock Papers LHA 6/23.
7. The Sherwood Rangers sailed from Alexandria for the UK on 17 November, only days before Bob arrived in Egypt.

Chapter 19

1. DEFE 2/710.
2. Letter from Bob to his father 14.6.44.
3. In May 1944, outbound from Lisbon to Philadelphia, the *Serpa Pinto* had been stopped by a U-boat, whose captain demanded that the crew and passengers take to the boats, whilst he sought permission to sink the ship. This was denied and they all boarded again and continued their voyage.
4. Letter from Bob to Angie 14.9.44.
5. The rest of the Dutch troop had been attached to 1 Airborne Division for Operation MARKET GARDEN, in which they largely acted as interpreters.
6. Churchill returned to the UK and was later given command of an infantry brigade. He had a distinguished post-war career, becoming a major general in due course.
7. Letter from Bob to Angie 26.11.44. Not very long afterwards, the Auchinlecks divorced following Lady Auchinleck's affair with her husband's RAF counterpart, Air Chief Marshal Sir Richard Peirse.
8. Letter from Bob to Angie 3.2.45.
9. Ismay, *The Memoirs of General Lord Ismay* p.387.

Chapter 20

1. Letter from Lovat to Bob 5.6.45.
2. Laycock Private Papers.
3. Letter from Bob to Angie 17.7.45.
4. *Memoirs* p.226.
5. Ibid. p.227.
6. 30 Assault Unit was disbanded in 1946, but its name has been subsequently recognized in 30 Commando Information Exploitation Group, formed in 2010, whilst 43 Commando Fleet Protection Group, formed in 2011, has revived yet another of the former RM Commandos. Moreover, there are now Army Commandos again, in the shape of 29 Commando Regiment RA and 24 Commando Engineer Regiment, all of whose officers and other ranks must pass the All Arms Commando Course.
7. Laycock Papers LHA 7/3.

8. There had long been antipathy between the two men, of which the major cause was an attempt by Tedder to have Montgomery sacked for his apparent lack of progress in Normandy.
9. Primmie Niven, Bob's niece, had died following an accident earlier in the year.
10. Letter from Bob to Angie 1.12.46.
11. Letter from Mountbatten to Bob 18.6.46.
12. Letter from Sturges to Bob 14.6.45.
13. The figure of a commando soldier is one of three, the others being a submariner and an airborne soldier.

Chapter 21

1. By a strange coincidence the *Saintes* was commanded by Captain Desmond Dreyer, the son of the Admiral in whose company Bob had first visited Malta in 1941.
2. Interview 19.2.15.
3. Letter from Bob to Angie 4.11.56.
4. CO 967/352.

Chapter 22

1. Letter from Bob to Emma 22.3.60.
2. Letter from Bob to Emma 23.10.57.
3. Now Welbeck Defence Sixth Form College at Loughborough.
4. Now A (Sherwood Rangers) Squadron, Royal Yeomanry.
5. In 1960 Head had been created Viscount Head for political services.
6. Later given the title of Director SAS and currently called Director Special Forces.
7. Mintoff regained power in 1971 and Malta became a republic in 1974.

Chapter 23

1. *Memoirs* p.159.
2. Macpherson, *Behind Enemy Lines* p.67.
3. Letter from Bob to Martha 17.10.66.
4. Letter from Bob to Angie 2.7.55.
5. Ibid.
6. Laycock Papers LHA 6/24.

Index